# Being and Becoming

## *Gender, Culture and Shifting Identity in Sub-Saharan Africa*

# Being and Becoming

*Gender, Culture and Shifting Identity in Sub-Saharan Africa*

Edited by

**Chinyere Ukpokolo**

Spears Media Press
Denver • Bamenda
7830 W. Alameda Ave, Suite 103 Denver, CO 80226

Anembom Consulting Building, Cow Street, Bamenda
P O Box 1151, Bamenda, NWR, Cameroon

Spears Media Press publishes under the auspices of the Spears Media Association.

The Press furthers the Association's mission by advancing the frontiers of knowledge in education, learning, entertainment and research.

First Published in 2016 by Spears Media Press
www.spearsmedia.com
info@spearsmedia.com
Information on this title: www.spearsmedia.com/africagender



Ordering Information:
Special discounts are available on bulk purchases by corporations, associations, and others. For details, contact the publisher at any of the addresses above.

ISBN: 978-1-942876-07-6 [Paperback]

To
Those who fought for equity
That others may live in liberty.

# *Contents*

## LIST OF FIGURES



## LIST OF TABLES

# Preface

## *Being and Becoming: Gender, Culture and Shifting Identity in Sub-Saharan Africa*

Gender inequity continues to feature prominently in discussions of governance, human rights, education, economy, violence, and development issues globally. Nowhere is the inequity more pronounced than in Sub-Saharan Africa where proponents of the unequal *status quo* advance reasons based on biological determinism or culture to perpetuate the existing structures. Decision making in the private and public domains is still skewed in favour of one gender and power, consequently, resides with those who hold it.

This book, *Being and becoming: Gender, Culture and Shifting Identities in Sub- Saharan Africa,* is an invaluable collection of papers by scholars across the continent exploring the intersections of culture, ethnicity, economy, religion, politics, sexuality and gender in the region. Contributors approach the issues from different ideological and theoretical perspectives and use a variety of methodologies deriving from various disciplines - Philosophy, Anthropology, History, Literature, and Sociology. This diversity of approaches facilitates the emergence of fresh insights and enables readers to come to a better understanding of the complexity of issues involved in gender dynamics in sub-Saharan Africa.

The editor's effort in attracting contributions from scholars in different countries with knowledge of the workings of gender issues in their situations is commendable. The contributors underscore the fact that gender cannot be ignored in exploring how traditional social structures, a history of colonization, globalization, Western education and economic policies have shaped and continue to reshape gender identities.

This collection contains valuable and intellectually stimulating materials on contemporary issues in gender in the region and raises debates which other researchers can explore constructively.

*Abiola Odejide* FNAL
*Professor, Communication and Language Arts*
*University of Ibadan, Ibadan, Nigeria*

# *Introduction*

Scholarship on women and gender issues in Africa has moved from 'footnotes' to exploring gender as a veritable area of research. The question of women's place in society remains a subject matter of debates across human societies and cultures, and at different historical epochs. For centuries, discussions as to whether a woman is a human being just like man persisted in the Western world. Efforts were made at understanding the woman's body, and subsequently define her identity and seal her destiny. In fact, Aristotle, the great Greek philosopher, has, in what came to be perceived as his biological theories, summarized his postulation on the woman's body with the 'concept of heat' (Weltz, 1998), and argued that 'only embryos that had sufficient heat could develop into *fully human form* (italics, mine), the rest became female' (cf Weltz, 1998: 3). For Aristotle, therefore, the woman was a 'misbegotten man', a not fully formed, and, thus, half-baked; a second class human. Aristotle's postulation was taken as 'scientific' truth and subsequently influenced discussions on the woman in the Western world for centuries, particularly between the fourth century B.C and the eighteenth century A.D.

'Nature' debates that anchored women's subordinating condition in most cultures to biology was based on this postulation. For biological determinists, Ortner (1974) noted, there is something inherently lacking in women, which has naturally placed them in a subordinate position to men, and disposes them to be "in general quite satisfied with their position, since it affords them protection and the opportunity to maximize maternal pleasures, which to them are the most satisfying experiences of life" (Ortner, 1974: 71). Sigmund Freud's psychoanalytical theory is also founded on this premise that women's subordination is biologically based. Sigmund Freud, in his work, 'Some Psychical Consequences of the Anatomical Distinction Between the Sexes' (Freud, 1925) noted that the female, anatomically, represents an incomplete version of the male sex in her development and, therefore, her subordination is an unchallengeable law of Nature (Durley and Edwards, 1986). The concept of 'castrated male' gave credence to and reinforced the perception of the woman as a second-class human being in Western societies. This position was, of course, rejected by the cultural determinists, most of them feminists. Feminism, a modern movement and an ideology, questions the classical Aristotelian theory of imperfect female nature, and Freud's notion of women's subjective nature.

Agitations by the feminists further generated interests in issues on women as the question of women's rights took centre stage in public discourses and social thoughts. Increasingly, women activists demanded for women's rights and inclusion. Accordingly, Ruth Sheila (1980) noted that feminism:

> Seeks to overthrow class/caste system in existence, the class system based on sex – a system consolidated over thousands of years, lending archetypal male and female roles an undeserved legitimacy and seeming permanence (Sheila, 1980: 23).

The feminists, claiming to speak for women across cultures and societies, demanded for the liberation of women from the constricting socio-cultural space, a view which also gained currency in feminist writings. Jonathan Culler, quoting Dorothy Dinnerstein, observes that:

> What women want is to stop serving as scapegoats (their own scapegoats as well as men's and children's scapegoats) for human condition. They want this so painfully and so pervasively, and until quite recently, it was such a hopeless thing to want, they have not yet been able to say out loud that they want it (Dorothy Dinnerstein as cited in Culler, 1982: 53 -54).

From the standpoint of feminist movements, the world has not been fair to the female gender. History has been written by the men from men's point of view, and the woman, 'the Other', excluded. Feminism, therefore, demands for a re-writing of history. The spectrum of writings by feminist scholars increasingly responds to this by revisiting earlier studies on women's place in cultural practices (see for instance, Oyewunmi, 1997; Ukpokolo, 2011a, b; Jell-Bahlsen 2014 in this collection).

Feminism however was in some quarters viewed with suspicion. Afro-American and African women criticised white feminists' attempt to generalize on women's subordinate condition. And, for Oyewunmi (1997), the rejection of Western-oriented feminism is informed by its inseparable connection, to biology, or what she terms 'biologic'. Torn apart by identity crisis, it was not long before feminism began to suffer both implosion and explosion, leading to different strands and schools of thought in the feminist theorizing, such as radical feminism, socialist feminism, Marxist feminism, liberal feminism among others. For the African feminist scholars, feminism as a school of thought lacks both the epistemological and ideological frameworks that capture the experiences of the African woman, which are anchored on the African realities. Concepts such as 'womanism', afro-centricism', among others, became options for the African feminists. More importantly also, many African women activists and researchers are conscious of the fact that most structural imbalances that undermine women's space and visibility in contemporary African society are products of colonial incursion into the continent. Employing Western-oriented theoretical and epistemological instruments to investigate the diverse socio-cultural, political and economic underpinnings unfavourable to the African woman's survival challenges, certainly, cannot adequately capture their marginality. Besides, gender issues, being products of culture, are bound by time and space, and as products of culture, changes with time. As culture is dynamic, gender issues are equally dynamic.

Nevertheless, cross-cultural studies on women demonstrate that power asymmetry remains a major issue that women, across cultures and societies, grapple with, though at varying degrees. As Ortner (1974) noted:

> The actual treatment of women and their relative power and contribution vary enormously from culture to culture, and over different periods in the history of particular traditions (1974: 65).

While the universality of female subordination is, therefore, not in doubt, its manifestations and degree vary across cultures and societies. Ortner identified three major considerations as indications that women are undervalued in any society. These, according to her, are: (1) "elements of cultural ideology and informants' statements that explicitly devalue women, according to their roles, their tasks, their products, and their social milieux less prestige than are accorded men and the male correlates, (2) symbolic devices, such as the attribution of defilement, which may be interpreted as implicitly making a statement of inferior valuation, and (3) social-structural arrangements that exclude women from participation in or contact with some realm in which the highest powers of the society are felt to reside" (Ortner, 1974: 69). In other words, for Ortner, to determine if women are subordinated in a particular culture, the researcher should look out for first, "explicit cultural ideology devaluing women – tasks, roles, products etc.; second, symbolic indications such as defilement, and three, female exclusion from the most sacred rite or highest political council" (Ortner, 1974: 65).

Women and men's identities, oftentimes, are circumscribed around 'being', a state which, however, places the woman in a binary opposition to the man. Change is a process which can transform 'being' to 'becoming', and initiate a shift in cultural paradigms. Values and norms respond to change as cultural flows across national boundaries interface, and cultural 'negotiations' fast-tract cultural mix and increasingly interconnect peoples transnationally. In these negotiations, gender issues are inescapable. In recent years, for instance, official recognition or rejection of gay marriage and homosexuality in some societies across the globe, including discourses emanating from the rejection of it, a case of homophobia, have generated 'violent' academic discussions and political condemnations, depending on which part of the globe one is located. LGBTQ, which is an acronym for lesbian, gay, bisexual, transgender and queer (for those who doubt their sexual identity), for instance, represents part of those indices of cross-cultural contact, currents and globality.

This book, is a collection of papers, which takes diverse perspectives in looking at different gender issues in the African sub-region across time and space. While more attention seems to have been given to women, generally, the volume aims at providing in-depth and critical analyses on diverse gender issues in the African sub-region. In chapter one, Abosede Pricilla Ipadeola provides a philosophical perspective and argues that radical feminists hold that the justification for women's freedom from male subjugation lies in their difference. This, for radical feminists, means that women could not be said to be inferior to men because they are fundamentally different from men. She contends that, in their struggle to explain the basis of the difference between women and men as a reason for their contestations, feminists sometimes drift into employing biology as an explanation for such difference, a strategy which is grounded in essentialism, the philosophical idea that everything functions or appear as a copy of its essence. In recent times, many feminists have rejected essentialism as a veritable instrument of contestation for women's freedom from male domination and oppression. For such anti-essentialist feminists, essentialism could even be a formidable justification for treating women differently and dominating them, a turn which undermines the basis of uniting as feminists to fight for women's liberation. African feminists are especially affected by this as they contend against patriarchy from a postcolonial stance. Ipadeola's paper maintains that even if biology does not provide the needed basis for uniting as African women in search of a common identity, strategic essentialism of Gayatri Spivak could provide such a basis. As African women resist patriarchal domination, complicated by their colonial experience, strategic essentialism, she suggests, becomes invaluable.

In chapter two, Sabine Jell-Bahlsen presents a case study of gender in Igbo culture focusing on the female side in the *Owu* complex of myth and masking of the riverine Igbo. Jell-Bahlsen notes that *Owu* masked performances have been described as events where "women cannot participate" and are instead "verbally and physically assaulted". Her paper is a specific case study of particular events in specific locations and at specific times, attempting to illuminate, share and interpret her personal encounters as an 'outsider-insider'. The paper focuses on the female side of the micro-cosmos of timed masquerade festivals celebrating *Owu-Okoroshi* masquerade festivals in select communities in the Oguta area of the riverine Igbo, bringing out their deliberate ambiguities, including women's involvement as active participants.

Chapter three illuminates the diverse ways of foregrounding the woman's 'being' and identity in Muganda, Uganda. Elizabeth Kyazike argues that the socialisation processes of a Muganda woman focuses on preparing her for her roles in society as a mother and wife, and entails the use of the Kiganda traditional education system, which prepares women to accept the *status quo*, and promotes the gender division of labour in which women control the production sector and not the distribution. Despite colonial socio-economic policies like Western education and religion or political pressure, socialisation and construction of a Muganda woman identity continues, as the cultural aspects are rather becoming stronger and stronger. The chapter, therefore, highlights what makes the Baganda attach to their culture in the 21st century when people are embracing modernity, this is foregrounded in their socialisation.

In chapter four, Oluwakemi Abiodum Adesina in her paper titled, "The Violence of Silence and the Limits of Community: The Ikale Woman in the Twenty-first Century Nigeria", examines gender relations among the Ikale – a sub-group of the Yoruba people of south-western Nigeria. She contends that gender issues cannot be understood in isolation from the peculiar structures existing in a particular epoch and place. While recognising that British colonialism in Nigeria affected every facet of the Nigerian society, she contends that the strong patriarchal nature of the Ikale society dictated what areas of their traditions were affected. No matter how much modern mechanisms tried to initiate structural changes in the society, Adesina argues, they met resistance in the countervailing power exerted by Ikale culture. The work highlights the limitations placed by tradition on Ikale women and how that has created for them a construction of an identity expressed in the overwhelming belief that silence is the greatest and most vital virtue for them in the age of modernity.

Taking a historical perspective, Aisha Balarabe Bawa argues in chapter five in her paper, "Gender, Identity and Change: The Case of Muslim Women in Northern Nigeria" that although most scholars situate the oppression of women in many Muslim societies within the context of Islamic laws on female code of dressing, a lot of changes have occurred in the lives of Muslim women in northern Nigeria over time. She examines these changes, focusing on three historical epochs: Hausaland before the Jihad, after the Jihad, and post-independence. The paper maintains that Islamic injunctions on women's rights have been distorted by local traditions to favour men, and in some cases, local customs have been confused with Islamic law because of ignorance.

Women in Nanka rural community, in a bid to survive the economic hardship in the rural areas, are shifting cultural paradigms and in the process redefining their identity while reconstructing gender ideologies. Chinyere Ukpokolo, in her paper in chapter six titled, "Economic Survival, Masculinity and Shifting Cultural Definition of the Woman's Identity in a Rural Igbo Society", contends that the economic condition of contemporary African countries raises survival challenges on the masses of the people. Prevailing poverty in rural areas challenges rural households to devise means of augmenting family income. In Nanka community, Igbo southeast Nigeria, rural women, in an attempt to cope with the new reality, re-invent the long distance trading activities characteristic of Igbo women in pre-colonial times. The study examines the nature of the current long distance trading and the implications of the new development on the household income and familial relations in the rural areas in Igboland, paying attention also to how this development affects cultural construction of masculinity and the woman's identity in the society. Dependency on the woman for financial provisioning has affected familial relations, with enhanced political power for such women at the home front, without commensurate power shift at the public space. Men's inability to meet the financial needs of their families has implications on their perception of cultural construction of masculinity. For the women, the emerging reality leads to shifting cultural definition of the woman's identity in this rural Igbo community.

In chapter seven, Samuel Oluwole Ogundele takes a look at indigenous palm oil production in Orile-Owu, Southwest Nigeria, and the gender implications of division of labour in palm oil production. The paper notes 'a tangled web of relationships' characterising palm oil production among a segment of the Owu sub-ethnic group of the Yoruba. He notes that the phenomenon of palm oil production in Orile-Owu is a large capsule of sociality, materiality and/or spatiality. These complex but robust metaphors can only be properly decoded through the lenses of thorough going researches enshrined in archaeo-anthropological disciplinarity. Contrary to popular thinking, this human adaptation to the challenges posed by the local natural environment is not exclusively female-gendered. Men also play certain important roles in the production process of this dimension of the Owu gendered material and to a lesser extent, the social world.

Tapiwa Praise Mapuranga in chapter eight, looks at "Religion and the Participation of Women in Politics in Zimbabwe: Changing Identities and Perspectives" and argues that the position of women in African politics and religion depends on whether one is focusing on patrilineal or matrilineal context, and on which particular practice is being referred to. She rejects the categorisation of all African practices as oppressive and dominating to women and thereby inhibiting them from participation in politics. According to her, there are some liberative aspects to be found within these African customs and practices. Looking at the values of women in the political sphere in Zimbabwe, she argues that there have been a slow but increasing number of women politicians. However, in order to appreciate this changing significance of women, the study notes that women generally suffered due to an oppressive background borne out of certain patriarchal and colonial attitudes within selected societies, which in most cases are stumbling blocks to the participation of women in the public spheres such as the political space. The study nevertheless seeks to find the liberating dimension that has brought change to the lives of selected women in Zimbabwe using African Womanism theory, which draws the attention of women to rejecting the status of victim, considering themselves as victors and sisters in charge of their own destiny, with their primary obligation being to make progress in their cultural way of life through the stability of family and commitment to community.

In chapter nine, Walter Gam Nkwi in "Contesting the Margins of Modernity: New Women, Migration and Consumption in British Colonial Cameroon", critiques the historical narratives and meta-narratives that have in time and space credited men as those who first felt the impact of colonialism in Africa. He tries to divert from that teleological and linear way of seeing men more in the colonial enterprise, and explores the preponderant role of women as cultural brokers and agents of modernity in the migration process. The paper notes that women's social engagements in various colonial traps, which included, *inter alia*: formal education, Christianity, plantations, anti-colonialism, and consumerism articulated and re-articulated, refigured and re-configured the boundaries of belonging, identity and social stratum in their societies. He argues that women became modern as well as the menfolk and also became conduits through which modernity passed to enter their remote villages, making women also purveyors of modernity. Nkwi, using empirical evidence informed by rigorous interviews, life histories of the women and corroborated with archival data and other secondary materials, contends that whether pursuing colonial education, adopting new dressing codes or hairstyles or even as housemaids, women fractured the traditional *status quo ante* and contributed to making themselves the privileged few, widening their mental horizons and enjoying enhanced and new prestige in the sub-region and in the process taking on a new identity hitherto unknown. The chapter addresses the dynamics which have been responsible for the contestation of modernity, and contends that what men can do women too can do.

Kwame Edwin Otu in chapter ten contends that the deluge of LGBTQ human rights politics and the growing political homophobia in parts of sub-Saharan Africa continues to be under-theorised and under-historicized. In his paper, titled, "Saints and Sinners: Rereading J. F. Faupel's *African* Holocaust as a "Clandestine Countermemory" against LGBT Visibility Politics in Postcolonial Africa" he argues, "while in the past decades, scholars with a focus on sexuality and gender in Africa have produced insightful works that have pointed to the complexity of sexual and gender formations in Africa, some have also justifiably questioned the claim that homosexuality is un-African", and notes that studies have elaborately shown that the "idea that homosexuality was imported to Africa is the product of a particular historical moment". This of course he notes, constitutes the erasure of particular historical episodes not as an accident of history but, rather the result of the tactical politics deployed by both LGBTQ organizations and the nation-state in mediating the tides triggered by neoliberalism in Africa. Closely examining two historical incidents — one historical and the other more contemporary — he elucidates the manner in which the 'neoliberal and neocolonial collusion,' to use Patricia McFadden's (2011) apt formulation, hones the matrix in which LGBTQ and nationalist politics get articulated. Mention is made of the incident in pre-colonial Uganda at the turn of the twentieth century. Then known as Buganda - a kingdom that had an established political organization under the absolute rulership of the kabaka—the king—before the onset of missionisation and colonisation. Analysing J. F. Faupel's narrative titled *African Holocaust* (1962), which captures the execution of the royal pages and other converts to Christianity in precolonial Uganda, in conjunction with the attempt by the Ugandan Parliament in 2009 to enact the "kill the gays' bill," he further explores how sexual politics in postcolonial Africa recalibrates the very conditions of possibility that stifle sexual decolonisation in particular, and decolonisation in general.

In chapter eleven, Anwesha Das, rethinks the concerns deeply enmeshed in the histories of human civilisation, questioning the politics which comes to play at the moment of encounter between diverse cultures, between people with divergent perspectives from within the same culture. Focusing on the Nigerian writer Thomas Obinkaram Echewa's novel *I Saw the Sky Catch Fire*, this chapter unravels the voices of women — Nne-nne and Stella — from generations apart, highlighting the encounter between Igbo women and a Western woman anthropologist, and that between Stella and her husband. What happens when people with such disparate view-points meet each other? This chapter invites one to rethink such delicate moments of encounter, which shape and reshape identities.

In chapter twelve, Omotade Adegbindin in his paper, "Gender Advocacy in Africa: An Insight from *Ifá* Literary Corpus" argues that there is a need to make advocacy a human, rather than a woman agenda, and discourages any separatist agenda or radical feminist approach to resolving gender issues in Africa. The paper maintains that the Yoruba pre-colonial understanding of the relationship between men and women was informed by gender complementarity, as the culture articulated clear visions of gender relations that challenge the current promotion of the need to create 'a separate world for women'. He concludes that the issues confronting Africa, including the problems that the African woman faces, require the efforts of both genders.

Finally, it is hoped that the diverse dimensions which the authors whose works are presented in this volume examined gender issues in Sub-Saharan Africa will robustly engage the reader to reconsider various forms and shades culture has interpreted, shaped and defined and redefined the African woman and man's identities and in the process shift or resist the shifting of paradigms and gender identity. While acknowledging the dynamics of history whether in terms of colonial encounter, globalization or intragroup interactions, gender, culture and identity in the Sub-Saharan Africa are, indeed, caught in between two paradigms – 'being' and 'becoming'.

## *References*

Bannon, I. Correia, M. C. 2006. Introduction. In: Bannon, Ian and Maria C. Correia (Eds.). *Men's Issues in Development: The Other*

*Half of Gender*. Washington DC.: World Bank. 219 – 244.

Culler, J. 1982. *Reading as a WOMAN: On Deconstruction: Theory and Criticism after Structuralism*. New York: Cornel UP. 53 – 60.

Durley, M. I. and Edwards, M. I.1986. 'Biology and Culture'. In: Durley, M. I. and Mary I. Edwards. *The Cross-cultural Study of Women*. New York: The Feminist Press at the University of New York. 3 – 25.

Freud, S. 1925. 'Some Psychical Consequences of the Anatomical Distinction between the Sexes'. In. Strouse, J. (ed.) *Women Analysis*. New York: Grossman. 25 - 37.

Ortner, S. B. 1974. 'Is Female to Male as Nature to Culture?' In: *Woman, Culture & Society*.

Rosaldo, Michelle Z. and Louise Lamphere (Eds.). Stanford: Stanford University Press. 67 – 88.

Oyewunmi, O. 1997. *The Invention of Women: Making an African Sense of Western Gender Discourses*. Minnesota: Minnesota University Press.

Sheila, R. 1980. *Issues in Feminism: A First Course in Women's Studies*. Boston: Houghton Mifflin Company.

Weltz, R.1998. 'A History of Women's Bodies'. In. Weitz, Rose (ed.) The Politics of Women's Bodies: Sexuality, Appearance, and Behaviour. New York: Oxford University Press. 3-11.

# Chapter One

## WHAT'S WRONG WITH ESSENTIALISM ANYWAY? AFRICAN WOMEN AND THE QUESTION OF IDENTITY

*Abosede Priscilla Ipadeola*

> Feminisms return to the problem of essentialism — despite their shared distaste for the mystifications of Woman — because it remains difficult to engage in feminist analysis and politics if not as a "woman" (Spivak, 1993:2)

### *Introduction*

Social identity is a crucial idea for the emancipation of African women from male domination and post-colonial enslavement. In the words of Hannum, social identity refers to "our way of thinking about ourselves and others based on social groupings. Social identity comprises the parts of a person's identity that come from belonging to a particular group" (Hannum, 2011: 3). In order for African women to resist patriarchal domination in Africa, as well as other peoples in some other places, there has to be a common or shared identity.

Questions regarding the definition of the 'woman' are at the heart of feminist theory. This is because, however anyone tries to define feminism, such a definition would be grossly inadequate if it leaves out the 'idea of woman'. Principally, feminists have, over the years, tried to address certain questions among which are:

> Are there certain attributes which characterise women? How are women similar to and different from men? What is significant about such similarities and differences? Are women's differences from men rooted in biology, or are they socially constructed? (Weisberg, 1993: 335).

The questions raised above are of extreme importance to the project of feminism, and how they are answered goes a long way in either strengthening or undermining the agitations of feminists with regard to women's emancipation, especially African women, from patriarchal domination. However, the task of defining the woman is a very difficult one; and the task of defining African woman is by no means an easier one too. Defining the African woman necessarily presupposes answering the questions: 'Who is a woman?' and 'Who is African?' To answer these questions, a possible response would be similar to that given in response to the question of who African feminists are. The response merely states that:

> We are African women – we live here in Africa and even when we live elsewhere, our focus is on the lives of African women on the continent. Our feminist identity is not qualified with "Ifs," "Buts," or "However." We are feminists Full stop (McGlotten and Davis, 2012: 189).

Nevertheless, the response above, or any similar response, may not suffice in defining who African women are and on what basis (or bases) they can come together to fight against gender molestation, subjugation and domination in this postcolonial era in Africa. The reason for this ambivalence is that 'to engage the construction of identity necessarily means encountering essentialism.' (Quashie, 2004: 2) Hence, African women's search for a common identity necessarily puts them at a standpoint where they are confronted with the challenge of essentialism. In order for us to answer the questions raised above, which are very central to the main concerns of this paper, the claims and flaws of essentialism as a philosophical and feminist idea would be considered with a view to adopting a version of essentialism that is considered invaluable in realising the identity needed by African women to fight marginalisation on the continent.

### *Women's Oppression, Marginalisation and Subjugation on the Continent*

Women have been viewed as the inferior sex in many parts of the world for a very long time. However, when marginalisation is considered in relation to African women, it assumes a sizable magnitude. In most parts of Africa, especially within families, family compounds and communities, preference for male children over and above female children is common. Right from childhood, it is made known to a girl that boys in the family are superior to her and are more useful in carrying on the name and chieftaincy titles of the family. For instance, Curry observes that:

> Women's subjugation begins at birth and is carried on throughout childhood, making girls feel like they are inferior beings. Perhaps the most compelling element in contemporary African female literature is the influence of proverbs as methods of initiation and instruction within the context of the authors' countries, specifically Nigeria and Senegal (Curry, 2004: 19).

Apart from patriarchy that keeps women under in the family, African women are also usually confronted with the reality of hegemony instituted by colonialism and globalisation, which further entrench gender inequality, oppression and subjugation of women in the larger society. Hence, marginalisation of women on the continent of Africa is as a result of different experiences before and after independence for most of the African countries. Taking the women of South Africa as example, Mabandla contends that:

> The life experiences of the majority of Black women in South Africa starkly show that, for them, oppression rests on the intersection of race and class with gender. As in most countries, Southern African society is patriarchal. Religious and traditional norms relegate women to an inferior position in both society and family. Institutionalized racism exacerbates the oppression of Black women by further encroaching upon their rights. Thus, the historic denial of civil and political rights to Black people, coupled with the historic oppression of women as a gender and as a class, has meant that Black women occupy the lowest rung of the social ladder (Mabandla, 1995: 67).

In essence, African feminists are mostly of the view that oppression, subjugation and marginalisation of women on the continent are not only consequences of tradition but also of the history of colonialist domination, which most of the countries in Africa have had, as well as the fact that most of the countries are still third world countries, characterised by unstable economic and political conditions. Hence, women's oppression is a hydra-headed monster. This is because "the reality of African women's oppression is criss-crossed by factors such as culture, nationalism, religion, globalization, colonialism and race" (Kelly, 2008: 111).

However, in these contemporary times, it is very essential for African women to come together to resist oppression, subjugation, marginalisation and every form of domination. This is very imperative in order for them to engender an egalitarian and equitable social order that can enhance their development as well as the development of their respective countries. It is important to stress the fact that unless African women come together to do the resistance, there is no other means of putting oppression, domination, marginalisation and subjugation behind them and generations of girls and women to come. Kolawole corroborates this by maintaining that: "The emphasis on women's *problems* also derives from the assumption that African women's refusal to speak loudly about oppression and inequality is an acceptance of marginality and minimalization." (Kolawole, 2004: 251) In order to "speak out loudly", therefore, African women must unite as this will give strength to their weak lone voices.

### *On the Idea of Essentialism*

Essentialism as a metaphysical idea has its origin in the ontology of the ancient philosopher, Plato. Plato, while addressing the problem of appearance and reality, argues that the individual entities and phenomena that we encounter in our everyday experiences are mere copies of real entities, and that these particular entities do not constitute realities themselves. As a matter of fact:

> Central to Plato's philosophy ... was his theory of Forms. This theory entailed a "two-world" cosmology. One world is our everyday world of change and impermanence. The other is an ideal world populated by ideal

> "Forms." The first, the "world of becoming," was in flux, as Heraclitus insisted, but the latter, the "world of Being," was eternal and unchanging, as Parmenides demanded (Solomon and Higgins, 1997: 37).

On the question of what the entities are, Plato claims that the entities that we come across everyday (including humans) are only appearances of the essences – that is, real entities – in the world of Forms. Furthermore, apart from using his theory of forms to distinguish between appearance and reality, Plato also uses it to differentiate particular entities from universal ideas. In the renowned dialogue of Plato's, *The Republic,* while differentiating a particular bed from the idea of bed, Plato says:

> And what of the maker of the bed? Were you not saying that he too makes, not the idea which, according to our view, is the essence of the bed, but only a particular bed? ... Then if he does not make that which exists he cannot make true existence, but only some semblance of existence; and if anyone were to say that the work of the maker of the bed, or of any other workman, has real existence, he could hardly be supposed to be speaking the truth (Plato, 360 BC: 459).

Underlying the idea of essences in Plato is the notion of participation. (Mensch, 1996: 18) In other words, Plato opines that the individual entities in this sensible world are related to the essences in the world of forms by way of participation. Hence, an individual woman in this world of appearance participates in the nature of the perfect, universal, timeless and immutable woman – or the idea of womanness – in the world of forms. According to Karl Popper, the idea of essence in Plato could be appropriately referred to as methodological essentialism. In Popper's own words:

> I use the name methodological essentialism to characterize the view, held by Plato and many of his followers, that it is the task of pure knowledge or "science" to discover and to describe the true nature of things i.e., their hidden reality or essence. It was Plato's peculiar belief that the essence of sensible things can be found in other and more real things – in their primogenitors or Forms. (Popper, 1995: 29)

It is important to note that Plato's dichotomy of entities into 'essence' and 'existence' pitiably implies a hierarchical arrangement or structure in nature. On the hierarchy, one entity, essence, which is in the world of Forms, is described as being superior to the other entity, appearance, in the known world. The shadow of Plato's dichotomy has since been haunting any and every formulations of methodological essentialism.

Also, apart from the methodological essentialism of Plato, there is a form of essentialism which has become very popular in gender discourse. This form of essentialism is known as 'biological essentialism.' Biological essentialism refers to 'a specific form of essentialism that conveys the idea that the essence of a person is rooted in their biology; that is, that their personality and characteristics are caused by something internal to the body (such as hormones or genes).' (Birke, 2002: 67) In their attempt to explain the basis of the differences between men and women, some feminists have employed essentialism as a viable explanation. For the essentialist feminists, women are fundamentally different from men and the difference is rooted in biology.

This line of argument was popularised in the second wave of feminism. In the first wave of feminism, equality between men and women was defined as sameness. It was argued that there were basically no differences between men and women, and so there was no basis for treating them differently or for one group to be dominating the other. However, when the renowned second wave feminist, Carol Gilligan published her pivotal feminist treatise, *In a Different Voice*, in 1982, the need to re-examine the concept of sameness and difference became popular in gender discourses. As a psychologist and researcher into the nature of morality, Gilligan embarked on finding out whether morality signifies the same thing for men as it does for women. She employed children as her subjects in a bid to encounter 'the natural woman and man' before being affected by conventional and societal influences. After probing to know how they would give moral judgments about certain issues, Gilligan noted that:

> It becomes clear why a morality of rights and non-interference may appear frightening to women in its potential justification of indifference and unconcern. At the same time, it becomes clear why from a male perspective, a morality of responsibility appears inconclusive and diffuse, given its

> insistence contextual relativism. Women's moral judgments thus elucidate the pattern observed in the description of the developmental differences between the sexes, but they also provide an alternative conception of maturity by which these differences can be assessed and their implications traced. ... Given the differences in women's conceptions of self and morality, women bring to the life cycle a different point of view and order human experience in terms of different priorities (Gilligan, 1982: 22).

Gilligan further notes that 'while the subject of moral development provides the final illustration of the reiterative pattern in the observation and assessment of sex differences in the literature on human development, it also indicates more particularly why the nature and significance of women's development has for so long been obscured and considered shrouded in mystery.' (Gilligan, 1987: 67-68) These observations – or better put, discoveries – of Gilligan were soon taken from the level of perception and judgment to a level as fundamental as nature. Hence, the idea that it is natural or essential for women to display care, love, concern and a spirit of self-sacrifice became popular in feminism. Men and women are deemed to be different, not only in terms of biological traits, but also in some other respects, which are even considered to be more fundamental than physical traits. For example, it is held that men and women are different with regard to psychological, emotional and social characteristics.

The issue of essentialism has, as a result of the beliefs stated above, become very controversial. This is because societies have held for centuries that women are fundamentally different from men. And men have been treating women differently in accordance with this belief. Therefore, feminists in the first wave held that their liberation as women lied in establishing that there is basically no difference between the two sexes. Meanwhile, when the different feminists sought to argue that there are actually certain fundamental differences between men and women and that such differences are essential, then essentialism fell into disrepute. As analysed in the subsequent section, right from the time of Plato, essentialism has been severely criticised. This is because, if Plato had only used essentialism to explain how we come to have a general or universal idea of bed or woman, or any other thing for that matter, in spite of the individual beds and women of our everyday experience, his idea would have been less problematic. Plato, however, complicated his idea by introducing essence as that which necessarily exists. Essence, in Plato's sense, is 'the belief in a single metaphysical nature that causally determines the identity and characteristics of a specific group of entities.' (Keltner, 2006: 188) The idea of essence, therefore, which is also commonly taken to be the basis of the difference(s) between men and women, is the crux of the objections raised against the different feminists, who mostly employ essentialism in pressing home their contentions for the liberation of the female gender from subjugation, oppression and marginalisation. For the radical and socialist feminists, there is an idea or essence of a woman that makes women different from men. For them, "woman" has a particular essence which defines woman as woman (Barnett, 1998: 158).

### *Critiques of Essentialism*

Plato's essentialism was quickly refuted by his contemporary and disciple, Aristotle. For Aristotle, to hold that the essences of individual entities exist on their own, either in the world of forms, or wherever for that matter, is to particularise or individuate the universal, which is self-contradictory. In other words, although Aristotle also agrees that there are essences or universals, yet his opinion is that they are found in individual entities in this known world.

Over time, essentialism has been popularly known as 'the idea that any specific group of objects or people (e.g a race, gender or class) is marked, identified, and defined by pure, immutable, and historical characteristics and essences that inhere in the specific group.' (Prasad, 2003: 25) Therefore, Nhanenge observes that, essentialism involves the idea that subjectivities have some similar universal and/or intrinsic commonalities, which brings about the danger of segregation (Nhanenge, 2011: 159). Going by Nhanenge's observation, it is not surprising that essentialism has been treated with so much suspicion and has been repeatedly criticised by some feminists. In fact, 'a number of writers currently are shifting the focus of feminist theory from the sameness-difference debate. They are part of a movement attacking essentialism in feminism' (Weisberg, 1993: 335). For instance, one very important point against biological essentialism is that raised by Dave Elder-Vass. In his idea, one serious implication of biological essentialism, in relation to females and males, is that it assumes that 'things fall *unambiguously* into kinds, that the members of those kinds are all the same, and therefore the members of those kinds are unchanging' (Elder-Vass, 2012: 124) However, if, as biological essentialism claims, people's personal and social identity are rooted in certain *unchanging* biological traits, then what happens when a transgendered person undergoes surgery to change his or her sex organs? In this instance, is such a person considered to be the same person or is the person considered a different person other than who he or she used to be? This, definitely, could not be answered by merely saying 'no' rather carelessly by a biological essentialist. This is because, for such a person, things like memory, beliefs and views about people and phenomena are likely going to remain unchanged.

In feminism, 'essentialism constitutes the view that all women are alike, sharing a common "essence" or certain "essential" traits that differentiate them from men (Weisberg, 1993: 335). Social constructionist feminists have seen essentialism as 'the idea of an irreducible immutable, metaphysical essence defining "woman"' (Fuss, 1989: 39). They, as a result, reject the idea of an essence of womanness. This is because, according to the feminist critics of essentialism, the idea serves to foreclose the discussion of women's specificity (Heyes, 2000: 51). On the other hand, essentialism has also been criticized for being politically exclusive and insensitive to power differences among women (Heyes, 2000: 51). Hence, some feminists, especially the third wave feminists, reject essentialism because of its alleged oppressive tendencies. For instance, some women have criticised certain feminists of foisting their ideals on other women. These groups of women include the black feminists and the lesbian feminists.

Finally, another important criticism of biological essentialism, according to Ellen Armour, is that it has the tendency to 'support biological reductionism' (Armour, 1999: 19). In all, it is doubtful whether biological essentialism has any hope of benefitting feminists' struggles for women's emancipation. Nevertheless, even if it indeed has any benefit, however little, it is rather unambiguously clear that its inherent threat to the liberty of women is greater than its benefits.

### *African Women and the Question of Identity*

For the African women to be free from male domination and segregation, they have to know who they are, and persons who are not African women ought to also know who the African women are. As said earlier, the question 'Who are African women?' is not as easy to answer as it seems. It is not easy to draw a clear-cut demarcation between African women and women of other climes without falling into the error and myopia of biological essentialism. Defining African women could be done along certain lines, each, however, inevitably has its limitations. For example, it is possible to see African women as a gender group with people who speak the same language. This means, in essence, that language would be the basis of identity among African women. This view, of course, is very problematic because Africa is known to be a multi-lingual continent. As a matter of fact, Doh points out that:

> Africa has over 1000 languages that are local to the continent, before those of the former colonialists that are also in use. … Some African languages that are well known out of the continent are Kiswahili, Hausa, Yoruba and Lingala. Within some African countries, there are hundreds of languages and dialects (Doh, 2009: 122).

There are as many languages as there are peoples in Africa. Therefore, using language as the denominator for who African women are fails from the outset, since there is no one language spoken by all African women. An attempt to identify with any particular language on the continent would be replicating what the colonialists did a few years ago when they superimposed their languages on the African peoples and many Africans, as a result, lost touch with their roots and history, and their sense of self-awareness.

Using location as a basis for identity would not do either. In other words, the idea that African women are women on the continent of Africa is also not totally inclusive of who African women are. This is because, apart from the fact that such definition takes the question of who a woman is for granted, it is also insensitive to the fact that a lot of African women are in the diaspora and this does not mean that they are not African women. The last definition of African women which would be considered, and which is considered very important in an analysis of who African women are, is that which views African women as the female descendants or wives of the male descendants of the people who were enslaved and colonised by the

West on the continent of Africa. Even the last definition is not adequate because slavery and colonialism were not experiences peculiar to Africans alone. If colonialism is employed as a basis of identity, all it could engender is a victim mentality, making one wallow in self-pity without showing the way out of one's predicament. In fact, none of the definitions stated above is adequate in defining African women. The reason for this is not far-fetched – each one of the definitions depict the African woman as a status which is conferred or which one merely inherits, with or without doing anything. A definition of African women which would work must rather see the term as an active concept and not a passive one. This is the difference between being and existing. An African woman without activity cannot be said to exist – she is just like the other lower animals and non-living things on the continent. To exist, however, is to exert active influence on one's society and environment. This clearly shows a significant failure of the methodological essentialism of Plato and the biological essentialism of radical feminism. Strategic essentialism is, however, viewed as a viable and active basis of identity among African women.

### *Gayatri Spivak's Strategic Essentialism*

Over the years in the history of gender and racial studies, the issue of essentialism has been very controversial. The disrepute that the notion of essentialism has been brought into currently makes many theorists avoid it like a plague. For instance, Marilyn Porter, who did an extensive work on maternal feminism, explains that rather than grounding the justification for maternal qualities that women share in some biological essence, she would rather ground them in experience – that  the experience of mothering. Meanwhile, in the light of the various criticisms levelled against essentialism, this chapter adopts the strategic essentialism of Gayatri Spivak, and so we contend that, in the light of strategic essentialism, essentialism does not always connote a negative concept. In other words, this paper considers Spivak's strategic essentialism important in African women's search for a common identity.

Spivak's theory of strategic essentialism explores the ways in which gendered subjectivity can be mobilised as part of political strategy (Morton, 2007: 126). In other words, if biology is not a logical basis of uniting to pursue a common cause in feminism, strategic essentialism is found a viable denominator in addressing the problem of the basis of African women uniting against oppression and domination. The idea of strategic essentialism accepts that essentialist categories should be criticised, but emphasises that one cannot avoid using such categories at times in order to make sense of the social and political world (Morton, 2003: 75). Spivak, therefore, recommends using the categories, which are instruments of oppression in the hand of the powerful, as a tool to be adopted by the oppressed, the minority and the marginalised in attaining their liberation. Hence, for feminists, 'Spivak suggests that "independent" definitions of woman always risks falling prey to the binary oppositions that perpetuate women's subordination in culture and society' (Morton, 2003: 74).

Spivak's strategic essentialism, though a form of essentialism, is opposed to the absolutism of the methodological essentialism of Plato and the biological essentialism of certain radical feminists. Strategic essentialism takes care of the formidable criticisms of essentialism as put forward by existentialism in philosophy. This is because strategic essentialism does not trivialise the idea of the existential condition of an individual woman. Strategic essentialism involves voluntary collaboration among women – African women – to repudiate oppression and domination. This, of course, is different from the view of biological essentialism which put women in the same category by some accident of birth or being. In other words, strategic essentialism succeeds where biological essentialism fails. One of the most serious problems of biological essentialism is that it leads to biological determinism, the idea that an entity or individual *cannot but* behave in a particular way because of certain inherent biological traits which determine the individual's perception and way of life. However, when confronted with exceptions, the whole idea of biological determinism collapses, and with it, biological essentialism which has employed it as an explanatory model. Meanwhile, strategic essentialism is not affected by the problem of biological determinism because it does not assume that there are essential or unalterable traits that all women possess or which any group of women possesses.

Strategic essentialism also takes care of the objection of existentialism in that it does not stampede the will of individual women. Put differently, existentialists object to the abstraction of humanity by essentialism. Abstraction of humanity de-emphasises the importance of the individual person's choices and actions. Persons are thereby passive as they are held, either to be determined by certain biological traits or are mere appearances, whose existence and individuality are merely secondary, or even inferior in comparison to their essence – that is, humanity. Since strategic essentialism requires that women unite to fight marginalisation, each individual woman has to be active as she decides or chooses to be part of the movement for emancipation and as she is active in realising the objectives of the movement. In line with Spivak's idea, therefore, strategic essentialism grounds the notion of identity among African women – hence, it is a tool for agency and liberation. Although, strategic essentialism still employs categories erstwhile employed by the dominant, oppressive and hegemonic group (patriarchy) namely, female, male, masculinity, femininity, African women and so forth, those categories are used against patriarchy and colonialism to affirm African women's agency and freedom.

## *Conclusion*

In conclusion, a problem never disappears just because it is ignored. Rather, decisive steps have to be taken if African women would overcome the problem of oppression, marginalisation, segregation and subjugation of women on the continent. A way of achieving this is by their coming together to fight against domination and oppression. In line with strategic essentialism, women need to come to the realisation that it is in their general and individual interest to unite in their fight against marginalisation. Women must speak out against all forms of gender molestation and domination. The fear of being called essentialists should not shut women up. Marginalisation, domination, segregation, oppression and domination by the patriarchal structure of many African societies are real. Therefore, attempts at putting the problem in check should also be strong, resolute and well co-ordinated.

## *References*

Anshuman, P. 2003. The Gaze of the Other: Postcolonial Theory and Organizational Analysis. In: *Postcolonial Theory and Organizational Analysis: A Critical Engagement*. Anshuman, P.

(Ed.). New York: Palgrave Macmillan. 3 - 46.

Armour, E. T. 1999. *Deconstruction, Feminist Theology and the Problem of Difference: Subverting the Race/Gender Divide*. Chicago: University of Chicago Press.

Birke, L. 2002. *Biological Essentialism*. In: *Encyclopedia of Feminist Theories*. Loraine, C. (Ed.). London: Routledge. 67-68.

Curry, G. 2004. *Awakening African Women: The Dynamics of Change*. Buckinghamshire: Cambridge Scholars Press.

Doh, E. F. 2009. *Stereotyping Africa: Surprising Answers to Surprising Questions*. Bamenda: Langaa Research and Publishing Common Initiative Group.

Elder-Vass, D. 2012. *The Reality of Social Construction*. Cambridge: Cambridge University Press. Fuss, D. 1989. *Essentially Speaking: Feminism, Nature and Difference*. New York: Routledge.

Gilligan, C. 1982. *In a Different Voice*. Massachusetts: Harvard University Press.

Gilligan, C. 1987. *Woman's Place in Man's Life Cycle*. In: *Feminism and Methodology*. Sandra, H. (Ed.). Indiana: Indiana University Press. 57-73.

Hannum, K. M. 2011. *Social Identity: Knowing Yourself, Leading Others*. New Jersey: John Wiley & Sons.

Heyes, C. J. 2000. *Line Drawings: Defining Women through Feminist Practice*. New York: Cornell University Press.

Kelly, C. 2008. White Men: An Exploration of Intersections of Masculinity, Whiteness and Colonialism and the Engagement of Counter-Hegemonic Projects. In: *Masculinities in Contemporary Africa*. Egodi, U. (Ed.). Dakar: CODESRIA. 110 – 132.

Kolawole, M. 2004. Re-Conceptualizing African Gender Theory: Feminism, Womanism and the Arere Metaphor. In: *Rethinking Sexualities in Africa*. Signe, A. (Ed). Uppsala: Nordiska Afrikainstitutet. 251 - 268.

Mabandla, B. 1995. Women in South Africa and the Constitution-Making Process. In: *Women's Rights, Human Right: International Feminist Perspectives*. Julie, P. and Andrea, W. (Eds.). London: Rouledge. 67-77.

Mensch, J. R. 1996. *After Modernity: Husserlian Reflections on a Philosophical Tradition*. Albany: State University of New York Press.

Morton, S. 2003. *Gayatri Chakravorty Spivak*. London: Routledge.
Morton, S. 2007. *Gayatri Spivak: Ethics, Subalternity and the Critique of Postcolonial Reason*. Malden: Polity Press.
Nhanenge, J. 2011. *Ecofeminism: Towards Integrating the Concerns of Women, Poor People, and Nature into Development*. Maryland: University Press of America, Inc.
Plato, 360 B.C. The Republic. Benjamin, J. trans. Available online at: http://classics.mit.edu//Plato/republic.html
Popper, K. R.1995. *The Open Society and Its Enemies: The Spell of Plato*. New York: Routledge.
Quashie, K. E. 2004. *Black Women, Identity, and Cultural Theory: (Un) Becoming the Subject*. New Jersey: Rutgers University Press.
Solomon, R. C. and Kathleen M. H. 1997. *A Passion for Wisdom: A Very Brief History of Philosophy*. Oxford: Oxford University Press.
Spivak, G. C. 1993. *Outside in the Teaching Machine*. New York: Routledge.
Weisberg, D K. 1993. *Feminist Legal Theory: Foundations*. Philadelphia: Temple University Press.

# Chapter Two

## GENDER IN OWU, A TIMED MASQUERADE FESTIVAL OF THE RIVERINE IGBO, SOUTHEAST NIGERIA

*Sabine Jell-Bahlsen*

### *Introduction*

This chapter presents a case study of gender in Igbo culture focusing on the female side in the *Owu* complex of myth and masking of the Riverine Igbo. Few scholars have examined women's participation in Igbo masquerades with the exception of Chinyere Okafor (2009) and Carol Lorenz (1989). While some portray the participation of women in Igbo culture generally as complementary to male activities (Nnaemeka 2003, Ezeigbo 1997, Ottenberg 1982, Jell-Bahlsen 1994, Ukpokolo 2011), others have interpreted masquerades solely as a vehicle for defining customary ideals of womanhood and relegating women to a subordinate place in society (Brink 1990: 271, cited by Okafor 2009).

*Owu* masked performances have been described as events where "women cannot participate" and are instead "verbally and physically assaulted" even though they are held in "a certain disdainful awe and are much respected" (Cole and Aniakor 1984: 187). Masquerades are spiritually motivated theatrical performances (Okafor 2009, Achebe 1984) that entertain, but are also important agents of education and social integration (Lawal 1996, Azogu 1997). The masquerade is the Igbo people's most prolific art form and largely deemed an exclusively male dominated activity (Okafor 2009: 308).

Adolescent male initiation was traditionally compulsory and a major component of Igbo masking. Its symbolism has largely been described as phallic and misogynist (Ottenberg 1989). However, in his seminal work, "Igbo Initiation: Phallus or Umbilicus?" linguist Victor Manfredi offers a philological critique of Ottenberg and exposes the common prevalence of Freudian presuppositions in ethnographic symbolic descriptions (Manfredi 1997). He counters "Ottenberg's claim that initiation involves Oedipal aggression against the mother" by citing the ritual context of birth and reincarnation as its "ideological context" (Manfredi 1997:182, 183). Manfredi emphasizes the importance of reincarnation in Igbo cosmology as expressed in initiation, and following Meillasoux (1981) designed to create equilibrium between the living and the dead. "From the complementary generational perspective, the same idea is found in a proverb cited by Ifemesia (1979: 97) *Ónye a mùlu amú jì úgwo òmumu* ('Someone who was procreated owes a debt of procreation'). In addition, assuming the ambiguity of *òmumu* ..., this last word of the translation of this proverb is alternatively 'initiation'" (Manfredi 1997: 189). Hence, Manfredi's "umbilical reanalysis of Ottenbergs's material" (185) on initiation and by extension the symbolism inherent in Igbo masquerades.

There are very few known incidents of female masking traditions among the Igbo, for instance, at Izzi (Okafor 1994, 2009) and Nsukka (Okafor 2009). A few male Igbo scholars would even go as far as claiming that "women are forbidden to see the masquerade," and as "gender-outsiders are even prohibited from researching Igbo masquerades" (Okafor 2009: 309-310).[1] Igbo masquerades are commonly based in men's secret societies, "women must not see the nakedness of a mask" (Achebe 2011), the institution of masking differentiates men from women (Onyeneke 1987) and moreover "regular men from full men" (Achebe 2011: 25). Yet, the unilateral identification of maleness and masking may be overtly simplified. Various male and female titles as well as varying levels and pretensions of secrecy are attributes of masking and furthermore, female audiences complement male masquerade performances. Gender and sex are not necessarily identical in Igbo society (Amadiume 1987, Achebe 2011). Yet the staging

---

[1] Okafor reports on an individual scholar's reaction to her research on women and masking at the University of Nigeria at Nsukka in 1985 (Okafor 2009: 302-310); a similar experience was shared by this author at the ISA meeting at Howard University in 2011.

of a masquerade by the female king, Ahebi Ugbabe, was a catalyst for her demise (Achebe 2011). Despite these paradoxes, multiple and ambivalent connections between women and masking, Chinyere Okafor holds that "female power (is) a cornerstone or central subject in Igbo mask performance" (Okafor 2009).

Okafor situates her examination of women's position in Igbo traditions within the wider discourse on Igbo women describing women's disempowerment, assertiveness, complementarity, and entitlements surpassing those of their Western sisters (Okafor 2009:307). While acknowledging the heterogeneity of Igbo traditions and the multiplicity, transitions and transformations of gender structures therein, Okafor illuminates " how female power works in a male-centered cultural activity like masking" and discusses "Women's Non/Involvement and omumu theory of begetting, Mother-figures and creative mothering, women and mask characterization, women audiences and masking illusions" (Okafor 2009: 319). Okafor's work is based on findings from her own ethnic insider field research in a wide range of Northern and Southern Igbo communities, as well as on comparative data from other ethnic groups such as the Yoruba, Senufo, Chokwe, Bini, Kalabari, Kpelle Bamana, and Poro people.

In contrast to a generalized discussion on the meta-level, the current chapter is a specific case study of particular events in specific locations and at specific times. I attempt to illuminate, share and interpret my personal encounters of an in-outsider, potentially corroborating Okafor and Manfredi. I am focusing on the female side of the micro-cosmos of timed masquerade festivals celebrating *Owu* in select communities in the Oguta area of the Riverine Igbo, examining these enigmatic phenomena and their apparent and deliberate ambiguities along the following lines: 1) the original *Owu* myth, 2) the *Agugu* festival and performance of balance 3) male and female titles 4) levels of learning and degrees of secrecy, 5) performance and manifestation of *Owu*, 6) agency, themes, messages and performances in *Owu-Okoroshi* masquerade festivals over time.

Based on my long-term field research experiences in the Oguta area 1978-2009, three cultural elements stand out: 1) the supreme importance ascribed to life and pro-creation; thus the equations of children with wealth, as expressed in Igbo birth songs (Chukwuma 1994) and in the name, *Kego* "Child is better than money," 2) the adoration of motherhood, as expressed in the name, *Nneka* "Mother is supreme," and 3) the ideal of balance, as expressed in the perceived need to strive for harmony, social and especially gender equilibrium, as expressed in many Igbo proverbs and symbols (Ilogu 1974; Nnaemeka 1998, 2003; Ukpokolo 2011). Mutual respect and collaboration between husband and wife was expected and perceived as a pre-requisite for a productive life. This is expressed in proverbs such as, "*Di na nwunye di nizu ofu ibe ji ezuelu ha ugani*", translated as: "when husband and wife are in accord, a slice of yam can last them for the months of scarcity, "*Aka nri kwoo aka ekpe, aka ekpe akwoo aka iri, ha abuo adi ocha*", translated as: "When the right hand washes the left one, and the left one washes the right one, the two will be clean;" or in names such as *Ibuadinma*, translated as: "togetherness ensures the good" (Ilogu 1974: 138); or in "*Ihe kwuru, ihe akwudebe ya*", translated as "when something stands, something else stands beside it" (Nnaemeka 1998); and *Ihe Uwa wu oke na nne* translated as "the things of the world have male and female sides; natural things are 'complementary binaries'"(Osuagwu 2012).

### *The Agugu Festival of Owu and its Complementary Performances*

Herbert Cole and Chike Aniakor have described *Owu* as "a major masking tradition of the Igbo." (Cole and Aniakor 1984). But *Owu* is also much more. The theatrical masquerade spectacle involves a wide range of visual, verbal, acoustic and kinesthetic artistic components; the performances are spiritually motivated, take place at very specific dates, and involve teaching, learning and entertainment.

In the Oru-Igbo towns of the Oguta area, *Owu* is performed during *Agugu,* a timed festival[2] in January-February around the New Year's first full moon cycle. The timing of the year is attributed to *Owu* (Cole and Aniakor 1984). At Oguta, the festival marks the beginning of the new farming season and the initiation of boys into the society of men. Different sections of the men's *Owu* society perform in secret and in public. Their activities are complemented by women's extremely secret rites and public activities.

---

[2] Oguta's usage of *Agugu* apparently differs from the Onitsha dialect where *agugu* generically translates as "festival". Williamson, Kay. *Igbo English Dictionary. 1972:11.*

The *Agugu* festival consists of complementary activities by men and women, by day and by night, in public and in secret.

The *Agugu* festival as a whole is complemented by *Omerife*, the New Yam festival taking place in July-August in the Oguta area. Orsu-Obodo is regarded as the most senior Oru-Igbo town and first to perform the *Agugu* festival. Oguta is next, and other towns celebrate one after the other, with some as late as July-August, when *Agugu* coincides with the New Yam festivals.

During *Agugu*, the highly organized performances of *Owu* (civilization/truth/order) are complemented by the chaotic appearances of *Nwo-nono* (chaos/madness/wilderness). The dichotomy of *Owu* and *Nwo-nono,* and its implications for gender roles will be discussed further below.

### *The Owu Myth and the Riddle of Chicken and Egg*

The question, "Which came first, chicken or egg?", has occupied the human mind over centuries. The myth of origin of the *Agugu* festival and the *Owu* masquerade told by the *Owu* society's bard may suggest an answer to the universal query (Jell-Bahlsen 1994):

> *There once was a woman, Ojeru, who was fishing in the local waters, when she caught something mysterious in her fishing basket. She showed her catch to her husband, Onyeura, and they decided to consult a diviner, Otugwa. He told the couple that Ojeru had found the ofo.*[3]
>
> *The diviner then told the mythical pair to produce the Owu masquerade. This brought them wealth/children.*[4] *Other members of the community soon joined to form the Owu society.*

[3] The *ofo* is *the* Igbo symbol of paternal authority (Ilogu 1964, Ejizu 1982), the foundation of society and cementing social integration. Yet, the *Owu* myth ascribes the origins of the *ofo* to a woman.

[4] The greatest wealth in this agrarian society was children. Children were regarded as surpassing or equal with wealth, as attested in many proverbs, names and birth songs. Most importantly, procreation/ children opened the door to re-incarnation (Manfredi 1997).

> *However, Ojeru's father wanted to claim the wealth/children his daughter had brought. Onyeura took him to court at the community's council of elders. They determined that Onyeura had paid to Ojeru's father what became known as "bride price."*[5] *Thus, the community resolved that Onyeura was entitled to the wealth/children his wife had brought into this world.*

According to this myth, the woman/mother who brought wealth/children to man clearly is number one. This notion is corroborated in the popular Igbo name, *Nneka*, "Mother is Supreme." The female body is a formidable source of power and correctly regarded as corner stone of not only the masquerade (Okafor 2009), but by extension, of society as a whole (Azogu 1998). This view contradicts the biblical perception of Eve as second human being "carved out of Adam's rib." The adoration of female fecundity furthermore contradicts the biblical notion of woman/Eve causing the "loss of paradise." By contrast, the *Owu* myth celebrates life and procreation; it reaffirms children as human being's greatest asset. The myth attests to the importance of woman to the foundation of Igbo society and the ritual authority that integrates it; for it was a woman who found the all-important *ofo-- the* Igbo symbol of paternal authority (Ilogu 1964, Ejizu 1986).

The myth further demonstrates indigenous knowledge expressed in an understanding of the ultimate importance of fresh water for the gestation of life. This knowledge is also expressed in proverbs such as *Ndu miri, ndu azu* – "So long as there is a living body of water, there will always be life fishes in it." (Nwauwa 2011).

Moreover, the *Owu* myth clearly rationalizes the identity of children: they belong to their father's *umunna* (patri)-lineage, not their mother's (father's) lineage. Following the myth, this arrangement is legitimized by the "child-wealth" arrangement, erroneously known as "bride-price;" this custom ensures every person of a place in the society as a member of his/her father's *umunna* (paternal lineage). The continued membership in this everlasting group is defined by and originates in uni-linear descent.[6] This

---

[5] "Bride price" is an anthropological misnomer and should more appropriately termed "child wealth."

[6] Different societies define kinship differently, resulting in different types of kinship

should prevent children from getting lost or being torn to pieces, when their nuclear family or entire social environment disintegrates, for the children's collective identity and social base are defined as permanent.

### *Male and Female Titles*

Like most Igbo masquerades, the *Owu* masquerade is based in a men's secret society. Its focus is the *Owu* spirit. There is a hierarchy of titles, ranks and initiation within the society. The *Owu* society's leaders are representatives of the three male founders who followed the mythical woman; other members represent those who first joined the newly formed society; and there are junior *Okoroshi* ranks and novices. Most importantly, yet often overlooked, there are male as well as female titles within *Owu.*

### *Male Titles and Gender Ambiguity*

The *Owu* society's leader serves as priest of the *Owu* spirit. He is a patrilinear descendant of *Onyeura*, *Ojeru*'s husband. The *Owu* shrine is located inside the society's secret lodge, the *Echina* house. It is owned by *Onyeura*'s patrilinear descendants, the *umunna* known as *Umuonyeura at* Orsu-Obodo where he is known as the *Omodi/Osere.* Yet, in an interesting twist of gender identity, *Omodi* is a female title at Oguta proper where the *Owu* priest is the *Osere.*

The title of the living representative of the mythical diviner, *Otugwa,* is *Ugbo Nta*, "Small Canoe." The title of the representative of *Ojeru*'s father's lineage is *Ugbo Ukwu*, "Big Canoe". When he dances, he moves his iron

---

systems. The European system radiates outward from the individual at the center and includes his/her relatives bi-laterally on the maternal and paternal side. However, the resulting kin-group fades out after two or three generations when relatives are no longer recognized and can no longer claim group membership or access to the group's resources. By contrast, unilateral kin-groups count from a founding ancestor down in either the male or female line only. The resulting group grows in size and can trace connections among the descendants down to 10 generations or more. Most Igbo communities recognize paternal descent groups known as umunna, as their constituents. There are also some matri-linear Igbo societies whose kin-groups are constructed through female links, and a few Igbo communities are based on dual descent systems.

staff like a paddle, and is then known as *Amala*[7], "paddle." The plain performance of "paddle" portrays a man who carries wealth as he paddles forward standing in his canoe. Yet, the word "*amala*" (LLL) carries gender ambiguity. It is translated as "paddle; broad-bladed oar used by canoe men," but also as "grace; mercy; favor; kindness" (Echeruo 2006: 22) —distinctly female qualities. [8] The gender ambivalence of "*amala*" is also interpreted in diverse mask performances: at Orsu-Obodo, paddle, *Amala* is performed by an undisguised man. In the nearby town of Izombe, paddle is *Okoroshi Amala*. This benign character is completely masked in white cloth, wearing a chiefly red cap, and carrying a paddle. Its bodily contours appear as a richly female figure with exaggerated buttocks who is modestly folding her arms holding her paddle. Her blessings are sought, for she is believed to protect and promote fertility (Cole and Aniakor 1984).[9]

The society's three leading titles correspond to the three mythical male founders surrounding the mythical woman, *Ojeru*. A group of eight men follows. They are the *Isa-ato* and represent the descendants of those who immediately followed the founders in joining the *Owu* society.

Beneath this rank/group are the regular society members, known as *Okoroshi* when in disguise. They are the enforcers who may ridicule, satirize and eventually punish social misfits. They may also be called upon to defend their town in war. Novice-*Okoroshi* are freshly initiated during the *Agugu* festival and are the society's most junior members.

### *Female titles: Ada Owu and Eze Nwanyi*

The female descendants of *Onyeura* are the *umuada*/daughters of Onyeura's *umunna*/patrilineage. According to the *Eze Nwanyi* of Orsu-Obodo, Madame Oroko, anyone of his classificatory daughters is entitled to take the title of *Ada Owu* (Jell-Bahlsen 1994). The lineage daughters' ability to

---

[7] Amala (LLL) is a noun translated as "paddle; broad-bladed oar used by canoe men" and also as "grace; mercy; favour; kindness." (Echeruo 2001: 22).

[8] The latter qualities are to be associated with women, because "women stand for compassion." Chinua Achebe, interview 2008.

[9] At Izombe, the Owu-Okoroshi masquerade is celebrated in July-August, and there are at least two Echina houses. Each of their Owu societies presents a huge variety of Okoroshi performances, characters and issues at festival time.

take up the *Ada Owu* title reaffirms women's inalienable place as female members, *umuada*, in their father's *umunna.*[10]

The late mother of my research assistant 1978-1998, Chief Francis Ebiri, had been from *Umuonyeura* village and was an installed *Ada Owu*. However, after she had died, nobody ventured to take up this title at Orsu-Obodo, "because of church and poverty." Yet, at the more affluent town of Izombe, I met and witnessed the performances of several women who were installed *Ada Owu* in August 2009. There, several female title holders, *Ada Owu*, acted prominently together. They guided and directed the public performances of certain masks in front of the dignitaries and general audiences.

The *Eze Nwanyi* is the title of the town's oldest woman. She performs an extremely secret and the most sacred ritual during the *Agugu* festival of *Owu* known as *Nchu-chu* at Oguta II (Jell-Bahlsen 1994, 2000, 2008, 2009).

### *Nchu-chu: Levels of Learning and Secrecy:*

The *Agugu* festival is characterized by successive levels of knowledge and degrees of secrecy. Knowledge is revealed only in stages, as is participation in the *Owu* society. My first encounter with *Agugu* was in January 1979, when I was living in the town of Orsu-Obodo also known as Oguta II for an entire year, involved in an in-depth field research toward my PhD in the USA. There was neither running water, nor electricity at that time, and communication with the outside world was extremely limited. The circumstances of my life on location awarded me an in-depth first-hand experience full of deprivations, yet also extremely rich in magic. Without a family, I felt lonely at times, despite the presence of my research assistants, many acquaintances, friends, and well-wishers.

Very few people spoke English fluently, and despite my serious attempts at learning the Igbo language, my language proficiency was still very limited

---

[10] The practice of burying women in their fathers' land has reaffirmed the inalienable identity and group membership of a woman in her fathers' umunna in the past. This has sometimes caused conflicts over portions of bride price payments still open at the woman's death. Today, women's inalienable descent group membership—and resulting entitlements—is undermined when wives are buried in their husbands' land. The new practice tends to reaffirm the husbands' property rights.

even after half a year of residence. In my research, I relied on participant observation and the help of research assistants, recordings and careful translations of interactions, conversations, inquiries, information, narrations, stories, speeches, proverbs, names, songs and prayers.

On one particular day in January of 1979, several people warned me intensely, not to leave my house at night under any circumstances. I was told to keep all of my windows tightly shut and that I would run the risk of being flogged or severely punished by the *Okoroshi*, if I ventured outside or even dared to secretly peep out of any cracks. It was the night of *Nchu-chu.* The reason given for its importance and secrecy was vague, but I obeyed. Shortly afterwards I found out that *Nchu-chu* was part of *Agugu* now in full swing, and soon witnessed several public performances and masquerades.

My research had been informed by Marxism, focused on political economy and left me little room to explore the arts. However, when I returned to Nigeria some years later my perspective shifted to a deeper level of enquiry; taking my clues from local encounters rather than academic discourse, I learnt more about *Ogbuide*, the Goddess of Oguta Lake (Jell-Bahlsen 2008). This became a turning point for my appreciation of the arts and the female side of the universe in Igbo cosmology. My new vantage point enabled me to recognize *Nchu-chu* as *the most secret and most sacred* part of the men's masquerade: Nobody is allowed to see *Nchu-chu,* no man, woman or child—whether insider, outsider, initiated into *Owu*, or not.

*Nchu-chu* is the masquerade festival's core and its most secret night ritual. At Oguta II, this is customarily performed by the town's oldest women *in the nude.* The women walk through town and greet all its major shrines. Without this extremely secret, sacred rite, the festival is not supposed to proceed, and the senior masks would not appear. *Nchu-chu* is truly at the core of the entire masquerade. Both, the ritual's phenomenon—female nudity—and its message—female power and the need for complementary action to sustain life—contradict the missionary-colonial complex.

Female ritual nudity is extremely powerful, perceived with awe, and also a taboo among traditional Igbo and in other African societies. Female nudity can be and was used as a form of protest, or even threat by several African societies (Amadiume 2008, Teboh 2007, Chuku 2001, Rogers 1980, Lawrence/Hanitsch 1937). Igbo women have used the politics of nudity to rein in their men in the past (VanAllen 1972, Chuku 2005), and have confronted colonial oppression in the nude during the Igbo women's war of 1929, when many of them were gunned down by the intimidated foreigners and their indigenous servants (Lawrence 1937, Jell-Bahlsen 2008); even today a woman may threaten her husband or unruly sons by "dropping her cloths." The female body is the most sacred, revered, and feared symbol of life and procreation (Amadiume 2008).

Madame Oroko was Orsu-Obodo's oldest woman, the *Eze Nwanyi*, who performed *Nchu-chu* in 1992 when I produced an ethnographic documentary there. She explained that her curse would be deadly for any transgressor who dared to confront her that night (Jell-Bahlsen 1994). She was highly respected and feared, and also possessed the ultimate authority to defend women and settle husband and wife conflicts. By 2009, Madame Oroko had passed away, and Madame Asu-ama-n'onyeoma had taken over as *Eze Nwanyi* to bless and protect women and the town, and to perform *Nchu-chu*.

The (female) *Nchu-chu* ritual of the town's oldest women is the *Owu* masquerade's most sacred and most secret event. Other (male) activities are also secret, yet to differing degrees: "very secret," "semi-secret," and "not secret" or public. Some rites are performed by the masking society's most senior ranking male members inside their secret lodge. They may be witnessed by—male and female—initiated members only. There are other episodes accomplished by the novices in their individual homes; these may only be witnessed by their individual fathers, coaches, and senior society members; other activities of the novices inside the secret lodge may only be seen by the initiated members; the *Okoroshi* and novices stage dances in the village square at one particular night, to be seen only by males—whether initiates or not; this semi-secret/semi-public appearance is complemented by the *Okoroshi*'s—and the novices' first—public performance in the village square in broad day light, to be seen by all—men, women and children. The festival culminates in a spectacle that thrives on the participation and interaction of mixed audiences and performers.

### *The Raw and the Cooked*

I could neither witness nor record the oldest women's secret night ritual. However, in 1992 the oldest women visited the society's bard at dawn right after *Nchu-chu*. On that occasion, the *Eze Nwanyi*, Madame Oroko and her assistant danced and sang a song about "the raw and the cooked" we recorded (Jell-Bahlsen 1994, 2008). According to Madame Asu-ama-n'Onyeoma (2009), the old women sing this song exclusively during the time of *Agugu:*

Kolanut makes you feel fine!
-- We know.
*Garri* is delicious.
-- Only when cooked!
-- We know.
Plantains are delicious!
-- Only when cooked!
-- We know.
Pounded yam with *ofé* (soup) is delicious!
-- Only when cooked!
-- We know.
Plantain chips are delicious!
-- Only when cooked!
-- We know,
Roasted cassava is delicious!
--Only when cooked!
We know[11] (Jell-Bahlsen 1994, 2008).

Cooking customarily is a woman's domain. Furthermore, cooking was used as a metaphor for sex in the traditional framework. If a woman refused to "cook for her husband" she also refused to share his bed and award him the opportunity to procreate. The song thus emphasizes the need for gender balance in order for man to fully enjoy the food cooked by women, together with women's power to procreate and sustain life.

### *Audiences, Performances and Levels of Secrecy:*

Various public performances involve participants and audiences to

---

[11] This important song and dance performed by the Eze Nwanyi of Orsu-Obodo and her assistant after Nchu-chu at the Owu society's bard's house at dawn was video recorded by my daughter, Saskia Jell, during the documentary film production of Owu: Chidi joins the Okoroshi on location at Orsu-Obodo, 1992.

different degrees during the *Owu-Okoroshi* festival. When the three most senior *Owu* masks dance in the village square they are facing the society's leaders and are surrounded by a mass audience of men, women and children learning, admiring, listening and watching.

Prior to the senior masks, the lower ranks of *Okoroshi* perform in public in the village square for a mixed crowd of men, women and children. The dancers are led into the arena in groups but perform individually. Each one is accompanied by an entourage of assistants who collect money and gifts thrown by cheering women and other admirers. Guards are keeping the crowd at bay, protecting the protagonists from those who might prey on the performers' loot or be offended by satirical performances. The interaction of the (male) actors and their (female) audience charges the atmosphere (Okafor 2009, Ottenberg 1982); the exchange gives contour to artistic images and scenes performed in masquerades like the color white becoming fully visible when contrasted with the color black, or as in the Igbo adage/ praise name, *Ikwa dugudugu* "the darkness that makes the moon relevant" (Njoku 2012).

Levels of secrecy enhance the interest in public events for performers and audiences alike. The *Owu* dance movements are difficult and require a very high degree of balance and of stamina acquired only through extensive practice. The novices exercise in secret and only gradually find enough courage to face the public, especially women, when dancing. The young men's goal is dancing in front of women and to be truly admired—rather than belittled or ridiculed—by those they admire and desire.

## *Manifestations of Myth, Sex and Gender*

There is a hierarchy of membership and of masking. The most senior *Owu* masks are manifestations of the ancestral spirits of the original myth. *Onyeura*'s mask is the most senior *Owu* mask. Its name is *Akarucha* translated as "After gossiping you still desire *it*." This mask features a semi-abstract, full, conical body covered in white lace, adorned with beads or corals, and crowned by a tall staff topped by a tiny, sun-like carved face surrounded by feathers. The mask figure carries a heavy load of unknown rattling objects on its back.

*Ojeru*'s father's mask is *Echarakecha,* translated as "father makes noise."

He has a rather realistically carved and slightly smiling male face topped by a chiefly red cap embellished by two chiefly eagle feathers. On his back, he also carries a heavy load of rattling objects.

The third senior *Owu* mask is the diviner's mask, known as "*Igbonnam-muo*" translated as "the Igbo's beauty." It is abstract and truly beautiful; its face is covered in white lace, garlanded by coral beads, and topped by a rich crown of eagle feathers. It dances elegantly with flowing movements of its richly robed wing-like arms. All three senior masks carry ceremonial horse tail whisks, a sign of their chiefly status.

### *Nwo-nono: Women's Agency and the Dichotomy of Order and Chaos:*

The classic *Owu* masquerade performances I witnessed at Orsu-Obodo (1979-1992) were highly balanced, choreographed and organized. They portrayed the social ideal of a customary order where every person had his/her place in society; where an individual's behavior corresponded to his/her identity; and where there was a gendered division of labour and behavior. The senior *Owu* masks represented Igbo civilization and the truth of its customary order (Osuagwu 2010, Jell-Bahlsen 2000). Okafor argues that the masquerade experience "is important for power relations, reflecting power, and maintaining stability through display of an ordered world." (Okafor 2009: 309).

Yet, Orsu-Obodo's *Agugu* festival goes beyond the "display of an ordered world." Its highly controlled, civilized performances of *Owu* are deliberately contrasted by the unpredictable appearances of the untamed *Nwo-nono*. The disparity between these events signals the dichotomy between civilization and chaos, and are expressed in the contrast of "normal/desirable gentle/modest" behavior of women on the one hand, and their "unusual/ wild/aggressive" actions on the other.

*Nwo-nono*[12] "hates feathers" and "must not meet *Owu*" whose bard

---

[12] According to Chidi Osuagwu, "… the Nwa-Nnono masquerade represents a chaotic motif. The name, Nwa-Nnono means, literally, "the bird." If the bird hates feathers, it represents a negation. But it probably represents a protesting bird, protesting against vain people who would acquire the bird's feather, at the expense of the bird to adorn themselves. It is a motif against natural injustice." E-mail to author, 2/20/2009.

praises "the tame bird that *Owu* brought." *Nwo-nono* is a very tall, semi-human figure. It wears a raffia costume topped by a flat wooden mask facing the sky. It emerges spontaneously throughout the town, is completely wild and aggressive, charges and is chased by the village youth. *Nwo-nono* has seemingly supernatural powers and a wild entourage throwing clubs at their persecutors, who in turn throw their clubs back at the *Nwo-nono* group; the parties are trying to stone and destroy each other. The wild chase goes back and forth throughout the town, all day long, and lasts four full days. It is very dangerous, people can get hurt, and babies and small children are kept in the homes. Picture taking is strictly prohibited and Nigerian Television Authority film crews are said to have lost their cameras on these occasions. If anybody gets hurt, there is no revenge or jurisdiction, for *Nwo-nono* and its chase are "above the law."

When I first witnessed the *Agugu* festival in 1979, women were commonly expected to wear wrappers or skirts down to their ankles. Yet, during the all-out, warlike *Nwo-nono* turmoil, young women would wear trousers, carry clubs, fight, and chase and be chased like men.

Today, young women wear trousers on many occasions in Southeastern Nigeria, especially to hitch a ride on an *Okada* (motorcycle), even in rural areas. Many things have changed for the better or worse. When Orsu-Obodo's *Omodi/Osere* died, his immediate successor was too poor to stage the *Agugu* festival and all of its *Owu* masked performances every year. When this man died, his successor by right was the oldest man of his lineage. But he refused to take up the title and its obligations "because of church." In 2013, a young man from *Umuonyeura* has stepped forward and accepted to be installed as *Owu*'s priest and leader of the society. He has yet to "find the money" to fully perform the *Owu* masquerade.

*Owu*—the "display of an ordered world"—has taken place only on and off at Orsu-Obodo over the past 34 years. Yet, *Nwo-nono*—chaos—always emerges. The village youths continue to strive on its performance of freedom and loss of constrictions, lawlessness, and uninhibited fighting. This may be an expression of the conflicting states of their personalities, community, and country. The festival's part that portrays social order, identity and harmony is largely lost. Yet, there is plenty of space, time and money for fighting. Classic *Owu-Okoroshi* performances have featured female power and the interaction and interdependence of men and women. In the past, men might portray female fecundity as focus of their fears and desires, and the basis of human society; they might also wear costumes portraying women in general, or gender expectations and relations, to make a point about women in general or raise specific issues about a specific character in town.

Today, the issues have shifted, and new existential problems are haunting especially the communities of or near the Niger Delta. Today's *Okoroshi* expose issues and portray such things like a high way cutting through town now suffering from heavy traffic, oil wells diluting local waters, helicopters, dangerous pipelines, and oil barges accompanied by new and unfathomable diseases, greed and all sorts of new trades, professions and evils. Some contemporary masquerade performances include realistic transvestites mimicking women in a highly realistic way. Their appearances are so realistically female as to transcend customary performance themes and blurring the differentiation between men and women. At Izombe, the beautiful transvestites who appear in women's attires as *Okoroshi* in August of 2009 were overly sweet and effeminate. One realistic trans-gender performer appeared with an entourage shaded by an umbrella carrier and holding/nourishing a (white/foreign) baby. These acts might be expressing the man's deepest personal desires and ambiguities, and could also be interpreted as commentaries on their own powerlessness and subordinate, passive position *vis a vis* contemporary global economic powers—rather than enigmatic portrayals of female power as a mythical source of life in customary, ordered society.

## *Conclusion:*

*The Owu-Okoroshi* masquerade is a complex series of events that involve men and women, and feature their interaction and interdependence. My study of the *Owu-Okoroshi* complex corroborates Okafor's general theory of "Female Power: Corner Stone or Central Subject in Igbo Mask Performance" (Okafor 2009), but also attests to the ideal of balancing female and male power, and to the expression of new issues. Popular masquerades involve both, men and women alike. *Owu* derives from awe for the gift of female fecundity and from understanding the value of life and its origins in water. Freshwater is a pre-condition for life as we know it. Masquerades are popular events and the Igbo people's most prolific art form. As theatrical spectacles, they teach and celebrate the culture's foundation, wisdom, history and identity. *Owu* acknowledges the supremacy of motherhood and once portrayed social ideals and customs; the *Owu-Okoroshi* complex once fostered complementary gender activity, harmony, and awe for the gifts of nature.

Today's *Owu* masquerades might still promote social integration. The *Okoroshi* expose social issues and punish misfits. *Owu* and *Nwo-nono* expose the danger of chaos and reassert the need for balance in a chaotic, spikey and violent contemporary world where the female side is largely ignored (Achebe 2008), or has become effeminate rather than complementary to man, and where the local people are increasingly disempowered by new economic and environmental challenges. As female power is eroded, so is the sustainability of local communities. Masquerades are naively defamed by fanatic Christians and some foreign educated Igbo men equally naively attempt to claim what has never been theirs alone. This study of the creativity expressed in the *Owu* masquerades attempts to counter the culture's denigration and to reassert its message of social balance and cooperation.

### *References*

Achebe, C. 2008. Chinua Achebe Turns 50 this year. An interview with Chinua Achebe for *The Village Voice*. Carol, C. *The Village Voice*. 19 February, 2008 http://www.villagevoice.com/arts/chinua-achebes-things-fall-apart-turns-50-this-year-7134303

Achebe, N. 2011. *The Female King of Colonial Nigeria, Ahebi Ugbabe* Bloomington: Indiana University Press.

Amadiume, I. 1987. *Male Daughters, Female Husbands: Gender and Sex in an African Society*. London: Zed Books.

Amadiume, I. 2008. African Women's Body Images in Postcolonial Discourse and Resistance to Neo-Crusaders. In: *Black Womanhood, Images, Icons, and Ideologies of the African Body*. Barbara, T. (Ed.). Seattle: University of Washington Press. 49-69.

Azogu, C. A.1998. *Oguta Cultural Heritage and Practices: A Handbook for the New Generation*. Port Harcourt.

Brink, A. E. 1990. Man-Made Woman: Gender, Class and Ideology of the Volksmoeder. In: *Women and Gender in Southern Africa*. Cheryl, W. (Ed.). Cape Town: David Phillips Publishers. 173-

192.
Chuku, G. 2005. *Igbo Women and Economic Transformation in Southeastern Nigeria 1900-1960.* New York: Routledge.
Chuku, G. 2003. The 'Untouchable Vultures?' Igbo Women in Resistance Movements. Paper presented at the 1st Igbo Studies Association (ISA) Meeting at Ithaca, Cornell University.
Chukwuma, H.1994. *Feminism, Fecundity and Igbo Birth Songs.* Feminism in African Literature.
Cole, H. M. and Chike A. (Eds). 1984. *Igbo Arts. Community and Cosmos.* Los Angeles: Fowler Museum of Art.
Ejizu, C. I. 1989. *Ofo: Igbo Ritual Symbol.* Enugu: Fourth Dimension Publishers.
Ezeigbo, T., A. 1997. *Gender Conflict in Flora Nwapa's Novels. In:Writing African Women: Gender, Popular Culture and Literature in West Africa.* Stephanie, N. (Ed.). London: Zed Books. 95-104.
Ifemesia, C. 1979. *Traditional Humane Living among the Igbo.* Enugu: Fourth Dimension Publications.
Ilogu, E. 1964. *Ofo: A religious and Political Symbol in Igboland. Nigeria Magazine.*
Ilogu, E. 1974. *Christianity and Igbo Culture.* Leiden: E.J. Brill.
Jell-Bahlsen, S. 2008. *The Water Goddess in Igbo Cosmology. Ogbuide of Oguta Lake.* Trenton, NJ: Africa World Press.
Jell-Bahlsen, S. 2009. Owu: Chidi Joins the Okoroshi Secret Society (video). Waterbury, MA: Documentary Educational Resources. www.der.org.
Jell-Bahlsen, S. 2000. Civilization, Wilderness, and Secrecy: Making two Films. *Visual Anthropology* 13 (4) Special Issue on Africa: 363-393.
Lawal, B. *The Gelede Spectacle: Art, Gender and Social Harmony in an African Culture.* Seattle: University of Washington Press, 1996.
Lawrence, C.T. 1937. *Memorandum; Appendix II and Quotations of Captain Hanitsch.* Great Britain: Colonial Office.
Manfredi, V.1997. Igbo Initiation: Phallus or Umbilicus? Cahiers d'Etudes africaines. 145.XXXVII-1:157-211 http://people.bu.edu/manfredi/OedipousOttenberg.pdf
Melliassoux, C. 1972. *Maidens, Meal, and Money: Capitalism and Community.* Cambridge: Cambridge University Press.

Njoku, Akuma-Kalu, Ticha. Praise Name Signature Posted to ISA-Google Group 20.4.2012 and in e-mails to this author 30.7. 2012, 10. 1. 2013.

Nnaemeka, O. 1968. Introduction. In: *Sisterhood: Feminisms and Power from Africa to the Diaspora.* Nnaemeka, O. 1968. (Ed.). Trenton, NJ: Africa World Press.

Nnaemeka, O. 2003. Negro-Feminism: Theorizing, Practicing, and Pruning Africa's Way. *Signs* 29 (2) 1-29.

Nwauwa, A. E-mail to this author, May 2011.

Okafor, C. 2009. Female Power: Corner Stone or Central Subject in Igbo Mask Performance. *Emergent Themes and Methods in African Studies. Essays in Honor of Adiele Afigbo.* Toyin F.and Adam, P. (Eds.). Trenton, NJ: Africa World Press. 307-323.

Okafor, C.1994. From the Heart of Masculinity: Ogbodo Uke Women's Masking. *Research in African Literatures* 25 (4). 7-17.

Osuagwu, C. 2002. Truth and Chaos: Dynamics of Truth within Igbo Cosmology. Paper presented at the Owerri International Symposium on Religion in a World of Change, Organized by the Whelan Research Academy, Owerri, December 2002. E-mails to this author February 2009 and September 2012.

Onyeneke, A.O. 1987. *The Dead among the Living. Masquerades in Igbo Society.* Nimo: Asele Institute.

Ottenberg, S. 1975. *Masked Rituals of Afikpo.* Seattle, WA: University of Washington Press.

Ottenberg, S. 1982. 'Boys' Secret Societies at Afikpo. In: *African Religious Groups and Beliefs.* Ottenberg, S. (Ed.). 170-184.

Ottenberg, S. 1982. (Ed.). African Religious Groups and Beliefs. African Religious Beliefs and Groups. Meerut: Archana.

Ottenberg, S. 1989. *Boyhood Rituals in an African Society: An Interpretation.* Seattle: University of Washington Press.

Rogers, S. 1980. Anti-Colonial Protest in Africa: A Female Strategy Re-considered. *Heresies* 1 (9) 22-25.

Teboh, B. 2007. Unruly Mothers, Combative Wives: Rituals, Women and Change in the Cameroon Grassfields c. 1889-1960. Paper presented at the African Studies Association Meeting in New York, November 2007.

Ukpokolo, C. 2011. Gender, Symbols and Traditional Peacemaking Among the Nanka-Igbo of South-Eastern Nigeria.

*Human Affairs* 21: 163-183.

Van Allen, J. 1972. 'Sitting on a Man': Colonialism and the Lost Political Institutions of Igbo Women. *Canadian Journal of African Studies* 6 (2): 165-181.

Williamson, K. 1972. *Igbo English Dictionary*. Benin City: Ethiope Publishing Co.

# Chapter Three

## GENDER, SOCIALISATION AND CONSTRUCTION OF A MUGANDA WOMAN IDENTITY

*Elizabeth Kyazike*

### *Introduction*

The Baganda are found in Uganda and their traditional Kingdom is Buganda while people are called the Baganda (plural) or Muganda (singular) and aspects of their culture are referred to as Kiganda or Gganda. Buganda is one of the richest kingdoms in Uganda in terms of values, norms, and traditions. The actual date for the establishment of the kingdom is not known due to the fact that the greatest part of it is stored in oral traditions. In relation to its origin, Kamuhangire (1993) cited Kaggwa (1901) and Ray (1991) who suggested that the first king of the Buganda kingdom was Kintu who came from heaven around the 14th and 15th centuries.

Before the coming of the British, Buganda kingdom was at the peak of its power, attacking and conquering the neighbouring states especially Bunyoro, Toro and Busoga. By 1890, an Anglo-German agreement was signed, which ceded Uganda to Britain. Prior to that, Buganda had had foreign contacts with the Muslims and the Christian missionaries as far back as 1840, who were invited through a letter written by the Kabaka (king) of Buganda to the Queen of England. This was followed by the arrival of the protestant missionaries of the Church Missionary Society (CMS) in 1877 and then the Catholic White Fathers in 1879 led by Father Lourdel Monpere and Brother Amans.

The invitation of the missionaries by the king of Buganda played a key role in bringing enlightenment and formal education in Uganda. This, also, aided the colonization of Uganda by the British who consequently used the Kiganda centralised system of administration as a basis for the British administrative system of indirect rule. This political role played by Buganda during the colonial era partly contributed to Buganda's dominance in Uganda, which some people regard as arrogance. The British lumped together Buganda and neighbouring communities to form what is Uganda today, which attained self-rule in 1962. However, despite the amalgamation with other ethnicities, the Baganda still stand out due to their large number and cultural identity. This chapter therefore seeks to discuss the processes of constructing the identity of a Muganda woman.

### *Geographical Location*

Buganda is located in the south central region of Uganda and this is where the capital city of Uganda is also found (Figure 1). Therefore Buganda lies in the southern part of Uganda in East Africa.

Buganda is the largest of all the traditional kingdoms in Uganda. According to the 2002 Uganda Population and Housing Census, the Baganda constitute 4,126,370 (17.3%) people out of the total Ugandan population of 24.4 million people. Buganda being in the central region is at an altitude between 4000-5000 feet above sea level. The latitude of land extends from 2° north to 1° south of the equator that positions Buganda at the centre of the African continent. In terms of longitude, Buganda is situated between 30° and 34° east of the Greenwich. The capital of the Buganda kingdom is Mengo where the Buganda parliament (Lukiiko) meets in the parliamentary building called Bulange (Figure 2).

Buganda lies along the northern and western shores of Lake Victoria near the headwater, about 200 miles along the lake shores. It extends in land to an average depth of 80 miles with an extension in the North West, reaching the southern shores of Lake Albert. The eastern boundary of Buganda is formed by the River Nile, on the far shores of the Busoga principality. In the north is the Bunyoro kingdom, and in the west are Toro and Ankole Kingdoms. Most of Buganda consists of lowland covered with savannah grasslands. Much of Buganda receives 50 or more inches of rainfall a year

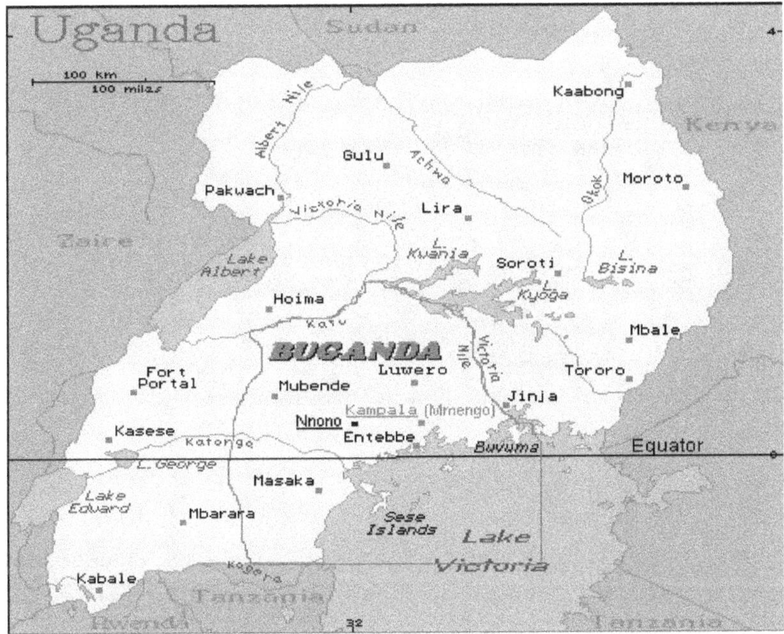


*Figure 1: Map of Uganda highlighting boundaries of Buganda in red*
*Source: http://www.buganda.or.ug/*

that is enough to sustain agriculture, which is the major activity of the Baganda. Buganda Kingdom has been developing in all aspects such as political, social, and economic spheres. It was because of this that Buganda was used by the British to extend and colonise the surrounding areas.

The Baganda traditionally have had and still have a richly organised culture. Their culture is heavily safeguarded by rules of avoidance and punishments. Most of these practices are very complex to explain and understand. The Baganda have customs and manners which are unique and create their identity. Most of these cultures are what are used to construct the Buganda identity and Buganda's glory (*Ekitiibwa kya Buganda*).

### *The Education System*

Education involved the numerous legends that were passed down with great skills from generation to generation. The key strategy for socialising a woman into womanhood was the education system using norms, taboos and traditions. This was done in a much organised system of education through observation, and correction whenever one made a mistake. In

*Figure 2: The Bulange at Mengo*
*Source: http://www.buganda.or.ug/*

Buganda, for instance, a woman was not allowed to eat products derived from animals and birds they reared themselves such as eggs, chicken, mutton and pork. Mukasa (2007) emphasises this by noting that, though women reared chicken and prepared eggs, these were reserved for men.

Women were not allowed to own land as they are excluded from inheritance of land (Southwold, 1956). It should be noted that inheritance was the major means of land acquisition besides getting it as gifts from the Kabaka and members of the royal family.

Decision making was another area governed by social norms and where, too, a Muganda woman's role was very minimal. Yet, women were comfortable and did not even complain or question it. This is because education begun from birth till death; nobody asked why these customs were followed and why and how they came into being (Wandira, 1971). Despite such, elderly women especially those that could predict the outcomes of wars or fore-told bad omens were accorded high respect. These were usually consulted and their advice respected by men. This therefore means that it is not in all cases that a Muganda woman was in an inferior position.

Another category of women who were respected were the Queen mother (Namasole) and princesses (Abambejja). This was demonstrated in greetings in which they were addressed as 'sir' (*ssebo*) and not 'madam' (*nyabo*) and they participated in decision making though this was done in the presence of chiefs or the King, who are men.

Generally, every woman in Buganda had to go through training where the home was the school and the fire place, the class room (Kenyatta, 1938).

This was because the security and wellbeing of any community depended on the efficacy and training given to members of the community from infancy. In the homes and farms, they were taught skills and behaviour that the society expected of its members.

Traditional education was multi-lateral and the end objective was to produce a balanced individual who was not only honest but also respectable, skilled, co-operative, intelligent and conformed to the social order of the society (Castle, 1966). Instructions normally took place around the fire place or whenever a girl committed an offence. These were done through stories, tales, and riddles. The mother or grandmother would alert the girls about what society expected of them as they grew up. While the mother was charged with the education of particularly girls, the father would, through proverbs, stories and direct instructions, teach the young boys their expected roles in society. The system of socialisation was similar but the subject matter differed depending on the particular needs and social values of the society and age.

In Buganda, there were special persons entrusted with recounting the history of these societies. The people were taught about their origins, their relations with their neighbours as well as common instances of rejoicing and suffering. The purpose of recounting people's historical and social traditions was to enable the society retain common heritage and tradition. The training centred on the cultural norms, traditions, values and taboos through a lot of '*dos*' and '*don'ts*', which were passed on from generation to generation. Social education was especially emphasised for a woman and the gist was based on mutual respect, skills, and wisdom in dealing with people especially her male counterparts. According to Fermia Namutebi personal communication on 1st and 2nd April 1998, a woman who excelled in this sphere was described as being good-mannered (*obuntu bulamu*). Such a kind of appraisal of one's behaviour would thus act as a re-enforcement for some other people to conform to certain norms of the society.

### *Aspects of the Socialisation Process (what was taught)*

According to Kyazike (2002) the following aspects of socialisation show what was taught to a Muganda woman.

### *History of the Society*

There were numerous legends and oral historical traditions in Buganda as each clan and family preserved its past in legends and stories, which were handed down from generation to generation with great skill. There were stories of great men and events, of the rise and fall of tribal leaders and of the daily exploits of men of the past. There was, for instance, the story of Kintu, the great ancestor and founder of the kingdom. What manner of man he was and where he came from remained matters of conjecture. Nevertheless, it was and still is the duty of every true Muganda to tell his/her children about this great ancestor and his significance to Buganda. After all, the Baganda are '*Baana ba Kintu*' (*Children of Kintu*) and it is pertinent that the children should know and revere their ancestors. Such stories suggested that man would not have been what he is, if someone had not risen above the ordinariness of life to lift others. As a result, each successive generation must have sufficient pride in its tribe's past in order to strive for its survival, progress, and glory.

Legends presented past actions and activities, changing pictures in which men and gods played their parts. This was the standard by which the present could be measured or contemplated. Children at an early age were exposed to values that had or had not stood the test of time. In a world facing the dangers of running adrift, 'cultural roots' offered anchorage (Kyazike, 2002).

### *Customs, Manners and Usage*

These can be summed up in what is referred to as '*Empisa y'ensi*', meaning manners and customs of the land. For instance, one is expected to shake hands with the right hand while greeting, and the younger person is expected to greet the elderly first. Girls/women had to kneel while greeting as emphasised by Roscoe (1911). In other words, no woman would think of saluting a man while standing and a woman carrying a load would excuse herself by saying: 'I am carrying a load and unable to ask how you are', meaning that she is unable to kneel down to greet. If a man greeted a woman carrying a load and the woman is unable to kneel, she would simply respond by saying: 'I am unable to answer because I have a load'. However, the wives of chiefs were treated differently. For instance, a wife of a chief would not kneel to greet a man of an inferior status (one who was not a chief) referred to as *omukopi* but they had to kneel for one of an equal or above the status of their husbands. Hence, values that are both transitory and permanent are handed down from generation to generation. The Baganda used different means to reinforce their customs and manners and also enforce their usage. These were fables, riddles, proverbs and music.

### *Fables*

There were a number of fables and stories told to the young through which the past influenced the present. Though some were for enjoyment, there were a considerable number of fables for the reinforcement of the Baganda customs. In using fables to pass on the customs of the land, besides the entertainment part, they also function as socialising agents. Most fables were about the cunningness of the hare who always came out triumphant.

### *Proverbs*

Wisdom was also condensed in proverbs. Proverbs provided commentary on a large number of topics such as shrewdness of judgement, kings and chiefs, the rich and poor, the family, clan and friendship, hospitality and visitors, herdsmen and their cattle, wild animals and occupations. The proverbs were not all directed in addressing the same thing and there were many that conflicted as observed by Rev Mugerere of Kisoga village (2nd April 1998). While one proverb warned against haste such as '*bbugu bbugu ssi muliro*' meaning that too much fire is not good for cooking, another encouraged haste like, *linda kiggweyo afumita mukira* literally meaning that the one who waits for the beast to be exposed may spear the tail or strike when the iron is still hot.

### *Riddles*

Another form of socialisation was through the use of riddles that could excite imagination. A riddle was staged according to known rules and a formal procedure. The challenger would invite another person or group of persons using formal phrase. *Koyi koyi* (this means a challenge but *koyi* means a wise person as well). The invitee(s) would accept the challenge by answering, *lya* (eat). The riddle was then set out and each of the group members had a go at it. If they all failed to answer the challenge then the challenger demanded to be given a village by asking that; *mumpe ekyalo* (give me a village). They would mention any village name by saying for instance that; *tukuwadde Nkonkonjeru,* meaning that we have given you Nkokonkeru. The challenger had the option of accepting the village or refusing it and so if he/she was not contented with the village one would then demand for another village by saying that, *mumpe ekirala* (give me another village). Each member of the group had the chance of setting a riddle. Kyazike (2002) noted that most challenges in the riddles were about ordinary things within the experience of most children. The set formula for their solution would become familiar to those who regularly participated. It was the duty of those who took part to think of a new challenge by exciting their imagination.

### *Music*

Socialisation was also promoted through music. Though songs were composed for entertainment, some songs had definite themes that aimed at teaching some moral and cultural standards. Ssempebwa cited in Wandira (1971) revisit eleven categories of folk songs in Buganda including: those concerned with historical happenings usually sung by harpists, those for succession ceremonies, semi-religious functions especially when one is sick, courtship and marriage, wars, commemoration of events, praise of rulers, children's songs (lullabies), those that commented about domestic life and those that were incorporated into folk tales and fables. It should be noted that the songs went beyond mere entertainment to enhancement of socialisation.

### *Social Values*

There were social values that were regarded as part of the law of the land (*mpisa ya nsi*) among these is emphasis on greeting. However, though greeting is emphasised, there are instances when one is not supposed to greet. For instance, people who are eating are not to be greeted or expected to greet in order to avoid being choked by the food, which the Baganda termed *empagama* (Anna Maria Nambi: 26th December 1998). Instead, those eating would invite passers-by by making signs, which which was a demonstration of hospitality and generosity. In line with this, emphasis is put on good neighbourliness demonstrated through caring for each other's child or children, calling on one another in times of sorrow. Essentially, neighbours are encouraged to live live in peace together and celebrate or commiserate with one another in times of joy or sorrow respectively. An example of this is in occasions of loss through death when people are expected not to engage in work especially digging. Therefore, whenever there was a dead body not yet buried, people would gather to mourn with the bereaved family till after burial. In Buganda, there is little or no belief in the occurrence of natural death as every death is believed to have a cause. This is shown in the popular saying, '*omuntu teyefiira*', meaning that a person cannot just die without a cause. So if one is found engaging in work especially digging when others are mourning, such a person would be suspected as part of the cause of the death (Magala, personal communication; 2nd April 1998) Therefore, in the case of death every member was supposed to regard the occasion as her/his own as is also true for birth or marriage (Nsimbi, 1956).

There were also numerous communal duties that people engaged in without pay regarded as *Bulungi bwa nsi,* that is, work for the good of the kingdom. Such tasks included cleaning of wells and clearing foot paths. The high degree of socialisation emphasised chastity. For instance, if a man went to war, he would entrust his family and especially the wife to the neighbour. His family stayed with the neighbour while the war lasted. The woman under this condition is expected to be faithful as it is believed that her infidelity would cause the death of her husband at the war front. In addition to this, pregnant women or those with suckling babies were not allowed to associate freely with men who were not their husbands. In case of misbehaviour in connection with the above, the pregnant woman would have difficulties in giving birth and would develop a tendency of wanting to eat the newborn baby. This is termed as *amakiro* meaning, 'desire to eat your own kid' (Nakyonyi Efranse, personal communication, 27th December 1998).

Another social value emphasised was sharing, which like all others begun from infancy. As noted earlier, if someone was passing by at a meal time such a person would be invited for a meal. The value of sharing is emphasized and extended to the extent that when one kills a fowl, a piece of it is given to the immediate neighbour. Also, children who displayed selfish tendencies are discouraged by mocking them through songs like *kirimululu nfa empewo,* which means that the greedy would die of cold. In the socialisation process the following principles were emphasised:

### *Physical Training*

This was done through music and dance. A child in Buganda is brought up with unlimited access to the stimulating rhythm of African music and dance. The first steps did not require any formal training but rather these were learnt mainly through observation and functioned as a platform for physical exercises and is one way of encouraging team work and group solidarity.

### *Character Training*

This is the cornerstone of Kiganda socialisation process. From infancy a girl was trained to be a good wife and mother. It should be noted that this was not the only the responsibility of the family members (mother, paternal aunt, and grandmother) but of the entire community. Some of the characters developed were respect, good eating habits, sharing, honesty, courage, humility, perseverance and good character at all times especially in relation with the male counterparts as relations between men and women were expected to be in accordance with the highest standards of decency (Moumoumi, 1968).

### *Intellectual training*

Reasoning, part of intellectual training, is highly encouraged and this is inculcated right from childhood through lullabies like those that taught how to count such as the famous; *kann'emu (one), kannabbiri (two), kafumba mwanyi(three), katta konkome(four) malangajja (five), kanna kwale(six), ofumba otya(seven), kambale(eight), bale (nine), ekkumi liweze (ten).*

A young girl, for instance learnt the local geography and history of her community. This was also through proverbs and riddles, believed to constitute a formidable intellectual exercise used for developing the child's reasoning capacity and skill in decision making. As the girl child grew up into adulthood she was exposed to a more advanced intellectual training. There were rhymes, riddles, songs, games and proverbs used to promote enumeration (counting), which offered room for mental development (Kyagalanyi, 1975). The socialisation catered for reasoning and through various ways helped its recipients in integrating their experiences into meaningful life patterns.

### *Vocational Training*

Three major vocations in the socialization of women were agricultural training, trades and crafts like weaving, smithing, hunting, carving, sculpturing, painting, carpentry, building, drumming, dancing, leather making, pottery making and many other highly valued vocations in traditional society; and professions like traditional medicine women, mediums, diviners, priests and village heads (Roscoe, 1911). Vocations like medicine were learnt while the young female apprentice moved with a practising medicine person observing the different grasses and trees as noted by Eseresi Namakula, a traditional healer in Sseira (personal communication; 8th December 1998). Vocational training in traditional Kiganda society was largely run on apprenticeship system and was significant for constructing identity in a Muganda woman.

### *Community Participation and Involvement*

In the traditional Kiganda socialisation system, a girl child was made to play her role as a member of a family that includes children, parents, grandparents, uncles, and aunties who also had their own children and other immediate relatives and neighbours. Emphasis on engagement in community work in both times of joy and sorrow started from the home where a woman/girl would get involved in taking care of the extended family and also do community service such as assisting elders to do household chores, taking care of the elderly's health such as removing jiggers and fetching water among others.

### *Promotion of Cultural Heritage*

Traditional education was an important vehicle for the perpetuation of the society's culture. The child grew up within the cultural heritage of her people. She imbibed it since culture in traditional society is innate. The child observed, imitated, and mimicked the actions of the elders and all the community people. That is why elders were careful not to make mistakes in front of young children for fear of encouraging bad behaviour.

### *The Socialisation Process*

Education in traditional Kiganda society in Mukono district went on throughout life, not being restricted to place or time. Before a child was born, the mother was taught what she was expected to do. From the time of pregnancy, she was not expected to be close to other men other than her husband. In case she committed adultery, it was believed, that she would get a disease called *amakiro* (an unnatural desire the newly born child).

The expectant mother was treated with care and would be given whatever she wanted to eat. However, a girl who got pregnant before marriage would have brought what the Baganda term as *amawemukirano* which means bringing disgrace to her parents and the entire family. In such a case, it is clear that all the shame and burden were heaped on the pregnant girl rather than the boy who impregnated her. A number of rituals were performed to cover up and discourage *amawemukirano* (disgrace). These entailed a pregnant girl having her own sleeping place at the extreme end of the parent's land where she lived in isolation, cooking and eating alone till she was delivered of her baby. She could not even share with her siblings who were also supposed to isolate her, which consequently discouraged others from associating with her. Even after delivery, such a girl was not given gifts by her parents or any other person. The boy responsible for the pregnancy would have to bring a goat and local beer to the girl's parents. The intention behind these measures was to discourage other young girls from getting involved in premarital sex, or pregnancy before marriage in order to avoid the suffering and shame involved.

It was the sole responsibility of the mothers to educate the new born babies as Moumouni (1968:17) observed: "Until she attains the age of six to eight, the Africa child remains in the shadow of women". This was seen from the fact that, it was the mother who breast feeds the child. It was also the responsibility of the mother to bathe the child or even put her to bed. Education during infancy involved whispering to the baby while it was breast feeding. For example, if a baby cried for nothing, the mother would slap it a bit and the baby would eventually learn that it was bad to cry without a cause. Whenever a child cried, the mother would give it the breast as a way to console it. Weaning only took place at a time when a child was old enough to understand the meaning of punishment and rebuke, which was in most cases, at the age of two. Mothers were blamed for their children's misbehaviour.

There were two most important skills that a child acquired during the early years of childhood. These are speech and movement. The beginnings were usually with words of greetings and farewell. Then the child acquired the words necessary for her needs such as food or water. The education at this stage was through living with many adults and older children, which gave the child the opportunity to listen, imitate, shout, or sing. The acquisition of skills of movement was encouraged. As soon as the child was old enough to sit, she was left to sit up and provided with plenty of things to play with. The first signs of crawling and eventually of walking were applauded enthusiastically. A devoted mother sat with open arms at one end of the yard and encouraged the toddler to walk towards her. There were special small bells (*endege*) tied at the ankles whose sounds encouraged the baby to put forward one leg after another. An older person could also lead the child by the hand while they walked from one end of the house to the other singing songs like, *Nswagiro alitambula ddi? Jjo, jjuuzi,* meaning, 'when will Nswagiro learn to walk? Maybe tomorrow'. When the child was able to walk by without aids, he/she moved freely around the vicinity since there were no walls or gates in the house that could constitute barriers. At this point also, the mother began to make the child aware of the social etiquette of the land. This is because etiquette was, and still is, an element in traditional Kiganda women education (Mair, 1934). Politeness in speech and cultivation of all other desirable values was emphasised. Attempts by the child to dominate adults and even fellow children were not tolerated and censored by parents. Young girls were encouraged to be considerate to other children at all times. Though seen as negative nowadays, the main roles played by young girls were targeted towards making them better mothers and home makers. Through such roles, they learned how to cook, take care of the younger ones, and care for the home. To drive home the importance of good behaviour, young girls were given lessons on morals through which they were advised to avoid all forms of vices such as betrayal, stealing, fornication, bickering, gossiping amongst others.

Awareness of spiritual values of the society was encouraged from an early age. In this, young girls participated in the Kiganda religious activities without any hindrance. There was no division between adult religious activities and those of children like the current Sunday school services. In this case, the child learnt by observation. For instance, when the religious sacrifices were offered or as the family head established communion with the ancestral spirits, the child was expected to observe the on goings. When she grew up, she was expected to follow the examples of the elders in the performance of the religious duties. In addition to this is learning by imitation in which the child would imitate until she got the meaning of what she imitated since there was no formal teaching at any time. Significantly, the role mothers played in the socialisation of children, especially the girl child cannot be over emphasized. The training of the girl child was not, however, restricted to her biological mother but was instead left open for other women to make their input. The reason is that when the girl child is useful, it will be to the good of the entire community.

As the girl child grew up, she gained mastery over a number of skills and acquired the potential for participation in a number of family activities. However, her attachment to activities was primarily to those of her mother's such as cooking, fetching water and fire wood, growing of food crops, gathering food from the garden, serving meals, making fire and taking charge of the preparation of meals. She also swept the house, washed the dishes, and kept the house in order. The girls' performance was the concern of the mother. So mother's guidance, instruction, and example were available at every stage. The girl was not expected to complain while she performed her chores. If she did not lend a hand in the discharge of household chores, she would be regarded as a failure. Likewise a parent who did not ask her daughter to do so was considered to be failing in preparing the girl for adult life. The girl was always reminded that it was the women who had to do so and that she would marry a man who would expect efficient discharge of those duties. It should be noted that the kind of activities girls did reflected the economic role they were to play in the future. For instance, girls accompanied their mothers to the plantain grove to weed or prune, they went to the fields to sow, plant or harvest, while boys went with fathers to fetch fodder for the goats, build houses, and carry out such activities as iron smithing and wood work.

Besides home activities, the child also participated in the clan and village activities like marriage, funerals, and religious observances, which brought together clansmen and neighbours. During such ceremonies, cousins were introduced to each other; links between great grandfathers explained and the child understood her relationship with other people. Funeral ceremonies took a long time during which the child had contact with various people. During these festivities, the blood ties that unite everyone were emphasized. Taboos of the clan were observed and explained. Taboos were a very significant method of social education in Buganda. Many of these taboos were justified in reference to the consequences of their violations. For instance, one was not supposed to sweep the house at night or else would become poor. The goal of this taboo was to encourage everybody to sweep their houses during the day for cleanliness and to avoid sweeping out important things unknowingly at night. Thus, social education of the child was made effective through the active and intelligent participation of the child in the affairs of the clan and the village. Entrance into this wide sympathetic human environment of the clan and village increased the child's chances of learning and practising.

Changes in the girl's physical appearance led to her initiation into adulthood. Such changes included increase in the size of the breasts and the onset of menstruation. At this stage, the mother started telling the girls that she was no longer a child. This was a time when the parent had more control on the adolescent as a means of training her for later life. But at the same time, she could be allowed some freedom to give her a feeling of maturity. At this time, the girl was under the supervision of her mother and maternal aunt and discharged duties of the women folk in the home. She was encouraged in cooking, fetching water and sweeping the house and all the varied jobs of the household. She always sat in company of other women, listened, and joined in their talks. The mother watched the girl's movements with a lot of care during this stage. The girl was no longer allowed to run off with groups of boys to play. A girl who played about with boys at this stage was considered spoilt. A lot of importance was attached to virginity at marriage and a girl who was not a virgin at marriage brought shame unto the family as observed by Afranse Nakyonyi (personal communication; 27th December 1998). It was, therefore, the duty of the mother to keep a watchful eye on the girl's contacts with boys and men. It was the girl's excellence in work and the desire of her mother to keep her 'good' that brought the adolescent girl more and more under the guidance of her mother and other women of her family. A girl who failed to show up the expected standards of skill and ability was often challenged with the reminder that womanhood was approaching. Hence, efforts were intensified in guidance and training for socialisation which shaped the Muganda woman's identity.

Unlike the boys who could build their own houses when they grew up, girls were not allowed. They either stayed with a married brother or an elderly aunt who had a house of her own (Kalyesubula, personal communication; 28th, December, 1998). At this stage, relationships became defined by custom. For instance, parents were not allowed to enter the daughter's bed room, and likewise the girl was not allowed to enter the parent's bedroom or use their bathing basins. The growing into adulthood and towards independence, which starts from puberty, culminates in marriage. The approach of maturity was marked by special ceremonies and dramatized by intense moral education. Much of the education required the young girl to take part in the daily activities of her family and community. Girls worked with their mothers on those things that enabled married women to run their homes. Now and again, conversations turned to what wives were expected to do. Parental conversations, hints, discussions with anybody, her personal contributions, all gave a picture of a young person formed for marriage and its responsibilities. There was formal detailed training for engaged girls. During this period the girl was prepared for the coming of her husband to settle marriage payments. Mothers and older female relatives gave detailed and sometimes formal instructions to the bride-to-be. Formal advice giving *(okuvuma)* also went on at this time. The girl was given instructions on the actual details of the sex act and on its significance in marriage. This was the speciality of paternal aunts. Since girls married while still very young This type of instruction was very important for girls who married while they were still young.

The circumstances in marriage called for qualities of tolerance and perseverance and could not be dealt with by insistence on rights and privileges for the woman. She could do this because much of the pre-marriage advice giving was devoted to an exhortation of the girl to give and sacrifice as much as possible for the success of her marriage. The ground was thus prepared for the demands of marriage. Divorce was greatly discouraged though there were customary laws through which marriage would be dissolved. A divorced woman found her position less comfortable at home than before she left. This was because divorce curtailed the woman's participation in her natural family and her relationships with her parents. For instance, she was not allowed to bathe from the same pot with her parents. Due to this sometimes she could be asked to go and live with her brothers or other relatives. The implications of social disapproval of a divorced woman discouraged women from divorce despite the great problems they encountered in their marriages. To avoid problems, women left marriage only when they were sure of entering another. Yet, this was also difficult.

Generally, the picture of marriage created by the traditional society was not of trial and error or convenience. It involved permanent responsibilities, sacrifice, and obligations. The question that every mother asked was whether her daughter would measure up to these challenges while enjoying the privileges in marriage. Newly-wedded couples called upon their elders for advice and counselling. Women fed up with their marriages sometimes took refuge with their in-laws before deciding whether to end the marriage. Thus, life was a long educative experience extending from the cradle to the grave, for during the marriage or adult life, a woman met experiences from which she learned and reshaped the education she gave to her children.

The socialization process also promoted division of labour between the two sex groups. Those for the men included salt making, trade, canoe building, and fishing, soap making, iron working, construction of houses, wood and leather works, while the women did crafts such as mat making, ropes, basketry, and pottery. Society had a negative attitude towards a woman who indulged herself in the so called men's activities such as trade and in most cases this was done by single women referred to as *nakyeyombekedde*. Actually they were scorned and referred to as prostitutes according to Namutebi Fermia (1st and 2nd April 1998).

The principal occupation of a woman was agriculture (Efranse; 27th December 1998), a number of crops were grown and cherished by the Baganda. To the Baganda the only food is *matooke* (plantain) otherwise the rest will be called by their names but if a Muganda asks for food it means plantain. But even the plantains have different types for instance those for eating as ripe bananas, while others are roasted (*gonja*). Other foods grown are cassava, sweet potatoes, ground nuts, sugar canes, and vegetables. Todaro (1977) cited Esther Boserup in her studies on women participation in agriculture in Africa who discovered that women do around 70% and in some cases nearly 80% of the total work load. However, these tasks are performed only with the most primitive tools and required many days of long hard labour simply to produce enough output to meet the family's subsistence requirements.

Cash crop production was for men and a number of cash crops were grown in the area for research which included: rubber, coffee, tea, and cotton. Animal husbandry was done too where both women and men participated but ownership and use was in the hands of men.

Land was and still is one of the major factors of production. Land in Buganda according to Mair (1934) was under the clans. Each clan head (*mutaka*) controlled land for the clan while some other land was in the hands of chiefs while the system was mailo land tenure but the Kabaka was regarded the Ssabataka meaning the controller of all the lands and clan heads. It should be noted that an unmarried woman would not own or inherit land due to the patrilineal system in Buganda. However, women like the princesses and Queen mothers owned land.

### *Discussion and Conclusion*

It should be noted that this chapter does not intend to equate gender to sex. This is because while sex is the biological classification of male and female, gender is socially constructed (Nelson, 1977) cited in Foluronso (2003). However, sex categories can be socially defined. In this chapter gender is related to sex because certain activities or behaviour are assigned based on the sex of the individuals. Socialisation begins from childhood to death, and is therefore a continuous process and this constituted the Muganda woman identity. However, the socialisation process had some weaknesses such as: denying women access and control over land, which made them more economically dependent on men. This led to an intensification of domestic patriarchy reinforced by the traditional institutions. Despite the fact that women were major food producers, they were denied direct ownership and control over agricultural lands. Speaking about African women in general, Seenarine, cited Sacks who explained that, the value of women's productive labour, in producing and processing food established and maintained their rights in domestic and other spheres such as economic, cultural, religious, social, political etc. (www. Impact-of-colonialism-on-african-women. WorldPress.com). In this case, the colonial policies that encouraged land alienation, wage labour and taxation made matters worse by depriving women of engagement in lucrative labour. Women were left to fend for the families as men moved on to towns to seek wage employment.

This means that colonialism worsened the situation. In this regard, Mukasa (2007) was of the view that through the colonization processes, women became invisible in Buganda kingdom.

Despite the loopholes in the Kiganda traditional system, there were certain positive aspects. In the past, Buganda had a dual sex political system that allowed for substantial female representation and involvement in governance and administration. The position of the Queen mother among the Baganda gave women prominent and visible political authority in running the kingdom. The education system prepared the women and the whole community and constituted the identity of the Baganda. It should be noted that if you train a woman you would have trained a nation. Therefore, by emphasising the education of women, the intention and aim are to train the whole community. It is because of this socialisation process that the Baganda could easily be identified from their behaviour as this constitutes their identity.

### *References*

Castle, E. B. 1966. *Growing up in East Africa*. London: Oxford University Press.

Chami, F.A. Pwiti, G. and Radimilahy, G. (Eds.). *Climate Change, Trade, and Modes of Production in Sub-Saharan Africa - Studies in the African Past 3*, Tanzania: University of Dar ES Salaam Press.

Folorunso, C. A. 2003. Exploring Gender in Tiv material Cultures: Ethno-archaeology in the Katsina-Ala Valley. *Studies in the African Past* 3:155-168.

Folorunso, C. A. 2007. Gender and archaeological site formation: Ethno-archaeological studies in parts of Nigeria. *Archaeology and Women: Ancient and Modern Issues.* Left Coast Press, Publications of the Institute of Archaeology, University College London, Walnut Creek, California. 353-372.

Kenyatta, J. 1938. *Facing Mountain Kenya*. London: Heinemann.

Kigozi, B. 2008. *An Evaluation of Music Education in Elementary Schools in Buganda; A Way Forward.* A PhD Thesis Submitted to the Department of Music, University of Pretoria.

Kyagulanyi, E. N. G. 1975. The Growth and Development of Education in Ssingo from Earliest Times. A Project Submitted to the Department of History for the Award of Bachelor of Arts

(History), Makerere University.
Kyazike, E. 2002. Culture and Development: The Case of Traditional Kiganda Women Education. Un Published M.A Dissertation submitted to the Department of History, Makerere University.
Mair, L. 1933. Buganda Land Tenure. *Journal of International African Institute*. 6 (2):187-205.
Moumoumni. 1968. *Education in Africa*. London: Andre Deutsche.
Mukasa, T. D. 2007. The State of Baganda Women: Invisible in Traditional Cultural Leadership. In: Ggwangamujje NY/NJ, Inc (eds.) Ttabamiruka 2007. The 3rd Baganda Ttabamiruka International Event. Hyatt Regency New Brunswick: New Jersey, USA August 31st- September 2nd 2007.
Nelson, S. M. 1997. *Gender in Archaeology*. London: Altamira.
Nsimbi, M.B. 1956. Village Life and Customs in Buganda. *Uganda Journal* 20 (1): 27-36.
Orwell, G. 1945. *Animal Farm: A Fairy Story*. London: Secker and Warburg.
Roscoe.1911. *The Baganda: An Account of their Native Customs and Beliefs*. London: Macmillan.
Southwold, M. B. A. 1956. The Inheritance of Land in Buganda. *Uganda Journal* 20 (1) 88-96.
Todaro, M. 1977. *Economics for a Developing World: An Introduction to Principles, Problems and Policies for Development*. London: Longman.
Wandira, A. 1971. Indigenous Education in Uganda. Department of History. Makerere University.

## *Informants*

| Name | Age | Date of interview |
|---|---|---|
| Mr. Kalyesubula Samuel | 78 | 28th December 1998 |
| Mr. Magala Fred | 68 | 2nd April 1998 |
| Ms. Nakyonyi Efranse | 76 | 27th December 1998 |
| Ms. Namakula Eseresi | About 80 | 8th December 1998 |
| Ms. Nambi Anna Maria | 63 | 26th December 1998 |
| Ms. Namutebi Fermia | 78 | 1st and 2nd April 1998 |
| Rev Mugerere | 67 | 2nd April 1998 |

# Chapter Four

## THE VIOLENCE OF SILENCE AND THE LIMITS OF COMMUNITY: THE IKALE WOMAN IN TWENTY-FIRST CENTURY NIGERIA

*Oluwakemi Abiodun Adesina*

> ...we should not overlook the fact that women everywhere are actively involved in working against social, cultural, racial, economic and political discrimination.[1]

### *Introduction*

It is presumptuous to believe that there is women resistance everywhere against social, cultural, economic and political discriminations. Such generalization will be subject to critique in this chapter. There are women who felt trapped by the walls erected by customs and traditions. There are also societies where women are not only objectified and repressed but are yet to find their individual or collective voices. They lived in a world provided by their social space. For historians, little attention is paid to the asymmetries of power contained therein.[2] The general neglect of pockets of areas and

---

[1] Richters, A. 'Introduction', Social Science and Medicine, vol. 35, no. 6, 1992. p. 749 as cited in Stein, Jane *Empowerment and Women's Health: Theory, Methods and Practice*, United Kingdom: Zed Books, 1997. p.1

[2] Moore, D. and Roberts, R. "Listening for Silences". *History in Africa*, Vol. 17, 1990, 319-325.

regions with attachment to age-old practices and values has robbed the intellectual terrain of the discrete particulars represented by such experiences as that of the Ikale people of south-western Nigeria.

The historical development of Ikaleland as well as its customs and institutions provide a deep insight into the dynamic development of a little-studied sub-group of the Yoruba.[3] Yorubaland has attracted an extraordinary amount of interest and attention in historical literature and has continued to do so due to the dynamic nature of the land and its people. However, in order to better appreciate the vivacious nature of the people and the land, it is imperative that more work of an historical nature be accomplished to bring into bold relief the breath and complexity that is the Yoruba country. In consonance with this idea, this work distinctively focuses on the South-eastern part of Yorubaland inhabited by the people identified as sub-groups of the Yoruba. This region extends from the coastal lagoons to the rainforest and contains peoples grouped together as Ijebu, Ondo, Itsekiri and Ikale. [4]The result is a collection of people that mirrors the diversity of the Yoruba group.

This work sets out to bring into focus both the general and specific circumstances of the Ikale people. It aims to fill a major gap in the knowledge of the dynamics involved in the history and development of Ikaleland and the consequence of all these for Ikale women. This work examines the impact of a community's ideals on the construction of women's identity within the ambit of gender relations. This effort also seeks to understand the relationship between women and men by examining their roles, status, and class within the traditional household and the community organization of the Ikale people of Ondo State. Gender is a construct within a people's living experience, embedded in the base of their philosophy and manifesting at the theoretical and pragmatic levels of their polity. Because gender is never independent of other social systems, it would be futile to consider it is a fixed and immutable construct; rather it is a process. Furthermore,

---

[3] Akinjogbin, I.A. and E.A. Ayandele, 'Yorubaland up to 1800', in Ikime, Obaro, Groundwork of Nigerian History, (Ibadan: Heinemann Educational Books, 1980), p.121.

[4] Obayemi, A. 'The Yoruba and Edo-speaking peoples and their Neighbours before 1600', in Ajayi J.F.A. & Michael Crowder, *History of West Africa,* Volume One', (London: Longman Group Ltd, 1971), p.220.

gender classifications permeate a people's cosmic perception and may be discernible in their language, wisdom storehouse, and philosophy. It thus, presents itself in every sector of a people's experience and philosophy of life.[5] This chapter identifies the parameters of social structure which developed along gender lines with the aim of recognizing the social dynamics and structures that emerged from the interaction of Western and Ikale cultures. In addition, it looks at aspects of continuity and change in Ikale tradition and culture within the contexts of social change induced by Westernization and the dynamics of post-independence Nigeria.

### *Ikale Women at the Dawn of the 20th century:*

Among the Ikale, polygamy was a fact of life. So also was working hard on the farm, even in the last trimester of pregnancy. Women worked without so much as a whimper and bore the tasks without complaint. The Ikale social and cultural conditions actively fostered this distinctive culture of 'silence' that bred the spirits of efficiency, hard work and ingenuity. An Ikale man, Chief Samuel Olukayo Akinnurun, born in 1939, lent credence to this in his autobiography. He reconstructed his mother's experiences: "... My mother told me that I was born in the first month of the year when they were harvesting yams from a farmland near a baobab tree popularly called "Opoipo."[6]

The socialization of the Ikale woman into the orthodox Ikale culture was very pronounced. Even when it was obvious an Ikale woman was going through certain tribulations in her home, she must grin and bear it. For instance, a man could lawfully construct a parallel relationship outside with another woman and to the knowledge of his wife without any consequence. She dared not say anything.[7] In the same vein, a man punished the wife or wives for any infraction committed by their children. The allowances of such women were withheld and in several cases while such women were

---

[5] Olajubu, O. *Women in the Yoruba Religious Sphere*, (New York: State University of New York Press, 2003), p.7.

[6] Akinnurun, S. O. *My Life.* (Lagos: Talent Publishers, 2008), p. 1.

[7] Interview, Madam Ruth Lagbayi, Teacher, 50 +, Ilutitun, April 26, 2007.

tongue-lashed publicly in front of their children and other wives. Whatever could be said and done would be done to maltreat such women before the other women and children.[8]

Socially and economically, the Ikale woman was subordinated and marginalised. Ikale men would give their women farmlands for their upkeep. Such women were also then given a separate portion to till for their husband in a practice known as '*Agban*'. Women were required to plant, weed, and generally take care of the farm. After harvesting, the products are sold and the proceeds surrendered to the man. To spend part of the money on oneself was a great taboo.[9] From the above examples, several common themes emerge about the Ikale woman: obedience, silence and conformity. These, for the women, became both a tool of prestige and means of survival.[10]

The cultural violence against women has been accepted as the norm and a way of life.[11] The tendency then, is for the Ikale woman to be silent. But in all these, the Ikale woman must develop a forbearance that has come to identify them with the 'muted group.'[12] Silence amongst Ikale women has therefore, not only become a survival mechanism but also a tool for upward mobility and peace of mind. This was inculcated in the Ikale people's rights from when they were young.

### *Social Systems: Hierarchies and Orientations*

The political, military and social organization in every Ikale district was based upon a system of '*otu*', or age companies. On reaching the age of eighteen, young men were banded together annually and one of them

---

[8] Bajowa, Olu, Spring of a Life – An Autobiography, Ibadan: Spectrum Books, 1992, p. 76.

[9] Interview, Madam Comfort Ikuejamofo, 100+, Ilutitun, April 16, 2008.

[10] Lashgari, D. *To Speak the Unspeakable: Implications of Gender*, "Race," Class, and Culture, in Violence, Silence, and Anger: Women's Writing As Transgression, (Charlottesville and London: University Press of Virginia, 1995), p.9.

[11] Lashgari, D. (Ed.), *Violence, Silence, and Anger: Women's Writing as Transgression,* Charlottesville and London: University Press of Virginia, 1995, p.1.

[12] Ardener, E. "Belief and the Problem of Women" in S. Ardener (ed), *Perceiving Culture,* (London: Dent, 1975), p.1-17.

was made the '*Oloriotu*', or 'head of the company' by the *Oloja* (the royal father) and his chiefs in consultation with the *Ifa* oracle. Men remained members of these companies throughout their lives unless and until such time as they acquired titles, in which case they forsook their position in the *Otu* and joined the company of *Ijoye* (chiefs). All communal work was carried out by the *Otu*, and in their military capacity they were employed by the community to enforce the collection of debts and exact the payment of compensation for adultery and other offences. The female gender did not belong to these age companies. They only gathered around their friends on wedding days, naming ceremonies, and burial ceremonies. Women were restricted to the private sphere and excluded from the public arena and governance (except in the market).

Patriarchy, as defined by Diane Richardson *et al.*[13] best describes the Ikale society. Patriarchy is defined as a political system in which men by force, direct pressure or through ritual, law and language, customs, etiquette, education, and the division of labour, determine what part a woman shall or shall not play, and in which the female is everywhere subsumed under the male. The word "patriarchy" has been defined by Jennifer Bathamley in the *Dictionary of Theories*[14] as either the argument that authority was derived by kings and aristocrats from God, whose fatherhood of all they represent on earth; or the view that power is divided along gender lines and in favour of men. She stated that the original theory of patriarchy was employed in 17th century Europe to justify the rule of monarchs and used by 20th century feminists to describe a division of power and advantage along lines of gender. The common usage of the term, thus, means rule by men in society. Ikaleland is a patriarchal society. The application of patriarchy to this work does not necessarily imply that no woman has power, or that women in Ikaleland may not have certain powers. Women exercised their powers in the private space on domestic issues and market related issues. A major feature of pre-colonial socio-economic life of Ikale people was the inter-sexual division of labour on farmlands and the sharing of profits

---

[13]Richardson, D. & Robinson, V. *Introducing Women's Studies*, (New York: Palgrave, 1993) p. 177.

[14]Bathamley, J. *Dictionary of Theories*, (New York: Barnes and Nobles, 1993).

between husbands and wives. Ikale society was not a monetised one, so proceeds from their farms that were traded by barter were shared by the household. In fairly rich families, the household was a large one comprising of a man and as many as three to ten wives and several children. Each wife was granted a sizeable proportion of the farmland from where she derived her own income to feed herself, her husband, and the entire household on days specifically allotted to her to take care of the household meals.

The head wife was a *primus inter pares* (first among equals), who was saved the rigours highlighted above as she was required to play the role of a 'husband' to other wives, settling disputes, allotting responsibilities, and generally taking care of the entire household. At the other end of the spectrum was the most junior wife upon whose shoulders rested many of the several chores in the compound. Because of the low status, it was not uncommon for such young wives to wish for another addition to the wives, so she could be freed from her heavy schedule.[15]

The birth and upbringing of a child was a very delicate issue among the Ikale. This is because, as in every Yoruba or African family, a child is important for the perpetuation of a family, a lineage and consequently a race.[16] Ikale children, just like in other Yoruba societies, were, therefore, given specialized training based on gender role. While fathers focused on the boy child, the mothers were expected to train the girl child on the cultural expectations. Sexual division of labour was most common in Ikaleland. The result was the ultimate formation of two complementary but separate gendered worlds for men and women. The father of the house, who was the head of the household, controlled the activities of his entire family and mobilised their labour at any given time. The wives and children of a man, unless exempted, must work for him. The boy child was socialized in the art of farming, craftsmanship, fishing, and hunting, depending on what the family orientation was. The girl child was trained in farming and domestic work such as to wash, clean the house and the environs and cook. She was taught to plant, harvest, process food for sale, and also taught to trade. It

---

[15]Interview with Mrs. Theresa Emehin, 84yrs of Igo-Aduwo Quarters 23/12/05

[16]Fasan, R. O. "*Transitional Ceremonial Song Performance of the Ondo, Ikale, Oyo and Ijebu.*" Unpublished Ph.D Thesis, Department of English, University of Ibadan, 2009, p.79.

was only after getting married that a son or daughter could claim to be independent of his/her father. In the case of the boy child, however, he got partial independence on getting married, while the girl child got full independence since she was no longer responsible to her family at marriage except attending to family celebrations and festivals at her husband's consent. Married women belonged to their husband's *ebi* (family) though without losing membership of their ancestral *ebi* (family). At most times, the Ikale woman at death is taken back to her ancestral home for burial except otherwise instructed before her death. To give a contrary instruction, she would have begged her family members to allow her remains to be interred at her husband's compound. The Ikale people do this to show the collection of dowry does not imply the sale of their daughters.

Full independence for the boy child was only attained after the father's demise. Thus, irrespective of the marital status of the son, he was expected to occasionally work for his father. In addition to the call on their labour, the sons were expected to cater for their parents in old age or during difficult times. Ikale *ebi* system found resonance in the economic organization. This was exemplified in the organization/division of labour and gender relations. The organization of labour was mainly based on kinship ties as each household was an economic unit. Characteristically, the Ikale *ebi* mode of production was organically linked with the kinship and social systems with the attendant division of labour between the sexes.[17] Also, access to the factors of production was conditional on one's membership of the *ebi*. Thus, as far as the mode of production was concerned, economic and family relationship and the social structure converged. These created an intricate network of relationships that served as the fundamental basis of Ikale social and cultural unity and identity.[18]

Marriage practices in Yorubaland were similar but with peculiarities in various sub-groups. However, among the Ikale there were three marriage types, namely: the *Olugbu* – the standard marriage practice in Ikale, sent-away or run-away marriages and through kidnapping. In pre-colonial

---

[17]Ekiran, M.A., *Marriage and the Family A Sociological Perspective*, (Lagos, Rebonik, 2002), pp.31-32.

[18]Interview, Chief Anthony Ibitoye, retired School teacher, Igbotako, December 23, 2005.

times, kidnapping for marriage was legal. This usually happened in very rare cases of rebellion exhibited by young women betrothed to men whom they considered unsuitable husbands. Hence, such young women were kidnapped with the permission of their fathers. After she had settled in her husband's home, the *Olugbu* rites were performed in her husband's home.[19]

The sent-away bride; a practice that is still in existence, is usually a lady who is sent out of her parent's house after she is confirmed pregnant before the *Olugbu* marriage rites. The lady's extended family (*ebi*) will fine her and her mother for this act and she is sent away with all her belongings or for fear of the consequences, she runs away to her suitor's home. The 'sent-away' or 'run-away' bride was usually punished by the bride's father's family together with her mother because it was believed that the mother had failed in her parenting duty or was in the know of the act. On the bride's arrival at the groom's family house, the man's family takes kolanuts, hot drinks, and an unspecified amount of money to inform the lady's family that she is with them and that they are ready to perform the marriage rites. However, before the matter is resolved, the lady will be fined a big live goat for violating the custom and tradition of her people, and her mother is fined for negligence, and members of her family are barred from having anything to do with her. At the settlement of the impasse, a date is set for the traditional marriage. How have Ikale women fared in the twenty-first century? That is the concern of the next section.

### *Tradition and the Modern Ikale Women*

The new culture introduced through colonial contact created an avenue for the Ikale woman to assert herself and to seek her freedom from traditions and customs. But cultural influences prevented a self-definition by the Ikale woman as witnessed in other Yoruba societies. This became a system of contradictions and a complicated set of dynamics. This is because the Ikale woman was not expected to reject the obvious gendered roles, sexuality and position epitomized by the ways and wisdom of the elderly women

---

[19] Akingbemi, G.B, *Ikale People and Culture*, (Lagos: Third World Media, 2007), pp.61, 71 & 73.

while trying to redeem herself or enhance her own ability to reposition or redefine herself.[20] The pre-established hierarchies and gender relations were left in place.[21] Thus, the notion of patriarchy survived in the power relations in Ikale society. Mrs. Temenu, in an oral interview, describes how the powers of the men were used to tame Ikale women. She says: "Gin and goat constituted and still constitute a potent force in keeping women in line."[22] Whenever a woman committed what is regarded as odious or an act of insubordination, she suffers a fine ranging from a bottle of gin and an *ikeegbe* (goat) to summoning her to the family house where she is subjected to other forms of sanctions including threats of divorce. In several instances, until such a fine was paid the woman was regarded as subsisting under a societal sanction that freezes her progress in the society. The longer she takes in paying the fine, the worse the situation gets."[23]

### *Limitations of Women's Power in the Community*

On the need to preserve Ikale culture, opposition is muted if ever it existed. Tradition to them, conveys a sense of safe nurture, warm growth, budding or ever-present wholeness.[24] Thus, in paying close attention to the existence of the Ikales in both their traditional and modern milieu, adherence to cultural and traditional practices have continued to have deep social, economic, cultural and political meanings and consequences, both in the private and public realms. Almost unanimously, all respondents share the conviction that becoming "modern" must not lead to the neglect of tradition and culture.[25] An insistent foregrounding of this is prevalent in many

---

[20]Interview, Mrs. Bukola, Omosola, teacher, 50+, Akotogbo, April 26, 2007

[21]Interview, Madam, Titilola Akinwalere, Teacher, 58, Okitipupa, April 26, 2007.

[22] Interview, Mrs. Ajike Temenu, Housewife, 70+,Okitipupa, April 27, 2007.

[23] Interview, Mrs Temenu, Housewife, 70+,Okitipupa, April 27, 2007.

[24] Fox, R. W. and Jackson Lears, T. J. The Power of Culture. Critical Essays in American History, (Chicago and London, The University of Chicago Press, 1993), p.1

[25] Interviews, Mr Akinyemi Omosola, Mr. Folorunso Akinmameji, Mr. Akinyemi Omosola, Mr. Morakinyo Olorunju, Mr. Festus Akingboju, Mrs Abosede Lagbaye, Madam Ruth Lagbayi, Madam Elizabeth Akinjahi and Mrs Yinde Sewo. These people were interviewed

Ikale people. While modern Ikales both in public and private have the right to participate in making decisions about the common or communal life, every member of the society also has the duty and task to continue to clarify and indeed affirm the basic values by which the Ikales have lived in the past and also strive to move the people and the society into the modern milieu without fundamental changes to the form and character of traditional Ikale culture.

Thus, in the era of re-definition of culture and values in the twenty-first century, the Ikale people have continued to bear true allegiance to their customs while also developing a rich network of personal loyalties to their family origins and communities. Ikale women are expected to defer to males and remain subordinate to them.[26] Ikale women are the major agency through which patriarchal control of women has continued to thrive by their acceptance of the framework of domination by men. As Glynis Breakwell noted, it is difficult for women and men to step too far beyond stereotypical behaviours without dire consequences.[27] Women, as a consequence of gender-power relations then, are more likely to accept the patriarchal/male version of their lives as their 'reality', although they experience and manifest contradictory responses. This has been succinctly put by Eva Figes:

> But woman is taught to desire not what her mother desired for herself, but what her father and all men find desirable in a woman. Not what she is, but should be. Man is a good deal more lenient with himself: he may say that men should be brave, unselfish, yet the fact that he is weak and egotistic is looked upon as a regrettable falling away from the ideal standard which is only to be expected in human beings. But since the standard of womanhood is set by men for men and not by women, no relaxation of

---

at different dates.

[26] Interviews, Mrs. Christianah Jimoh, Trader and Woman Politican, 50+, Okitipupa, December 14, 2007; Mrs. Eniola Igbasan, Teacher and Woman Politician, 50+, Okitipupa, December 15, 2007.

[27] For details, see, Breakwell, G.B., The Quiet Rebel: Women at Work in a Man's World, (London: Century), 1985.

standards is allowable, she is either an absolute woman or nothing at all… [28]

Thus, many women come to believe that child care and home-making are their destiny, or that, despite intellect and competence, they are not suited for senior management.[29] This does not imply that Ikale women are not educated or do not occupy senior management positions. They do. However, the patriarchal culture among the Ikale came to represent a set of pervasive and ossified structure that privileged maleness/masculinity over femaleness/femininity. This inevitably resulted in persistent failure by the average Ikale man and woman to challenge assumptions underlying everyday experience and belief. Thus, it is clear that, while Yoruba culture may be patriarchal and male dominant in certain practices and ideological statements, it also emphasises very frequently and importantly the androgynous reality of existence, making central the importance of the female principle as life's mainstay; and, thus, Yoruba culture tends to be integrative of the sexes and gender roles.[30] This is fundamental and underpins gender relations among the Ikale people.

In the modern period, many entrenched obstacles have hindered addressing even practical gender needs, not to mention the more structural changes needed to redress power imbalances in gender relations.[31] The Ikale situation under colonialism has been confronted with dominant decision-making structures within the community, resulting in little change to social relations. The context in which an understanding of the status of the Ikale woman is constructed revolves around male power and perceptions, and the problems and experiences of women. Their subordination has also been understood within the context of Yoruba women's experiences in general. Yoruba women occupied a significant position in pre-colonial political

---

[28] Piges, E. *Patriarchal Attitudes: Women in Society*, (London: Virago, 1978), p.17.

[29] Nicolson, P. Gender, Power and Organisation:…, p.11

[30] Ogundipe, O. "Indigenous and Contemporary Gender Concepts and Issues in Africa: Implications for Nigeria's Development." CBAAC Occasional Monograph No. 2, (Lagos: Malthouse Press Ltd., 2007), p.41.

[31] Guijt, I. and Shah, M. K. (eds), The Myth of Community. Gender Issues in Participatory, (London: ITDG Publishing), 2001, p.3.

organization, religion, family life and economy.[32]The private domain, that is, domesticity and motherhood, seems to be the space of women in most cultures. Private and public spaces are, however, linked. Women, for instance, shape the lives of those who occupy the public space in their capacity as mothers and people who nurture.[33]

However, certain common parameters do manifest in any consideration of women in society cross-culturally. Despite this, limitations on women's functions in the public space are usually manifestations of local gender constructs. The relationship between men and women in several societies are based on fundamental inequalities. The roots of this profound dis-aggregation are traceable to patriarchal control of society. In several cultures, Yorubaland inclusive, men control economic, political and cultural power while women take a subordinate position. In other words, while men control public life, women occupy the resigned marginal spaces of private life and domesticity. But how did the Ikale woman negotiate her way in the developing cross-currents? It is important to understand the changes taking place in the country that significantly affected the people and society of Yorubaland in general and in Ikaleland specifically.

### *Structural Adjustment Programme (SAP) and the Ikale Woman*

Nigeria's military government embarked on the politics of adjustment in 1986. The Structural Adjustment Programme (SAP) introduced in Nigeria by the Babangida administration in 1986 sought to enthrone more market oriented policies. SAP was the economic recovery measure proffered by the World Bank and the International Monetary Fund (IMF) for the ailing economies of the sub-Saharan African countries.[34] The military regime was

---

[32] Denzer, L. "Yoruba Women: a Historiographical Study", *The International Journal of African Historical Studies,* Vol. 27, No.1 (1994), pp.1-39.

[33] Olajubu O. *Women In the Yoruba Religious Sphere*, (New York: State University of New York Press, 2003),p.10

[34] Ojo, M.O. and Akanji, O.O. "The impact of macroeconomic policy reforms on Nigerian agriculture" Economic and Financial Review, Central Bank of Nigeria, vol. 34(2), 1996, p. 549-570; Moser, G.S. Rogers and R. van Til, 'Nigeria: Experience with Structural Adjustment', Occasional paper 148, International Monetary Fund, Washington D. C,

forced to accept the programme as a condition to the rescheduling of the nation's foreign debt. The objectives of SAP adopted in June 1986 were:

- to restructure and diversify the productive base of the economy in order to lessen the dependency on the oil sector and import;
- to achieve fiscal balance of payment viability over a period of time;
- to lay the basis for sustainable, non-inflationary or minimum inflationary growth; and
- to lessen the dominance of unproductive investment in the public sector, improve the sector's efficiency and intensify the growth potential of the private sector.

The programme of adjustment, however, came with a number of preconditions including the devaluation of the local currency, freezing of wages, imposition of numerous taxes on workers and peasants, privatization of public enterprises, government-reduced spending on education, health and transportation services, removal of subsidies and the deregulation of the price of petroleum products.[35] Before the introduction of SAP, the government was a major employer of labour. It also implemented policies such as foreign exchange control measures to regulate and protect the value of the local currency in the international market. Accordingly, the population was able to access foreign goods and services at minimal costs. Cost of living was also minimal and allowed most families to have a moderate quality of life. But surprisingly, under SAP, the economy dramatically worsened, resulting in the impoverishment of many Nigerians, particularly women.[36]

---

1997; Titilola, S.O., "The impact of Structural Adjustment Programme on the agriculture and rural economy of Nigeria," in Phillips, A. O. and E. C Ndekwu (eds.), Structural Adjustment Programme in Developing Economy: The case of Nigeria, Ibadan, NISER, 1987, pp. 150-166; Akintola, J.O. and J.T.O. Oke, "Impact of Macro- economic policy reforms on the output and prices of food grains in Nigeria", The Nigerian Journal of Economic History, No. 4, 2001, pp.70-80; Nigerian Institute of Social and Economic Research (NISER), Social Impact of the Structural Adjustment Programme, Ibadan, NISER Monograph Series, No.1, 1988.

[35] Bonat, Z and Abdullahi, Y., ""The World Bank, IMF, and the Nigerian Agricultural and Rural Economy', in Bade Onimode (ed) The IMF, the World Bank, and the AfricanDebt: the Social and Political Impact, (London: Zed Books, 1989), pp.167-70

[36] Omorodion, F.I. "Rural Women's Experiences of Micro-Credit Schemes in Nigeria. Case Study of Esan Women", *Journal of Asian and African Studies*, Vol. 42 (6), pp. 479-494.

The process of adjustment became one of the greatest threats to the basic foundations of African societies by creating social tensions and ineffective action. It had the capacity to widen gender differentiation as husbands and wives pursued different goals for different reasons. Prior to this, the process of modernization that increased the demand for formal education eventually had its own backlash. The substantial rates of educational dropouts in Ikaleland became a factor in gender relations. Similarly, the result of the rapid expansion of the educational system and the subsequent saturation of the labour market began a phenomenon of graduate unemployment in the 1980s.[37]

It has been asserted that the process of change has been defined by the structure of a system. The educational system proved significant in this regard. As noted by Lesthaeghe, "education…allows younger men social mobility through new channels, threatening the gerontocracy, and because it encourages closeness between spouses and hence undermines lineage power and control."[38] The large army of unemployed and disgruntled youths began to question certain orthodoxies not only in their communities but also in their country in general. These began to weaken, in some respect, the hold of custom on the new generation. People began to move out in search of greener pastures. The contemporary realities dictated by SAP were self-reliance and productivity. But there were other unstated realities. According to Lawal:

> By and large the operators of S.A.P did not consider the interests of the majority of the people who lived in the rural areas. Since rapid urbanization continued without any check, population explosion in the cities compounded the problems. Already the majority of people in the urban centres were poor. When they were joined by the waves of the rural poor, the gravity of social problems they precipitated could only be

[37] Oni, B. "Education and Alternative Avenues of Mobility: A Nigerian Study", *Comparative Education Review*, Vol. 32, No. 1 (Feb., 1988), pp.87-99.

[38] Lockwood, M. "Structure and Behavior in the Social Demography of Africa", *Population and Development Review*, Vol. 21, No.1 (March 1995) pp.1-32; Lesthaeghe, R. "On the social control of human reproduction", *Population and Development Review*, 6, No. 4, 1980, pp.527-548 (see, p.541)

imagined than experienced.[39]

A large Ikale Diaspora developed in Lagos, Ibadan and other Nigerian towns and cities that became a significant statement on how a new generation can begin the process of relocation and adaptation to change. This generation also wanted to distance itself from the control of tradition and culture. P.C. Lloyd has identified and commented on such reactions:

> In their turn, the young educated men and women are sometimes intolerant and impatient of traditional ways and values. A few are ashamed of them. It is among these that one finds the rare case of the man who returns from overseas with a complete Western outfit for his mother, so that she can be a 'civilized' woman and not an embarrassment to him. But such rejection of indigenous society, more common in earlier decades, has usually been succeeded by a repudiation of assimilationist tendencies. The African seeks the roots of his own culture; he endeavours to preserve in it the elements which seem distinctly African. His parents in many cases represent this traditional culture, and he thus respects their way of life. Indeed many seek from their elder kin a fuller appreciation of their heritage, the learning of which was denied to them at school and by their long absence from home.[40]

But the formation of the Ikale hometown associations began the process of reining in the youths who might have wanted to severe the umbilical relations with the homeland. For instance, at the University of Ibadan, a strong Ikale association emerged that served as a uniting force for Ikale students, teachers and workers.[41] Many of the young men within the association began to seek out their female counterparts for a future together.[42]

However, back home in the traditional milieu, the division of labour

---

[39] Lawal, A.A., "The Negative Impact of Structural Adjustment Programme on Agriculture in Nigeria", *The Nigerian Journal of Economic History,* No. 4, 2001, pp.61-69.

[40] Lloyd, P.C., *Africa in Social Change: Changing traditional societies in the modern world,* England: Penguin Books Ltd., 1967, pp.185-6.

[41] Interview, Mr. Festus Akingboju, 52, Zoologist, December 23, 2005.

[42] Ibid.

that characterised Ikale gender relations did not relent. With the broader policies and programmes of SAP buffeting the rural areas folks engaged in informal productive activities as those in the formal and urban sectors, the rural economies were at a disadvantage in reacting to their biting effects. This even began a process of disaggregating the units of social action within the framework of the survival of the fittest. The subordination of women in production and consumption not only continued, but it even became more predatory. Nevertheless, the women became more enterprising. They combined farming with trading and other vocations. The Ikale woman had to take care of the house and the children as part of the 'division of labour.' Nevertheless, several husbands began to take "soft loans" from their wives without being willing or able to pay back.[43] It is obvious that even with SAP, the Ikale traditional institution's self-perpetuating mechanism of domination still managed to reposition itself.

### *Better Life for Rural Women: Gbebiro*

A major and fundamental development in Nigeria between 1986 and 1992 was the inauguration of what the people of Ondo State, to which the Ikales belong, knew and addressed as *Gbebiro.* This was the Better Life Programme for the Rural Women (BLP), a poverty alleviation programme. This was one of the strategic institutional arrangements designed to raise the standards of living of the rural woman. It was one of the most ambitious programmes mounted for the improvement of the lot of women in Nigeria.[44] It was created in 1987 by the wife of the then president, Mrs. Maryam Babangida. The objectives[45] of the BLP were:

a. To stimulate and motivate rural women to achieve better living standards and to sensitize the rest of the Nigerian population to the problems of women

b. To mobilize women collectively in order to improve their general

---

[43] Interview, Mrs. Busola Omosola, Trader, 60+, Ode Irele, February 24, 2009

[44] Apollo, R. African Women and children crisis and response, Greenwood Publishing Group, 2001, p. 267.

[45] Ibid, pp. 146-147; Federal Republic of Nigeria, 1992, A361

lot and ability to seek and achieve leadership roles in all spheres of society.

c. To educate rural women in simple hygiene, family planning, and the importance of child care and to increase literacy rates.

d. To raise consciousness about the rights of women, the availability of opportunities and facilities, and their social, political, and economic responsibilities.

e. To inculcate the spirit of self-development, particularly in the fields of education, business, the arts, crafts, and agriculture.

In order to achieve the lofty goals set for the programme, the organization set forth the following strategies[46]:

1. Enlightenment campaign, study tours, and visits
2. Radio broadcasts and television discussions educating women and the general public about BLP's objectives.
3. Organizing Seminars and Workshops.
4. Field days - BLP fairs and cultural displays at both the district and village levels, aimed at generating interest.

Thus, in order to further strengthen the framework for the programme, other institutions partnered the BLP in its programmes. These included the Directorate for Social Mobilization (MAMSER) and the Directorate of Food, Roads, and Rural Infrastructure (DFRRI). These were government agencies established for the mobilization, education and re-orientation of Nigerians toward economic recovery, development and a new social order. Despite the novelty of participatory development, such as the BLP in Nigeria, it is not a new phenomenon. Many earlier initiatives that stress empowerment and collective local action include, among others, the New Deal in India in the 1930s and community – development programmes in Latin America in the 1950s.[47]

What social realities did BLP portend for the Ikale woman? For the first time in Nigerian history, the wife of a Nigerian Head of State was not

---

[46] Ibid

[47] Gujit, I. and Shah, M. K. T*he Myth of Community: Gender Issues in Participatory Development*, (London: ITDG Publishing, 2001 ed), p.3

content with the traditionally ceremonial and honorary role of the 'First Lady'. Mrs Maryam Babangida not only transformed the position into an intensive supportive mechanism for the presidency, but also used it as a tool for national campaign to change the lot of women in the country. Ultimately, she turned her ceremonial position as First Lady into rallying point for the aspirations and contributions of the disenfranchised in the country. Through the BLP she encouraged women to improve their lives through the programmes in education, health, agriculture, craft and food processing as well as trade.[48]

The programme, which believed in advocacy and gender mainstreaming, was widely received with women organised into segments to take advantage of it. The *modus operandi* adopted was novel. It recognised the diverse ways African men and women perceive and deal with women's issues and it, as a matter of fact, incorporated these into its development paradigm. It must be stated here, that Ikale men and indeed men of Ondo origin in general were farmers just like the women. Along the line, however, "the men virtually abandoned certain aspects of the economy which appear not too lucrative (food crops) for high yielding ones (the cash crops); the women have taken up the challenges of supplying these very essential life-sustaining, though ulcerative services, for the sustenance of the economy".[49]

It is worth noting, however, that before the BLP, there was never a time when women farmers were made objects of assistance through government programmes. Rather, Ikale people, both male and female, were organized into cooperative farmers groups, who supported one another in the planting, harvesting, and processing of cash crops, foodstuffs and palm oil.[50] With the existence of women cooperative organizations before the establishment of

---

[48] *The Nation* (Lagos), January 2, 2010, p.10

[49] Afolabi, M.M., "Women As Pillars of National Economy In Nigeria: A Study of Economic Activities of Rural Women in Six Local Government Areas of Ondo State", https://editorialexpress.com/cgi- --bin/conference/download.cgi?db_name=IAFFE2008&paper_id=240, p.1.

[50] Afolabi, M.M., "Women As Pillars of National Economy In Nigeria: A Study of Economic Activities of Rural Women in Six Local Government Areas of Ondo State", https://editorialexpress.com/cgi- bin/conference/download.cgi?db_name=IAFFE2008&paper_id=240, p.7.

the BLP, the programme helped the female farmers to have easy access to the Ministry of Agriculture to improve their yields, and access to micro-credits. Through the DFFRI programmes the infrastructural needs of the farmers were ameliorated. Food was produced in abundance and exported to other states. The programme also promised huge trade and investment potentials for the women. The leader of the women organizations at the village level represented their interest at the local government level in Okitipupa. The major products of these women were cassava and palm produce. Usually, they got loans from the BLP to plant cassava on communal farmlands of about 30 to 40 acres of land. After harvesting, the cassava is processed into *garri* and *pupuru*. They sold them together with the products from the palm farms they had bought. The BLP assisted them in the sales and transportation of their wares and, at the end of sales dividends were shared.

Unfortunately, the desire to restructure the condition of the Ikale woman was to be sacrificed on the altar of political expediency. Since the women were already organised into groups and guilds, it became easy for the political elite to take advantage of them. The women were 'encouraged' to sew uniforms (*anko*) and to parade for visiting dignitaries or were taken to the state capital like objects of display on the nation's independence and other anniversaries. The Ikale women baulked at this as it was considered anathema for the hard-working Ikale woman who believed so much in spending quality time with her family and in other more utilitarian pursuits to gallivant all over the place wasting valuable time and resources.[51] The elitist nature of the programme left the women almost hapless. It increased their visibility, confidence and even sophistication without a corresponding rise in their standard of living. Unfortunately, the programme further exacerbated women's unequal opportunities and access to power. Some husbands even abdicated their responsibilities, choosing instead "to send their wives to BLP for means of sustenance."[52] The women's experiences with BLP unfortunately precluded them from embracing the Family Support Programme (FSP) that came as the successor to the BLP.[53] The FSP

[51] Interview, Madam Bose, Ayebusuwa, School teacher, Igbotako, March 27, 2007.

[52] Interview, Mrs Peju Akinrogunde, Trader, 60+, Igbotako, March 27, 2007

[53] Interview, Mrs. Comfort Adetula, Retired School Teacher, Ode Aye, January 29, 2009.

was the brainchild of Mrs Mariam Abacha, the wife of the then Nigerian Head of State, Gen. Sani Abacha.

### *Conclusion*

It must be noted that Ikale women are the major agency through which patriarchal control of women has continued to thrive by their acceptance of the framework of domination by men. Ikale women's sense of reality persuades them that their success is subject to their acceptance of domestic inequalities. The sense of 'emancipation', for the Ikale woman, is a transformation process of moving to the next level with the support of her husband, kins, affines, and community. Therefore, traditional gender roles among the Ikale limit the social possibilities for the women and were in a way established and sustained by an interlocking system of domination. It is therefore likely that despite all the information and propaganda produced by feminists and gender activists, Ikale women may not be able to find their 'voices' as dictated by modern realities. They are likely to retain for a long time their voices in their silences. Perhaps, in the silences, there is voice. For the Ikale woman, silences coincide with what a poet referred to as "the blueprint to a life."[54]

**_Newspapers, Periodicals and Pamphlets:_**
*The Nation* (Lagos), January 2, 2010.

**_B. Oral Sources_**

- Interview: Mr. Festus Akingboju. Agirifon Quarters. 52. Zoologist, December 23, 2005.
- Interview: Madame Theresa Emehin. 84. Igo-Aduwo Quarters. Trader. 23/12/05.
- Interview: Chief Anthony Ibitoye, retired School teacher, Igbotako, December 23, 2005.
- Interview: Mr. Benjamin Ikuejamofo, Community leader, 70 +, Igboegunrin,

---

[54] Falk Jones, L. "Breaking Silences in Feminist Dystopias", *Utopian Studies*, No. 3 (1991), pp. 7-11.

May 25, 2008.

. Interview: Mr. Folorunso Akinmameji, trader, 60+, Okitipupa, February 25, 2006.
. Interview: Pa Akinyemi Omosola, Community leader, 70+, Akotogbo, April 26, 2007.
. Interview: Mr Morakinyo Olorunju, Tailor, 60+, Ikoya, April 27, 2007.
. Interview: Madam, Titilola Akinwalere, Teacher, 58, Okitipupa, April 26, 2007.
. Interview: Mrs Temenu, Housewife, 70+,Okitipupa, April 27, 2007.
. Interview: Mrs Yinde Sewo, trader, 60+, Ilutitun, April 26, 2007.
. Interview: Madam Elizabeth Akinjahi, Businesswoman, Okitipupa, 60+, April 17, 2007.
. Interview: Madam Ruth Lagbayi, Teacher, 50 +, Ilutitun, April 26, 2007.
. Interview: Madam Comfort Ikuejamofo, 100+, Ilutitun, April 16, 2008.
. Interview: Mrs. Abosede Lagbaye, 40, Teacher,Okitipupa, April 26, 2007.
. Interview: Chief Ademola Lagbayi, Community leader, April 27, 2007.
. Interview: Mrs Bosede Aiyebusuwa, retired school teacher, 70+, Irele, May 30, 2008.
. Interview: Mrs. Comfort Adetula, Retired School Teacher, Ode Aye, January 29, 2009.
. Interview: Mrs Peju Akinrogunde, Trader, 60+, Igbotako, March 27, 2007
. Interview: Mrs. Christiana Jimoh, Trader and Woman Politican, 50+, Okitipupa, December 14, 2007.
. Interview: Mrs. Eniola Igbasan, Teacher and Woman Politician, 50+, Okitipupa, December 15, 2007.

### *Books And Chapters In Books*

Ajayi, J.F.A. & Crowder, M. 1971. *History of West Africa* Vol. I. London:Longman Group Ltd.

Akingbemi, G.B. 2007. *Ikale People and Culture*. Lagos: Third World Media.

Akinjogbin, I.A. and E.A. Ayandele. 1980. Yorubaland up to 1800. In: *Groundwork of Nigerian History*. Ikime, O. (Ed.). Ibadan: Heinemann Educational Books.

Akinnurun, S. O. 2008. *My Life*. Lagos: Talent Publishers.

Ardener, E. 1975. Belief and the Problem of Women. In: *Perceiving Women*. Ardener, S.( Ed.). London: Malaby Press.

Bajowa, J. O. 1993. *Ikale*. Lagos: Newswatch Books Ltd.
Bathamley, J. 1993. *Dictionary of Theories*. New York: Barnes and Nobles.
Bonat, Z and Abdullahi, Y. 1989. The World Bank, IMF, and the Nigerian Agricultural and Rural Economy.In: The IMF, the World Bank, and the African Debt: the Social and Political Impact. Bade, O.( Ed) London: Zed Books: 167-70.
Cole, C. M., Takyiwaa, M. and Stephan, F. M. (Ed. ). 2007. *Africa After Gender?* Bloomington and Indianapolis: Indiana University Press.
Ekiran, M.A. 2002. *Marriage and the Family: A Sociological Perspective*. Lagos: Rebonik.
Guijt, I. and Meera, K. S. (Eds). 2001. *The Myth of Community: Gender Issues in Participatory Development.* London: ITDG Publishing.
Lashgari, D. 1995. *Violence, Silence, and Anger: Women's Writing As Transgression*. Charlottesville and London: University Press of Virginia.
Moser, G.S. Rogers and Van Til, R. 1997. Nigeria: Experience with Structural Adjustment. Occasional paper 148. Washington D. C: International Monetary Fund.
Nicolson, P. 1996. *Gender, Power and Organisation: A Psychological Perspective.* London: Routledge.
Obayemi, A. 1971.The Yoruba and Edo-speaking peoples and their Neighbours before 1600'. Ajayi J.F.A. & Michael C. History of West Africa. Volume One. London: Longman Group Ltd: 196-263.
Ogundipe, O. 2007. Indigenous and Contemporary Gender Concepts and Issues in Africa: Implications for Nigeria's Development." *CBAAC Occasional Monograph* No. 2. Lagos: Malthouse Press Ltd.
Ojo, Afolabi. 1966. *Yoruba Culture: A Geographical Analysis*. London: University of London Press.
Olajubu, O. 2003. *Women in the Yoruba Religious Sphere*. New York: State University of New York Press.
Phillips, A. O. and Ndekwu, E. C. (Eds.). 1987. *Structural Adjustment Programme in Developing Economy: The case of Nigeria*. Ibadan. NISER.
Piges, E. 1978. *Patriarchal Attitudes: Women in Society*. London: Virago.
Plant, M. A. 1990. *Aids, Drugs, and Prostitution*. London & New York: Routledge.

Richardson, D. & Robinson, V. 1993. *Introducing Women's Studies.* New York: Palgrave.

Stein, J. 1997. *Empowerment and Women's Health: Theory, Methods and Practice.* United Kingdom: Zed Books.

Titilola, S.O. 1987. The impact of Structural Adjustment Programme on agriculture and rural economy of Nigeria. In: *Structural Adjustment Programme in Developing Economy*: The *case of Nigeria.*

Phillips, A. O. and Ndekwu E.C. (Eds.). Ibadan. NISER: 177-184.

### *Journal or Magazine Articles*

Akintola, J.O. and Oke, J.T.O. 2001. Impact of Macro-economic policy reforms on the output and prices of food grains in Nigeria. The Nigerian Journal of Economic History. No. 4: 70-80.

Denzer, L. 1994. Yoruba Women: A Historiographical Study. *The International Journal of African Historical Studies.* Vol. 27, No. 1: 1-39.

Lawal, A.A. 2001. The Negative Impact of Structural Adjustment Programme on Agriculture in Nigeria. *The Nigerian Journal of Economic History.* No. 4: 61-69.

Lesthaeghe, R. 1980. On the social control of human reproduction. *Population and Development Review.* 6. No. 4: 527-548.

Lockwood, M. 1995. Structure and Behavior in the Social Demography of Africa. *Population and Development Review.* Vol. 21.No.1: 1-32.

Lloyd, P. C. 1968. Divorce among the Yoruba. *American Anthropologist,* Volume 70 Number 1: 67-81.

Moore, D. and R. Roberts 1990. Listening for Silences. *History in Africa,* Vol. 17: 319-325.

Ojo, M.O. and Akanji, O.O. 1996. "The impact of macroeconomic policy reforms on Nigerian agriculture. *Economic and Financial Review, Central Bank of Nigeria,* vol. 34(2): 549-570.

Omorodion, F. I. 2007. Rural Women's Experiences of Micro-Credit Schemes in Nigeria. Case Study of Esan Women. *Journal of Asian and African Studies.* Vol. 42 (6):479-494.

Oni, B. 1988. Education and Alternative Avenues of Mobility: A Nigerian Study. *Comparative Education Review.* Vol. 32. No. 1: 87-99.

Richters, A. 1997. Introduction. Social Science and Medicine. Vol. 35,

No. 6. as cited in Stein, J. *Empowerment and Women's Health: Theory, Methods and Practice.* United Kingdom: Zed Books.

***Unpublished Works, Theses and Long Essays***

Fasan, R. O. 2009. Transitional Ceremonial Song Performance of the Ondo, Ikale, Oyo and Ijebu." Unpublished Ph.D Thesis, Department of English, University of Ibadan.

***World Wide Web (WWW) Resources***

Afolabi, M.M. Women as Pillars of National Economy In Nigeria: A Study of Economic Activities of Rural Women in Six Local Government Areas of Ondo State. https://editorialexpress.com/cgibin/conference/download.cgi?db_name=IAFFE2008&paper_id=240 25 October 2005.

# *Chapter Five*

## GENDER, IDENTITY AND CHANGE: THE CASE OF MUSLIM WOMEN IN NORTHERN NIGERIA

*Aisha Balarabe Bawa*

### *Introduction*

The status of Muslim women in contemporary society has generated a lot of controversies and is still generating serious debates and discussions in scholarly studies. Most scholars consequently situate the oppression of women in many Muslim societies within the context of Islamic laws on female code of dressing. They also identify the veiling of Muslim women with bitter suppression and therefore conclude that the veil is a constraint to the emancipation of women.[1]

Leila Ahmed is of the view that the pre-occupation with the code of conduct of women by Islamic organizations borders on issues of cultural identity, resistance against Western domination, class struggles and opposition to the empowerment of women that was effected by the teachings of Islam among the conservative Arabs. Ahmed further argues that the Christian West tainted the feminist struggle in the Muslim societies with their colonial and missionary assaults against the veiling of women and other "backward" practices. According to her, opposition towards the matter came

---

[1] Ibrahim Olatunde Uthman, *Contemporary Feminist Movement*. Cambridge: Cambridge Scholars Publishers, 2009, p. 1.

from the Islamists, who focused on women conduct, as a form of resistance to the colonial crusade against the so-called backward position of women.[2]

On the other hand, Amina Wadud denies the claim that Islam establishes a patriarchal society or female subordination. She grounds her views in Fazlur Rahman's hermeneutic approach to the Qur'an and concludes that the Qur'an only teaches non-authoritarian male responsibility so as to assist women. She submits that this balances the important contributions of women, as mothers, because one of the guiding Qur'anic principles in gender relation is equality.[3] In Northern Nigeria where Islam is the dominant religion, the perception or understanding of Muslim women in this region is their subordination by men arising from socio-cultural factors associated with Islam. But with the literacy campaign of the Northern Element Progressive Union (NEPU) political party in the 1950s under the leadership of Malam Aminu Kano, Northerm Women Movement (*Jam'iyar Matan Arewa*) as well as the influence of globalization has greatly changed the lives of women in this part of the country. However, despite the surge of women in development literature, Northern Nigerian women have received comparatively less attention than their Southern counterparts. The aim of this chapter therefore, is to examine the changes that have taken place in the lives of Muslim women in Northern Nigeria over time. The chapter will focus on three historical epochs: Hausaland before the Jihad, after the Jihad, and post-independence.

### *The Position of Women in Hausaland Before 1804*

The area referred to in this chapter as Northern Nigeria was formerly known as Hausaland with almost half of it in present day Niger Republic. The area designated as Hausaland according to Adamu is the original territory of the Hausa States of Gobir, Kabi (Kebbi), Daura, Katsina, Zamfara,

---

[2] Leila Ahmed, *Women and Gender in Islam: Roots of a Modern Debate*. New Haven: Yale University Press, 1992, 225 – 237.

[3] Amina Wadud-Muhsin, *Qur'an and Women: Rereading the Sacred Text from a Woman's Perspective*. New York: Oxford University Press, 1999, p.3 – 74.

Kano and Garun Gabas (the Eastern Wall) or Biram as it is called.[4] Before the influx, at different times since the 15th century, of the Fulani from the West, the Tuareg from the Sahara, and the Barebari and the Felata Borno from the East, this was the area in which the majority of the people spoke Hausa as the first and only language, and the socio-cultural traits often associated with the people predominated.[5]

Hausaland has long been a place of creation, exchange, and conflict – not only internally but also with other regions of the world. This deep and dynamic history is seen in the various Hausa social structures, cosmologies and identities that have emerged and changed over time. One of the major changes that occurred in Hausaland during this period, which has impacted on the lives of women was Islam. Certainly, Islam has been influential in all spheres of social and political life in some of the major Hausa centres since at least the Fifteen Century. From the end of the Fifteen Century to beginning of the Sixteen Century, Shaikh Abd al-Karim al-Maghili, of Tlemen in modern Algeria, was teaching in Kano, and the century witnessed the expansion of Islamic intellectual activity and the growth of Islamic literature in classical Arabic written by Hausa *ulama* (scholars).[6]

The 18th century marked the rise of Islam in many of the Hausa States and King Muhammadu Rumfa of Kano (1463 - 1499) played a critical role in its emergence.[7] During this time, women were prevented from directly participating in government. Callaway and Creevey stress that, by the end of the reign of Rumfa, women of high social status were secluded, and a very orthodox form of Islam had been firmly established.[8] This precedent

---

[4] Mahdi Adamu, "The Spread of the Hausa Culture in West Africa, 1700 – 1900". *Savanna*, 5(1): 3 – 13, 1976, p. 3.

[5] *Ibid.*

[6] Anne Haour and Benedetta Rossi," Hausa Identity: Language, History and Religion" in Anne, H. And Benedetta, R. (eds) *Being and Becoming Hausa: Interdisciplinary Perspectives*, Boston, Brill.2010. p.14.

[7] Kari Bergstrom, Legacies of Colonialism and Islam for Hausa Women: An Historical Analysis, 1804 – 1960. *Women and International Development*, 2002, p. 2.

[8] Callaway, Barbara J. and Lucy Creevey, *Heritage of Islam: Women, Religion and Politics in West Africa*. Boulder: Lynne Reinner Publishers, 1994.

of removing women from many public positions, secluding women and introducing Shari'a law marks the beginning of substantial changes in women's status in many of the Hausa states.

It is interesting to note that, historical and diachronic studies have shown that Hausa women in pre-Jihad periods had enjoyed a good deal of participation in the public space. For example, Herdi Nast's extensive research on the history of the royal palace in Kano around 1500 shows that there existed important public positions for women as tax collectors, market administrators, and religious leaders through the *Bori* spirit cult.[9] In the history of Daura before the 9th century AD, women officials like Magajiya of Daura played important role in the political set up. Also, in pre-colonial Bornu, especially among the Kanuri, the Kokoto and the Bagirmian, women occupied the highly respected offices of Magira (Mai's mother), Magara (Mai's senior sister) and Gumsu (Mai's first wife). The extent of the Magira's power was demonstrated in the imprisonment of Mai Biri (1151 - 1176) and that Magira Aisa Kuli controlled Kanuri political life before the coming to power of Mai Idris Alooma in 1572.[10]

The 16th century Hausaland also witnessed the emergence of powerful female rulers. Queen Amina (the oldest child of Bakwa Turuku) not only took over the throne of Zazzau (Zaria) in 1576 but she emerged as warrior queen who built a high wall around Zaria in order to protect the city from invasion. She also extended the boundaries of Zazzau kingdom beyond Bauchi and up to some parts of Zamfara and Kebbi Kingdoms. Her exploits are still widely recounted in Hausaland. However, the time from the Seventeenth to Eighteenth Centuries was the period of moral decadence in most parts of Hausaland and this affected the lives of Muslim women most. During this period subservience to husbands was emphasized at the expense of obedience to God. Men used the opportunity to over-burden women with domestic chores like gathering of firewood, cooking, washing of clothes and the like. Women were also used on farms for manual

---

[9] Nast, Heidi J., "Islam, Gender and Slavery in West African Circa 1500: Spatial Archeology of the Kano Palace, Northern Nigeria." *Annals of the Association of American Geographers*, 86(1):44 – 77.

[10] Michel Crowder, *The Story of Nigeria*. London: Faber and Faber, 1976, p. 29.

labour which uplifted the social status of men. Islam as a religion has a comprehensive package of rights for women which includes the right to enter into contracts and legal agreements; the right to earn an income and dispose her property as she wishes; the right to express her opinions on all issues private or public; the right to education; the right to inherit and be inherited by her next of kin; the right to contribute to the development of the society in all spheres. However, Islamic injunctions on women's rights have been distorted by local tradition to favour men. In some cases, local customs have been confused with Islamic law because of ignorance.[11] It was at the midst of this situation that Shehu Usman Danfodiyo emerged as a revolutionary leader in Hausa society from the beginning of the 19th century. Shehu Usman Danfodiyo organized a religious movement aimed at reinvigorating Islamic values and establishesd a socio-political system that would protect Islamic moral values from disintegrating.

### *Women's Position After the Jihad: 1804 – 1960*

The Jihad Movement of the early 19th century Hausaland, which culminated into the establishment of an Islamic State, the Sokoto Caliphate, had far reaching impact on women. One of the dramatic changes during this period was on the position of women. The role and position of women became an area of contest and concern among the Jihadist.[12] Barbara Cooper remarks that, "the identity of those following Shehu Usman Danfodiyo came increasingly to coalesce around issues and conflicts related to gender and dress."[13] In this regard, Islamic scholars began to voice disapproval of the Bori spirit possession cult, women's dress and public interaction between

---

[11] Bawa, Aisha Balarabe, Culture, Islam and Women in Northern Nigeria: Some Historical Investigations. Paper Presented at the Toyin Falda Annual Conference (TOFAC) held on 2nd – 4th July, 2012 at Excellence Hotel, Ogba, Ikeja, Lagos.

[12] Fatima L. Adamu, Women, Islam and Development in Northern Nigeria. Report Submitted to the University of Birmingham and Nigerian Institute of Social and Economic Research (NISER), 2006.

[13] Cooper, Barbara M., "Reflections on Slavery, Seclusion and Female Labor in the Maradi Region in the Nineteenth and Twentieth Centuries", *Journal of African History*, 35:61-78, 1998, p. 24.

sexes. For instance, it was deemed inappropriate for women to hold public office and they were increasingly secluded in their homes. Free Muslim women's status became associated with seclusion and veiling. After the Jihads, women began disappearing from agricultural work, as this type of work was associated with slave status.[14]

In order to protect the modesty of women, female seclusion was strictly enforced. During this period (1804 – 1903), increasing number of Muslim women, both rural and urban, have entered into seclusion, irrespective of class at least partially associated with the emancipation.[15] However, Shehu Usman Danfodiyo has devoted at least three of his works to emphasizing the rights of women to education. The ideas of rights made women eligible for formal education, including business education, though the emphasis was on religion. Shehu was very blunt about the literacy and ignorance of women for which he squarely blamed men. According to him:

> Men treat these beings like household implements which became broken after long use and which are then thrown out on the dung heap. This is an abominable crime. Alas! How can they shut their wives, their daughters and their captives in the darkness of ignorance while daily they impact knowledge to their students?[16]

He further stressed that:

> Muslim women – do not listen to the speech of those who are misguided and who sow seed of error in the heart of another, they deceive you when they stress obedience to your husband and without telling you of obedience to God and to His Messenger (May God show him bounty and grant him salvation), and when they say that the woman find her happiness in obedience to her husband. They seek only their own satisfaction, and

---

[14] Callaway, Barbara, J. and Lucy, Creevey, *Heritage of* Islam, *Op.* cit, p. 191.

[15] Smith, M.G., The Kano Chronicle as History, In: B.M. Barkindo (ed.) *Studies in the History of Kano.* Ibadan: Heinemann Educational Books, 1983.

[16] Hodgkin Thomas, *Nigerian Perspectives: An Historical Anthropology.* London: Longman, 1975, p. 254.

> that is why they impose upon you tasks which the law of God and that of his Prophet never especially assigned to you. Such are the preparation of food stuffs, the washing of clothes and other duties which they like to impose upon you.[17]

Therefore, women education was given prominence during this period, which influenced the emergence of Nana Asma'u, the daughter of Usmanu Danfodio. She played a significant role through her organization of itinerant women (the *Yan Taru*) in the development of education.[18] Before the formation of the *Yan Taru*, Nana Asma'u began teaching the children and women of her household, which was later extended to neighbourhood and then to the community as a whole. Considering the plight of women, Asma'u, later on, started massive mobilization for women's education. In the 1860, Asma'u died and her sister Maryam, a learned scholar as well, took over the teaching of the '*Yan Taru*. At her demise, her daughter Maryam Tamadi continued with the *Yan Taru*. This system has survived till today, in the hands of each *Maidaki* in the Hubbaren Shehu who continue to handle the affairs of the *Yan Taru* as they come on occasion such as the beginning of new Islamic calendar. Therefore, looking at the issues outlined above, it is clear that Islam attaches a lot of importance to knowledge and encourages its acquisition.

Politically, it was apparent that women made their views known on the way the Islamic state was run, indicating that they were recognized and their views on governance mattered. In fact at certain time, women served as arbiters to whom critical issues on succession were referred. Nana Asma'u, as one of the survivors of the Hijrah, intervened during the caliphate of Abubakar Atiku on the appointment of Wazir when Khalilu was appointed as Wazir and Muhammad Lema refused to acknowledge the appointment. She consoled Muhammad Lema and succeeded in getting him appointed as Dangaladima Waziri to Khalilu, thus assuring him of the vizierate after Khalilu. Maryam, her sister, was once asked by the Emir

---

[17] *Ibid*, p. 255.

[18] The 'Yan taru was primarily a system for imparting knowledge particularly to women living in villages.

of Kano Uthman bin Dabo, on the situation of people who migrated from Hausaland to the East assuming that Mahdi was about to appear.[19] She replied him that those people were liars and have strayed from the right path. The same Maryam suggested the appointment of Muhammad Bello as the Emir of Kano when controversy started after the death of former Emir Abdullahi. The Gombe emirate was given to Nana Asma'u and her descendants to administer.

In addition, women have also played vital roles in the preservation of history of the Jihad and the caliphate. For example, Nana Asma'u composed poetry in Fulfulde on the history of the Jihad which dated back to 1840. She also wrote on the family of the Shehu Usman Danfodiyo, while her sister Maryam composed a poem on the success of the Jama'ah when they dispersed the army of Yunfa of Gobir. Their deep knowledge of Arabic enabled them to compose poems both in Arabic and Hausa as tribute to late relatives.

It is interesting to note therefore, that despite the fact that women were secluded under the caliphate system of administration, they are not only educated but were involved in decision making particularly as advisers and constructive critics. Another remarkable change that occurred in the lives of women in Northern Nigerian was colonialism. The advent of British colonialism, like in any other society, impacted negatively on the status of women in Northern Nigeria. The British and the French made several treaties in the latter parts of the 19th century before deciding how to divide Hausaland between them. In the end, the partition roughly corresponds with the already existing divisions between the Sokoto Caliphate and the northern kingdoms outside of the caliphate such as Damagaram, Maradi and Tsibiri.[20] Thus, the Islamic polity that ruled Northern Nigeria since 1804 was replaced by the British colonialist in 1903.

One major impact of British colonialism on women in this region was in the area of Western education. The British gave limited encouragement

---

[19] The migration to the East was as a result of Universal Proclamation of Muhammad Ahmad B. Abdullahi in June 1881 as the Mahdi (Messier).

[20] Kari, Bergstrom, *Legacies of Colonialism and Islam for Hausa Women: An Historical Analysis, 1804 – 1960*, p. 6.

to Western education in the North. Although the policy of the British in the Protectorate was to discourage missionary activity, but it would appear that the policy was more in keeping with the desire to maintain northern development strictly on native lines.[21] It was only in the 1920s that western education began to emerge in the north. Fearing Islamic opposition, the British introduced secular education instead of Christian missionary education, yet Western education was never popular among Muslims. In 1922, the British established the Katsina College as the first Western educational institutions of "higher learning" that trained the first generation of Muslims to rise to senior positions in the colonial administration. The British colonial administration however, paid little attention to the education of women. This neglect of enrolment of northern girls in western education has contributed in creating a great disparity between the women in the south and in the north. It was much later in the 1950s that education of northern women was given attention.

Although adult education had existed in the area for decades, it was in the 1950s that the late Mallam Aminu Kano, leader of the Northern Element Progressive Union (NEPU) and later Peoples' Redemption Party (PRP) political parties was committed to education and raising the status of women. He was remarkable for promoting women's education.[22] In another development, the Women's Wing of NEPU under Gambo Sawaba was in the vanguard of the emancipation of northern women from the shackles of male dominance as well as inspiring other women in the north to emerge as women activist in the post-colonial period.

### *Northern Nigerian Women and Change: The Post-Independence Period*

The post-independence era ushered in some dramatic changes in the integration of women in this region in the developmental process. Although the numerical strength was insignificant as compared to their southern

---

[21] Abubakar, S., "The Northern Province Under Colonial Rule", In: O. Ikime (ed.) *Groundwork of Nigerian History*. Ibadan: Heinemann Education Books, 1980, p. 474.

[22] Balkisu Yusuf," Hausa-Fulani Women: The State of the Struggle", In: Catherine Coles and Beverly Mack (eds.) *Hausa Women in the 20th Century*. USA: Wisconsin Press, 1991, p. 94.

counterpart, what is important is the transformation. Several factors culminated into these remarkable changes. The first and most important was the emergence of women's movement in the north under the umbrella of *Jam'iyar Matan Arewa* (Northern Women's Congress) in 1963. It was a group of 60 women who sought to "bring together all women in the north in order to teach the reading and writing of English and general domestic science." It was an organization set by northern wives and mothers to speak and act for women and children, work with men to improve lives and bring relief and hope for the under-privileged. The association includes: Hajia Laila Dogon Yaro, Mrs. Comfort Dikko, Hajiya Bamanga Tukur, Mrs. Zakari and Hajiya Aishatu Jeda.[23] With the active support of their husbands and the late Sardauna of Sokoto, Sir Ahmadu Bello, they achieved many results and distinction. The association was based in Kaduna and had branches across the whole length and breadth of the North. The *Jam'iyar Matan Arewa* built schools and orphanages to train women in basic literacy and provide welfare for orphans. The Association also incorporated wives of northern military leaders. Prominent among them were Mrs. Victoria Yakubu Gowon and Mrs. Maryam Sani Abacha. These women mobilized other women from all classes and circumstances to stand up against any injustices meted out against them. Men were made to sit up and take note, and accord the pressure of women the attention and credit it deserved.

The declaration of the International Women Day by the United Nations Organization (UNO) in 1975 and of 1976 to 1985 as a decade for women, also served as a clarion call for women in Nigeria. The declaration was followed by a series of conferences on women: Copenhagen, Denmark (1980), Nairobi, Kenya (1985), and Beijing, China (1995). The world conference in Kenya attracted the attention of Non-Governmental Organizations (NGOs) in making viable changes in the lives of women in society.[24]

In 1987, the Federal Government of Nigeria under General Babangida launched the Better Life Programme for Rural Women (BLPRW). Mrs.

---

[23] Aisha B. Bawa, "Examination of Policies and Programmes of General Ibrahim Babangida Regime on the Women Folk in Nigeria, 1985 – 1993." *Sokoto Journal of History*, 1(1):80-94, 2012, p. 81.

[24] Sani H., *Women and Development, the Way Forward.* Ibadan: Spectrum Books Ltd, 2001.

Maryam Babangida was identified as having conceived the idea for the programme through her vision. In this regard, women were educated on the basic literacy of reading, writing and calculation. It is not wrong, therefore, to say that, literacy could be one of the first steps in a process of enabling women to take control of their lives to participate on a more equal basis in society and eventually to free themselves from economic exploitation and patriarchal oppression.

Odi argued that literacy skills empowered the women because the skills gave the women a new pair of eyes with which they used to see their plight, their lives and how to improve on their situations.[25]

Literacy skills therefore, empowered the women to organize themselves to fight for their rights and privileges. In Kano State for example, six centres were established in Bichi Gumel, Dutse (now Jigawa State), Gwaram, Minjibir and Gaya on the basic literacy training of women, in addition to agricultural studies, home management, leather works, poetry, food processing and nutrition.[26]

Apart from the knowledge acquired by women to deal with their marketable products through literacy, the programme improved the political consciousness and awareness of rural women. This achievement was best demonstrated by the increased interest and participation of women during the transition to civil rule and in their massive turnout during the subsequent local government, state, federal and presidential elections between 1989 and 1993.[27] It was in 1987 local government elections that, for the first time in Kano State, women contested and won elections. Mallama Yelwa Hauwa'u and Ladi Gwaram became councilors in Wudil and Dutse respectively.[28]

---

[25] Odi, U.J. "An Education of the Literacy Component of the Better Life Programme for Rural Women in Ohaozara L.G.A. Nsukka." Unpublished B.Ed. Project, UNN, 1993.

[26] Babangida, M., *Four Years of the Better Life Programme for RuralWomen.* Abuja: A Publication of the National Organizing Committee of the BLPRW, 1991.

[27] Sani Hajo, *First Ladyship: An Empowerment Programmes in Nigeria*. Ibadan: Spectrum Books Limited, 2010, p. 71.

[28] Sani Hajo, *Women and Development: The Way Forward*. Ibadan: Spectrum Books Limited, 2001, p. 127. The period also witnessed the election of two women into the National Assembly. They were Hon. Rabi Allamin from Borno State and Hon. Mariya Abdullahi from Katsina State.

Although the administration of Babangida has received serious criticism particularly on the Better Life Programme and the Structural Adjustment Programme (SAP), the latter had considerable impact on the family, and the society at large.[29] The former was viewed as more of elite than the targeted group (rural women). However, despite all this, the administration has done more than any previous administration in the country to reverse the trend of marginalizing women by empowering and integrating them into the mainstream of national development.

Since then, successive administrations have tried to introduce policies and programmes that have direct bearing on improving the situation of women. In 1993, when General Sani Abacha emerged as the military Head of State in midst of widespread political crises that followed the annulment of the June 12 election, he introduced quite a number of policies that helped in raising the status of women. Amongst other things, he upgraded the National Commission for Women (NCW) to a full-fledged Ministry of Women Affairs and Social Development in January 1995. The NCW in all States of the Federation were upgraded to state ministries of Women Affairs with a woman as a commissioner to head the ministry.

General Abacha appointed women as ministers in the Ministry for Women Affairs, which provided the opportunity for many women in Northern Nigeria to serve in those capacities. In addition, some women were also appointed to head government agencies and they equally distinguished themselves. These women include Hajiya Hadiza Sani Kangiwa, Commissioner and Chief Executive of National Commission for Refugees, Hajiya Amina Az-Zubar, former Senior Special Assistant Advisor to the President on MDGs and now Special Adviser to the UN Secretary-General Mr. Ban Ki-Moon on post-2015 Development Planning.

In politics northern women have shown great interest in contesting for elective public offices. In the aborted transition programme of the late General Sani Abacha, there were few women who contested election. Hajiya Mairo Habib and Hajiya Fati Tagwai contested the gubernatorial elections in Kaduna and Kano States respectively. In Kano State, Hajiya Naja'atu

---

[29] Uche Isiugo-Abanihe, "*Impact* of Economic Adjustment on the Family", In Kassey, P. Garba, Bala Akanji and Ifeoma Isiugo-Abanihe (eds.) *Women and Economic Reform in Nigeria*. Ibadan: WORDOC, 1997, p. 186.

Muhammed emerged as the first female elected Senator under UNCP.

Another important and significant international response to the UN Decade for Women was the Convention on the Elimination of all forms of Discrimination Against Women (CEDAW). The Convention identifies women's rights as human rights and demands their inclusion in all spheres of national life. Nigeria ratified CEDAW in 1985, but while the provisions of the treaty enjoy international law status, they are not yet part of Nigeria's domestic framework[30]. Although the Convention is not legally enforced in domestic legislature, by nature of the ratification, Nigeria has accepted the obligation to be assessed in terms of its respect for the rights of women and also in terms of its progress since ratification. In this regard, Nigeria had formulated and approved a National Policy on Women. The policy is an attempt to incorporate women fully into national development as equal partners, decision makers and beneficiaries of Nigeria, through the removal of gender-based inequalities.[31] The policy aspires to include women in all spheres of national life, including education, science and technology, healthcare, employment, agriculture and industry, environment, legal justice, social services and the media. It aspires to eliminate the negative aspects of Nigerian culture which serve only to harm women.

***Table 1: Profile of Northern Nigerian women in ministerial appointment (1997 - 2013)***

| S/N | Name | Ministry | Year |
|---|---|---|---|
| 1. | Hajo Sani | Women Affairs | 1997 – 1998 |
| 2. | Dr. Laraba Abdullahi | Women Affairs | 1998 – 1999 |
| 3. | Mrs. B. Ibrahim Musa | Education | 1999 – 2001 |
| 4. | Dr. (Mrs.) Amina Ndalolo | Health | 1999 - 2001 |
| 5. | Hajiya Aishatu Ismail | Women Affairs | 1999 – 2001 |
| 6. | Mrs. Maryam Ciroma | Women Affairs | 2001 – 2003 |

[30] Comfort Chukuezi, "Socio-Cultural Factors Associated with Maternal Mortality in Nigeria" *Research Journal of Social Sciences,* 1( 5): 22-26. 2010.

[31] Ibid. p. 24.

| 7. | Mrs. Fatima Balarabe Ibrahim | Energy | 2007-2009 |
|---|---|---|---|
| 8. | Mrs. Saudatu Usman Bungudu | Women Affairs | 2007-2009 |
| 9. | Mrs. Salamatu Suleiman | Women Affairs | 2009-2011 |
| 10. | Prof. Ruqayyat Rufa'i | Education | 2010 – 2013 |
| 11. | Hajiya Hadiza Mailafiya | Environment | 2010 – 2013 |
| 12. | Hajiya Zainab Kuchi | Energy (Power) | 2010 -2013 |
| 13 | Hajiya Zainab Maina | Women Affairs | 2011- 2015 |

### *Conclusion*

This chapter examined the changes that have taken place in the lives of Muslim women in Northern Nigeria over time. Northern Nigeria, like any other society, is a dynamic and subject to change and development. Women in this region have experienced a lot of changes in their lives. Starting from the pre-Jihad period, women were denied some of their rights that were supposed to be enjoyed according to Islam. In the aftermath of the jihad, women were secluded in their homes but were also allowed to seek for knowledge of their religion. However, in the post- independence, as a result of increased in awareness, both from within and outside the country, women have been sensitized, mobilized and integrated into the national development. There is evidence of change in their lives through their participation in social, political and economic activities of their nation, though there is still a wide gap between them and their counterparts in the south in terms of their involvement in decision-making and high level illiteracy. Therefore, for change to be effective there must be continuity. There is need for government and all stakeholders in Northern Nigeria to ensure that women are given the necessary education to enable them to fully participate in decisions that affect their lives in the society.

### *References*

Abubakar, S. 1980. The Northern Province Under Colonial Rule. In: *Groundwork of Nigerian History*. Ikime, O. (Ed.). Ibadan: Heinmann Education Books. 447-483.

Adamu, F. L. 2006. Women, Islam and Development in Northern Nigeria.Report Submitted to the University of Birmingham and Nigerian Institute of Social and Economic Research (NISER).

Adamu, M. 1976. The Spread of the Hausa Culture in West Africa, 1700 – 1900. *Savanna*, 5(1): 3-13.

Ahmed, L. 1992. *Women and Gender in Islam: Roots of a Modern Debate.* New Haven: Yale University Press.

Bawa, A. B. 2012. Culture, Islam and Women in Northern Nigeria: Some Historical Investigations. Paper Presented at the Toyin Falola Annual Conference (TOFAC) held on 2nd – 4th July, 2012 at Excellence Hotel, Ogba, Ikeja, Lagos.

Bawa, A. B. 2012. Examination of Policies and Programmes of General Ibrahim Babangida Regime on the Women Folk in Nigeria, 1985 – 1993. *Sokoto Journal of History*, 1(1): 80-94.

Babangida, M. 1991. Four Years of the Better Life Programme for Rural Women. Abuja: A Publication of the National Organizing Committee of the BLPRW.

Callaway, B. J. and Lucy C. 1994. *Heritage of Islam: Women, Religion and Politics in West Africa.* Boulder: Lynne Reinner Publishers. Cooper, B. M. 1998. Reflections on Slavery, Seclusion and Female Labor in The Maradi Region in the Nineteenth and Twentieth Centuries.*Journal of African History*. 35:61-78.

Crowder, M. 1976. *The Story of Nigeria.* London: Faber and Faber.

Hodgkin, T. 1975. *Nigerian Perspectives: An Historical Anthropology.* London: Longman.

Ibrahim, O. U. 2009. *Contemporary Feminist Movement.* Cambridge: Cambridge Scholars Publishers.

Isiugo-Abanihe, U.1997.Impact of Economic Adjustment on the Family. In: *Women and Economic Reform in Nigeria.* Kassey, P. G.

Bala, A. and Isiugo- Abanihe, I. (Eds.). Ibadan: Women's Research and Documentation Centre (WORDOC): 186-203.

Kari, B. 2002. Legacies of Colonialism and Islam for Hausa Women: An Historical Analysis, 1804 – 1960. Working Paper, USA. 1 – 23.

Nast, H. J. 1996. Islam, Gender and Slavery in West African Circa 1500: Archeology of the Kano Palace, Northern Nigeria *Annals of the Association of American Geographers.*86 (1).44-77.

Odi, U.J. 1993. "An Education of the Literacy Component of the Better Life Programme for Rural Women in Ohaozara L.G.A. Nsukka"

Unpublished B.Ed. Project, UNN, Education Department.

Sani H. 1992. *Women and Development: the Way Forward.* Ibadan: Spectrum Books Ltd.

Umoden, G.E.1992. *Babangida Years.* Lagos: Gabuino Publishing Company Limited.

Sani, H. 2010. *First Ladyship: An Empowerment Programmes in Nigeria.* Ibadan: Spectrum Books Limited.

Smith, M.G. 1983. "The Kano Chronicle as History" In: *Studies in the History of Kano.* Barkindo, B.M. (Ed.).Ibadan: Heinemann Educational Books: 31-56.

Wadud-Muhsin, A.1999.*Qur'an and Women: Rereading the Sacred Text from a Woman's Perspective.* New York: Oxford University Press.

Yusuf, B. 1991. Hausa-Fulani Women: In: *The State of the Struggle. Hausa Women in the 20th Century.* Coles, C. and Mack, B. (Eds). USA: Wisconsin Press: 90-109.

# *Chapter Six*

## ECONOMIC SURVIVAL, MASCULINITY AND SHIFTING CULTURAL DEFINITION OF THE WOMAN'S IDENTITY IN A RURAL IGBO SOCIETY

*Chinyere Ukpokolo*

### *Introduction*

Economic hardship characteristic of post-colonial African states has continued to take its toll on individuals and households, and undoubtedly changing the people's lifeways. Increasingly, basic necessities of life remain luxuries to many homes. The development at the global arena including open market economy and neoliberalism has also led to survival of the fittest at the regional and inter-regional levels. Indeed, government policies in Africa, beginning with Structural Adjustment Programme (SAP) in the 1980s to the current reliance on the dictates at the global market, have all crippled chances of survival for most people in underdeveloped economy, especially in the sub-Saharan Africa. These have challenged African leaders to begin to imagine more collaborative and rewarding economic alignments, both regionally and intercontinentally, for better positioning of the continent in their dealings with development partners and the developed nations, with the view to increasing their economic chances and enhancing better life for their people. One of these efforts, for instance, is the New Partnership for Africa's Development (NEPAD), aimed at integrating the economic potentials of the region for better negotiation at inter-continental level, particularly in dealing with the developed economies of Europe and America (see Adesina *et al.*, 2006). Peer review mechanisms and encouragement of intra-regional collaborations among African nations, were intended to enhance performance and reduce poverty in the region. Yet, over a decade down the line, NEPAD has not been able to address the challenges of poverty in the continent. Perhaps what has come to be regarded as 'technological gap' has even further crippled the chances of African regions catching up with the rest of the world, and in this milieu, indices of poverty reverberate in other forms. For instance, according to the British Council Report (2012), an average of 54% of Nigerians live in poverty, albeit with geographical disparities.

Poverty gap in Nigeria varies along the rural-urban divide. In 2010, while poverty is estimated at 61.8% in urban areas, it was 73.2% in the rural areas. Further, geographical disparities indicate that poverty is more prevalent in northern Nigeria than in the south. For instance, human development outcome for women and girls are worse in the north than in the southeast (British Council Report, 2012: 4). At the general level, women and girls in Nigeria have worse life chances than men and boys. Women's situation is worsened by the prevalence of gender-based violence. The British Council Report notes that "violence compounds and reinforces this [women's] disadvantage and exclusion" (British Council Report, 2012: 5). It further argues that though the government has excellent policies and intentions, this has not translated into budgets or actions to make changes required if women are to contribute effectively to Nigeria's development. Although the country has gender policy, this too has not successfully transformed the lives of majority of women in the country.

Unemployment is still prevalent in the country, and this has gender dimensions as a lesser number of women than men are likely to get employed in the formal sector of the economy. Women are disproportionately concentrated in the informal sector (Kolev *et al.*, 2010: 23). Interestingly also, of 80.2 million Nigerian women, 54 million live and work in rural areas, indicating that there are more women in the rural areas than in the urban centres, with majority experiencing grinding poverty, as they enjoy little of government attention and interventions that could translate into positive economic transforming experience. Although there are internal regional variations in gender disparities, indicating northern Nigeria as the worst affected, with 72% in the northeast of the country compared to 26% in the southeast, by and large, poverty in the country is worrisome. The lower level of poverty in the southeast may not be unconnected with the struggle of men and women to increase household income and women breaking cultural barriers to improve on the financial security of the household. Indeed, reports indicate that economic empowerment of women, coupled with their economic autonomy, also impact more directly on the lives of children in the areas of children's health, nutrition, education and future growth (British Council, 2012: 4).

At the household level, the current economic condition in African countries has brought about the challenge of financial insecurity as, increasingly, many low income families are thrown into abject poverty, leading to more and more children dropping out of school. And, for those who complete their secondary education, the chance of higher education is bleak, both in terms of access and completion due to lack of funding. Recent statistics indicate that 10.5 million children in Nigeria are currently out of school, with 9.5 million of this number from the northern region of the country. Households are therefore confronted with the challenge of survival as they device means of augmenting family income. Rural Igbo women, in an attempt to confront the challenge of grinding poverty, re-invent the long-distance trading activities characteristic of Igbo women in pre-colonial times, as inter-state trading. This study examined the nature of the current long-distance trading and the implications of the new development on familial relations in rural Nanka society, southeast Nigeria, paying attention to how the woman's identity as '*oriaku*' (consumer of wealth) is shifting to '*okpataku*' (generator of wealth), with attendant implications on the woman's identity in the society. The paper further explored how the emerging reality redefines the boundaries of masculinity and femininity, and culturally reconstructs the woman's identity. The study established that in families where women participate in long-distance trading, role overlap has also occurred. Dependency on the woman for financial provisioning has affected power relations in the family, making the woman core in family decisions without commensurate power shift at the public space. For the man to maintain his relevance, his ability to perform such roles defined culturally as women's roles is necessary, with implications on the people's cultural construction of masculinity, and their definition of the woman's identity in this rural Igbo community.

### *Research Context and Methodology*

The location for this research is multi-sited. Although Nanka community is the study area, participants were also selected from three market sites in two other towns namely: Eke-Ekwulobia Market in Ekwulobia; Nkwor-Igbo Market in Igbo-Ukwu town, and Afor-Udo market in Nanka; the three major places where the research participants trade their goods (see Figure 3). The three communities were originally in Aguata Local Government Area (LGA). Today, however, Nanka is in Orumba North North LGA following the last local government creation in Nigeria in 1991, while Ekwulobia and Igbo-Ukwu remain in Aguata LGA. The essence of drawing participants from these other markets is to capture how goods are distributed to final retailers and/or consumers at the selling points. The fieldwork for this study was carried out between January and July, 2013. A total of 65 traders participated in this research, employing qualitative methodology and such research methods as Key informant interview, Focus group discussions, and in-depth-interview. As the study focuses primarily on women, 60 of the participants were women while five men were interviewed to ascertain their attitude to rural Nanka women's participation in long-distance trading. The interviews were conducted in Igbo Language. The collected data were analysed descriptively. The names of the research participants have been fictionalised to protect their identity, without jeopardising the scientific content of the study. This strategy has been used in Ukpokolo (2013; 2010), and Wallot (2009) among other studies.

Nanka is a patriarchal society with patrilineal descent system, and also operates patrilocal residence pattern. Men are traditionally heads of households. Although polygyny was prevalent in pre-colonial times, the introduction of Christianity in the late 19th Century changed the marriage landscape as monogamy has become the norm. Christian patriarchal values further enhanced men's powers and their control of their wives and children. Nanka is an agrarian community even though this is at a subsistence level. Arable land in large scale is scarce due to gully erosion, which has washed away large expanse of land that could be cultivated. The family traditionally depends on the man for financial security, particularly in agrarian economy

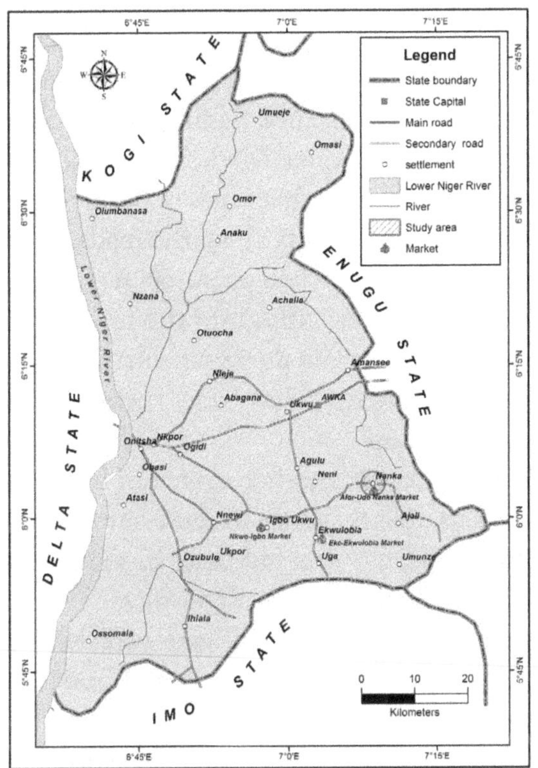


*Figure 3: Map of Anambra State showing the study areas.*
*Source: Ministry of Land and Housing, Anambra State*

where subsistence farming subsists despite soil leaching that has led to soil infertility and low productivity. Nanka people engage in *olu ugbo* (farming), rearing such farm animals as goats, sheep and poultry while a few people rear cows. They also plant such crops as yam, cassava, cocoyam, maize, and assorted types of vegetables like *ugu* (pumpkin), melon, okro, tomatoes, and pepper, all at subsistence level using simple farming technology like hoes and machetes. While men concentrate on planting yam, women tend to plant cocoyam, cassava, melon, and vegetables, though no taboo concretises such norms. Women have their portions of land, which they possess by lease and, through the method of shifting cultivation, they cultivate the land available to them. Such economic trees as palm, breadfruit, mango and pear are sparingly planted on farmlands. Other trees like coconut, kolanut and orange are mainly planted within the family compound. Some men also travel to towns like Ndiowu, Ufuma, Ndikelionwu, and Umunze within

Anambra State, and to such towns as Abakaliki and Nsukka in Ebonyi and Enugu states respectively, where large tracts of land are available for the cultivation of yam. In recent decades, many rural Nanka women are beginning to engage in long-distance trading, or inter-state trading. This is the subject matter of this chapter. Medicine stores, mini supermarkets, beer parlours and restaurants are other types of business activities common in the town. These are located mainly along the roads, and business usually boom during the festive periods when operators record higher sales due to the influx of indigenes from the cities into the town, particularly around Easter and Christmas holidays and during the month of August when the indigenes return home for *Iwa ji* (New Yam) Festival and mid-year meetings termed 'August Meeting'.

Transportation business is another source of livelihood for the rural people of the town. Bus drivers engage in intra- and inter- states transportation travelling to and from towns and cities in southeastern Nigeria and beyond. These include: Ekwulobia, Oko, Igbo-ukwu, Ufuma, Umunze, Aba, Enugu, Port Harcourt and Benin City. Bigger vehicles such as trucks and luxury buses convey goods and passengers to and from more distant cities and states of the country, particularly to the western and the northern parts of Nigeria. Some also travel to neighbouring West African countries such as Ghana, Cameroon and Benin Republic among others, conveying goods and passengers. Only men are engaged in public transportation business. Recently, motorcycle transportation (popularly known as *okada*) has been introduced into the economic life of the people. Okada riders are readily available and convey passengers to the remotest parts of the locality and neighbouring towns. Nanka people place high premium on Western education and the town has produced several PhD holders and successful men and women in different fields such as pharmacy, engineering, accountancy, and the teaching profession. Several others have equally done well in business.

While many Nanka people have migrated to urban areas in search of higher education, business opportunities and employment in the formal and informal sectors, majority of the people, particularly women and children, remain in the rural areas eking a living in an ecology threatened by gully erosion and low productivity resulting from soil infertility. Undoubtedly, for those residing in the rural area, their economic condition shapes their socio-cultural reality and informs their responses to their immediate challenges, and the meanings they give to the difficulties that threaten their existence and redefine their lifeways. Although an attempt to change cultural practices in an indigenous community is often resisted, in this rural community, when such a change aids human survival in a harsh economic reality, the acceptance of such culture change seems inevitable. Women in particular are responding to survival challenges that threaten the quality of life of the members of the rural households, and they do this through their engagement in long-distance trading or inter-state trading.

### *Nanka Rural Women and Inter-state Trading: Trades and Trade Routes*

According to Afigbo (1972, reprinted in 2005), Igbo people are associated with two dominant stereotypes which are: first, the people are notoriously religious and, second, the Igbo people are ubiquitous as a result of their involvement in diverse economic enterprises that necessitates their migration to different parts of Nigeria and Africa in search of better economic opportunities. Afigbo further reports that Igbo socio-religious ethics reflect the intricate relationship between wealth and religion, which is a product of the people's conception of salvation. To the Igbo people, the Supreme Being bequeaths economic success to an individual. This God, represented by the Earth goddess, mediates between man and man, man and woman, as well as man and the universe. God, through the Earth goddess, rewards a morally upright person with wealth, such as a good harvest, as the Earth Goddess is endowed with power over fertility in humans, animals and in crops. Besides, the Igbo people's belief in the life hereafter also implies that a wealthy man in this world will retain his status in the world to come (Afigbo, 1972, reprinted, 2005: 298). Thus, Afigbo concludes:

> It was not only that the traditional Igbo man perceived *chukwu* as the source of wealth and prosperity, but that he also saw economic activity and the pursuit of material wealth as a form of religious activity, a form of worship (Afigbo, 1972, reprinted 2005: 299).

Poverty therefore, to a traditional Igbo man is an aberration and could indeed mean lack of right standing with and approval of one's life by the Supreme Being. An average Igbo, accordingly, strives to acquire wealth and abhors poverty as the people believe that poverty is a deviation from the true desire of the Supreme Being for his people, and is in fact a sign of affliction or punishment of some sort on an individual. The Christian religion introduced into Igboland in the 19th century did not significantly alter this belief system with regard to wealth acquisition and distribution. As the Bible states: 'It is God's desire that 'You shall prosper as your soul prospers' (3 John 1: 2), and at another place, 'Whatever you lay your hands upon shall prosper' (Deuteronomy 28: 8). Thus, the Christian religion also re-echoes the Igbo traditional belief that God blesses his worshipers with wealth.

With Western contact, Igbo people embraced Western education through which people acquire diverse skills needed to gain semi-skilled and skilled employment in the emerging capitalist economy. While men have been privileged in availing themselves of the opportunity offered by Western education, due to cultural practices enshrined in the Victorian notion of the woman in society, transferred to African societies through colonialism, women remain peripherised in the scheme of things. These values contribute to women's marginalization in decision making in the post-independence political structure. Despite the appreciable progress recorded in recent decades, a lot is yet to be achieved in the area of political participation which can bring about structural changes needed for women's economic transformation. For instance, the 2007 election in Nigeria indicates that women's representation in key state structures is marginal, as indicated below:

*Table 2: Women elected to public office in Nigeria: 2007*

| Office | Seats available | Women | Men | % |
|---|---|---|---|---|
| President | 1 | 0 | 1 | 0.0 |
| Senate | 109 | 9 | 100 | 8.3 |
| House of representatives | 360 | 27 | 333 | 6.9 |
| Governor | 36 | 0 | 36 | 0.0 |
| State House of Assembly (SHA) | 990 | 57 | 933 | 5.8 |
| SHA Committee chairperson | 887 | 52 | 835 | 5.9 |

| LGA Chairperson | 740 | 27 | 713 | 3.6 |
|---|---|---|---|---|
| Councillors | 6368 | 235 | 6133 | 3.7 |

*Source: British Council Gender Report, 2012*

The indication from Table 2 above is that women's representation in decision making in the country remains marginal, which has implications on agenda setting and prioritisation. With regard to economic empowerment, women in rural communities still struggle with abject poverty as they make a living from subsistence farming and small scale trading activities.

With the economic depression that began in the 1980s in Africa, many Igbo rural women began to seek alternative means of increasing household income, and in Igboland, re-invention of long distance trading activities, popular in pre-colonial times, provide a viable option. In the earlier period, trekking was the major means of movement from one location to the other, and the income from such economic activities was quite meagre. In the recent decades, with the explosion of technological inventions and innovations, big trucks, popularly known as *911,* have gained popularity, making it easier for the traders involved to travel to longer distances across the country. As an informant noted: "The economic situation in Nigeria is a problem; so, it has made it difficult for men alone to cope [financially]" (Mrs Louisa Okoye, personal communication, July, 2013).

Indeed, trading activities across cultures and peoples have a long history in Africa. As far back as the ninth Century, the Arab traders had begun their trading activities across the Western Sahara, trading in such goods as slaves, elephant tusks and gold among others items (Lavers, 2004, first printed, 1980]. In southwest Nigeria, people like Madam, Tinubu of Lagos, and Iyalode Efunsetan Iyaniwura of Ibadan became popular as a result of their involvement in economic activities with people of Yorubaland and the Europeans, particularly the Portuguese, at the coast of what is known today as Nigeria. Trading activities in recent decades among rural Igbo women involves travelling across states and regions of Nigeria for farm produce. The duration of each business trips varies from one to five days, depending on the choice of destination.

The above map (Fig. 3) indicates the route of trading activities. From Anambra State (marked in orange colour), the traders travel to Edo, Delta and Niger states to the left, and to the right to Enugu, Ebonyi, and the northern states of the country where the greater part of the trading takes place (see the map for details).

Findings indicate that major trade items are farm produce namely yam tubers (genus *Dioscorea*), Nigerian rice, fresh tomatoes (*lycopersicum esculentum* or *solanum lycopersicum)*, beans (legumous plant, *vicia faba*), dried meat, smoked fish, groundnuts (genus *arachis*), wheat (genus *triticum*), [processed] cassava (genus *manihot*) in form of the local staple food known as *garri* and parboiled *fufu*, among others (see Table 3 below), which are mostly produced in large quantities outside Igboland. The women travel to farm settlements and local markets to purchase these goods in large quantity. According to Mrs Ojiakor, she engages in yam business as long as yam is in season and switches over to *oji* (kolanut) business when out of season. This could entail a change of trade route.

***Table 3: Selected Items of Trade and Places of Purchase***

| S/N | Items(s) of trade | Town/market | State |
|---|---|---|---|
| 1 | Yam tubers, groundnuts | Zakio Biam; Ugba; Gboko; Kadorko | Benue |
| 2 | Processed cassava (garri; par-boiled fufu) | Uromi; Ilushi; | Edo |
| 3 | Beans; soya-beans; wheat; 'dawa'[millet] | Mararba-Mubi, Marte, Damboa | Borno |
| 4 | Nigerian rice (Ebony Rice/ Abakaliki Rice) | Abakaliki | Ebonyi |
| 5 | Yam tubers; kolanuts; turkeys; local rice | Eha Alumana; Ibegwa; Akpo-opi; Nsukka; Adani, | Enugu |
| 6 | Processed cassava (garri and fufu); | Umunede; Asaba | Delta |
| 7 | Yam tubers | Ukari; Sarkin kudu; Yauwa | Taraba; Adamawa |
| 8 | Yam tubers | Lambata; Kwakiti; Suleja; Paiko (near Minna); | Niger State/ Abuja Fed. Capital Territory |

*Source: Author's Fieldwork, 2013*

Those travelling to rural markets around Nsukka in Enugu State or Abakaliki in Ebonyi State, leave home around 9 pm after supper, and sleep at the motor park. As early as 4 or 4.30 am, the vehicles leave for these states. A trip could last for 4 hours, as they arrive at their destination between 8.30 am and 9 am. Buying of the items could last from this time to 2 pm, after which loading of goods begins. The return journey to Anambra State terminates at the local market namely Afor-Udo, Eke-Ekwulobia, and Nkwor-Igbo markets in Nanka, Ekwulobia, and Igbo-ukwu towns respectively (see Figure 3).

Often the local farmers, from whom the traders purchase their goods, through established networks, coordinate and assemble the goods awaiting the women traders. The popular trade destinations located in northern Nigeria are found in such states as Borno, Katsina, Adamawa, Niger (near Abuja, Nigerian's Federal Capital Territory), Taraba and Benue; Delta and Edo states in the south-south; and Ebonyi and Enugu states in the south-east. The variability of the business is reflected in the manner the women switch from one trading item to another, depending on the item of trade in season and the availability of funds. The age range of the traders varies between 30 and 55 years. A few of the participants are literate as they either hold secondary school certificates or are college of education graduates. It was also discovered that some of the traders are former primary school teachers who voluntarily retired from service due to poor remuneration. This category of traders travels to neighbouring states such as Enugu, Ebonyi, Delta and Edo.

On arrival, the distribution of goods begins the same day, depending on the time of arrival. Most of the traders primarily engage in wholesale trading, selling their goods to the final retailers, while others are equally retailers themselves, particularly those who purchase their goods from neighbouring Igbo states. Perishable goods such as fresh tomatoes are easily sold off in baskets on the day of arrival, while other goods like tubers of yams, bags of groundnuts and processed cassava, may take more days. In any case, the traders may not await the total disposal of the goods before embarking on another trip, as long as they have collected a reasonable amount of money from their customers.

### *'Crisis of Normative Masculinity' in the Context of Rural Nanka Commu-*

***nity***

Both scholarly discourses and social perceptions are dominated with the view of women's oppression and subjugation by men. Correia and Bannon (2006: 245) contend that this approach is only 'half of the story', as men are also objects of subjugation by other men. Indeed, since the 1980s when research on gender issues took centre stage in the discourses on women's positioning in society, men remained under-studied, if researched at all. While recognising what Correia and Bannon (2006) call 'hegemonic masculinity where men are categorised as a monolithic entity, and agents of women's subjugation, it is also important to engage in the categorization of men and masculinity to discover, if any, the diverse ways which give significant indication that there are instances where women domination exists, particularly among low income and poor households, where women have assumed the role of 'household head'. In such instances, the dominant model of men subjugating women is challenged, as masculinity as a monolithic cultural construct fails in the face of more critical analysis.

The notion of masculinity as a socio-cultural construction varies across cultures and societies, giving room for diverse manifestations of masculinity. Masculinities have been recognised as "configurations of practice structured by gender relations", which are inherently historical, and "their making and remaking is a political process affecting the balance of interests in society and the direction of social change" (Women's Commission for Refugee Women and Children, September, 2005: 5). Such cultural shifting blurs the boundary of masculinity/femininity divide. If gender construct is culture-centric, then, how society constructs maleness is also culture specific. In other words, what may be culturally acceptable as the manifestations of masculinity in a particular cultural context and time may not necessarily apply in a similar way elsewhere. Uchendu (2008) reports that, among the pre-colonial and colonial Zulu, abstinence from premarital penetrative sexual encounter with females and ability to show expertise in domesticity, were marks of manliness. To a large extent, this is understandable as the Zulu society in that era was a martial society. Citing Bryant (1974), Uchendu noted that other qualities expected of a real Zulu man include "loyalty, aggression, a sense of responsibility, courage, self-reliance, athleticism, endurance, and absence of emotions" (Bryant, 1974, cited in Uchendu, 2008: 8). Across most cultures

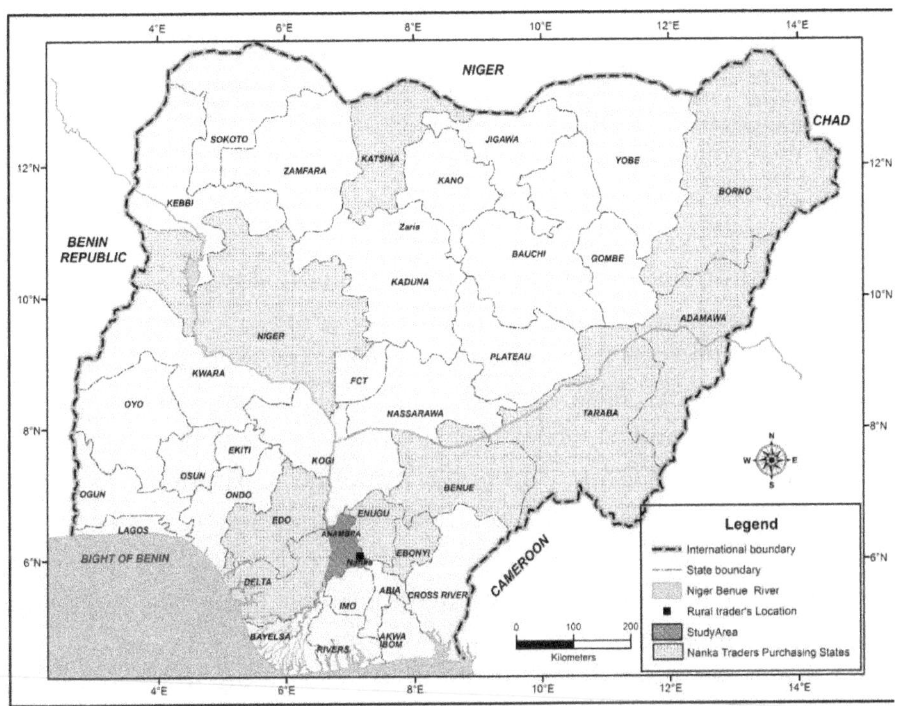


*Fig 4 : Map of Nigeria showing the various states and locations from which rural Nanka traders purchase their goods*

of the world, the dominant ideals of manhood is constructed around 'man the breadwinner', and the fact that men achieve social recognition and self-actualisation by what they 'do' rather than what they 'are'. Even in classical anthropology, the concept of 'man the hunter' dominated the discourse on economic anthropology, until 'woman the gatherer' was included, but with the assumption that even in that 'hunter-gatherer' economy, men provided the household needs and nutrients more than the women. This thesis, of course, came under powerful criticism decades later, as studies have proven that women actually provided the household nutrition more than men, as men did not always bring in game each time they went hunting.

The dominant narratives for a long time were centred on those activities that projected men, even at times giving them undue credits that collapse at the face of more scientific analysis. Thus, across human cultures, while perceptions about men centre on their 'doing', that is, activities, and what they do in those activities, which again helps to differentiate men from men and categories of men, women's perception centres on their 'being'. The cultural perception of the woman could be an impediment to her contributing to her society, or even obscures such contributions from recognition and rewards where they exist. Little wonder that her culturally defined identity of whom she is such as mother, nurturer, caregiver, housekeeper among others, remains central in the evaluation of her role and positioning in society. Any other aspiration the woman has must be contained within the limit the culture places on her gender. 'Being' and 'doing' are in a binary opposition in the context of women and men's place in society. 'Being' in this context could connote 'static', 'unchanging', 'traditional', ancient', 'archaic', 'resistant to innovation' and, in fact, devoid of agency hence lacking the capacity to initiate a change. By implication, maintaining a particular, acceptable *status quo* is a sure way of 'being' a woman. For the man, his ability to work and achieve financial independence defines what it means to be a man, and not to have these is an indication of the loss of his means of affirming his identity and achieving masculinity (Carreia and Bannon, 2006: 246).

Perhaps it may be relevant at this point to draw attention to how the conception of 'manliness' is constructed in patriarchal agrarian rural Nanka society through an appellation ascribed to a maternal grandfather. My late maternal grandfather was greeted with the appellation, "*Nwoke nwanyi n'enye nri, ogbugbu ka ya nma*", translated to mean, "A man that a woman feeds, it is better if he were killed". Such appellations encapsulate the cultural definition and perception of 'manness' in this rural community, and symbolises how the culture constructs manliness as enshrined in a man's ability to work and feed his household, and being able to effectively do this implies that one is living up to cultural expectation. Women, on the other hand, are referred to as '*oriaku*', that is 'the consumer of wealth', although this is prevalent in most Igbo communities as well. Nevertheless, in Nanka, this shapes women's positioning in the people's consciousness. As 'wealth consumers', women's economic contributions may go unrecognized, and consequently unrewarded with accruing social prestige. This feigned ignorance of women's economic contributions to the household seemingly gives the impression of docility and domesticity, and portrays the woman as one who merely consumes, and her agency is denied. While women acknowledge such appellation, they nonetheless perceive themselves beyond the 'notion of consumerism'. For instance, '*odozi aku*', meaning one who 'takes care of or conserves wealth' seems to be what many women would rather prefer to be called.

In recent times, women are shifting from 'being' to 'doing', transgressing the masculinity-femininity boundary. The present scenario indicates a shift to what I may term '*okpata aku*', meaning 'one who accumulates wealth'. As an informant noted, "Because, if you check, these days, it can be said that women carry more household [financial] responsibilities than men" (Bridget Ezebudike, personal communication, 4 June, 2013; translation, mine). The informant further argued that the era of women depending on men to provide for the household has gone.

The movement from agrarian to cash economy and capitalism occasioned by colonial encounter in Africa, initiated a change, which disproportionately favoured men. Women's access to the formal sector of the economy was hampered by cultural constraints both at the labour market and at the home front. This of course is changing in response to diverse issues, which include more access to education, and the poverty challenge. Yet, a considerable gap still remains to be filled. With regard to poverty, the promise of rights and empowerment by neoliberal democracy in Africa, to say the least, has brought about frustrations and failed expectations on the part of the populace. What is obvious is the increasing popularization of a greater number of the people, and on the part of the women, what has come to be known as 'feminisation of poverty'. Situated within the discussions in this paper, we are therefore witnessing in the words of Amuyunzu-Nyamomgo *et al.* (2006), a 'crisis of normative masculinity' particularly in developing economy such as in Africa, where it has become increasingly impossible for men alone to provide financial supports for the household. This development has psychological and socio-cultural implications, including 'culture shift' and subsequent erosion of men's roles in the family. In their study of rural Kenya, Amuyunzu-Nyamongo *et al* identified various factors that can give rise to the erosion of men's role in the family namely: decline in agriculture and pastoral economy; collapse of market and marketing institutions; high exposure to risk; and, women's increasing contribution to the economy (Amuyunzu-Nyamongo *et al* 2006: 222). In the rural areas in Igboland, cultural beliefs are changing in a dramatic way in response to contemporary economic difficulties that challenge human survival. At the micro (household) level, there is a greater recognition of the contributions of women to household economy, and at household economy, and simultaneously bringing to the public consciousness the enormity of these contributions. While this change has become obvious, it is interesting to underscore not only how the changing milieu is affecting men and women's positioning in the family, but also the societal attitude to the cultural shifts occasioned by the new development. Notably, how is economic survival shaping the cultural construction of masculinity in the rural Igbo society? Women's increasing contributions to the household income in the rural society is also shaping the way they are perceived, and thus, redefining their identity. How does this shift from 'being' to 'doing' shape and reshape familial relations and redefine the woman's identity?

### *Shifting Cultural Construction of the Woman's Identity*

Rural Nanka women who participate in long-distance trading are breaking cultural barriers. For most research participants, their husbands participate in housekeeping by playing supervisory role. According to an informant, "The man must show interest because he is the one being helped; the man oversees things from a distance" (Mrs Agnes Odinagbo, personal communication, July, 2013; translation mine). This suggests that, though the women recognise their new key role in household economic provisioning, they also perceive this development as 'filling the gap' or 'standing in' for the man, because as the informant stressed, "*Maka noo isi ya ka ana ese*", that is, "*because it is his 'head' that is being secured*".

The loss of self-esteem on the part of the man is suggested in such statements as, "But, you know, the man will be answering her [the wife] 'sir' because she is the one that brings family income; the man will be answering her 'sir' so that she will continue to bring" (Mr Felix Okuzo, personal communication, July 2013; translation mine). Invariably, as women gain more financial autonomy, there is also a shift in power relations within the home front. Ascribing the honorific 'sir' to the woman as the informant, Mr Felix Okuzo, observed, demonstrates the woman's 'assumption' of masculinity; of being 'a man' occasioned by her increasing financial support to the family. The use of 'sir' for the woman seems to suggest a kind of mockery of the woman's new positioning, which again, could be an indirect rejection of her current position, yet, not explicitly expressed; a revolt, and an indication of a psychological war raging on in the mind of the man for a failed masculinity.

Scholars like Sanday (1979) have argued that woman's economic empowerment results in political empowerment at the public space. Findings from the current study do not seem to suggest a similar conclusion. While it is obvious that the woman's decision-making power is enhanced at the home front, there is no corresponding indication that this results in more access to decision making spaces in the public sphere in this rural community, beyond what has been traditionally ascribed to the woman through the diverse women's groups and associational ties. Several reasons can account for this. First, the income these rural women generate does not make much direct impact on the larger society, compared to the financial contributions from wealthy women with Western education from the urban centres who have higher economic power base and social networks. Second, it was discovered that most of these women hardly have time to participate in the socio-political life of the community as a result of time constraint, besides lack of higher formal education. From all indications, the attitude of members of this local community with regard to women's contribution to household income through their participation in long-distance trading has been that of acceptance and understanding, while for some men, tolerance. Kin group members such as the woman's younger siblings, mother, or mother in-law assist by providing care to the children in the absence of the mother. With social support, many more women continue to join in the trade.

Emerging from this study also is the fact that women's economic empowerment directly affects the family as income generated is utilised in addressing those problems that affect women and children directly. Research participants maintain that the income from the business is used to address pressing family needs that impact on the lives of their children, and the entire family (see Table: 4 below). Needs such as feeding, children's school fees and health, receive priority of attention. As one of the informants captures it:

> The income from the business is used to meet family needs. I use it to train our children in schools; the one that is not schooling but is an apprentice to a businessman in town, whatever you have will be used to assist him [when he is settled by his master] (Source, Mrs Odinaka Akuejika, personal communication, June, 2013; translation mine).

As Igbo people are predominantly traders, the possibility that some children may rather opt for trading than education is high. Boy-child drop-out of school in southeast Nigeria is a problem that has drawn the attention of UNICEF. Available statistics (see Table: 4) indicate that there is higher female enrolment in primary, junior and senior secondary schools in Anambra State, southeastern Nigeria, for instance.

***Table 4: Expenditure indicator (in percentage)***

| **S/N** | **Item** | **No of Participants** | **% of participants** |
|---|---|---|---|
| 1 | Children's education | 60 | 100 |
| 2 | Supporting capital for children's businesses | 50 | 83.3 |
| 3 | Healthcare | 60 | 100 |
| 4 | Food | 60 | 100 |
| 5 | Family house (building/renovation) | 45 | 65 |
| 6 | Community levies | 45 | 65 |

*Source: Author's Fieldwork, 2013*

This socio-cultural peculiarity necessitates women's contribution to ensure the boy-child has a good head-start in his chosen profession. Financial assistance is given to those who have opted for trading rather than formal education, particularly immediately after apprenticeship. Another informant, Mrs. Bridget Ezebudike, who has engaged in the business for over 20 years noted with pleasure that, with the income she makes from her business, she is able to pay the school fees of five of her children in tertiary institutions.

> If you come to my house now, I have five children in the university. They are five. One is in UNIBen [University of Benin]. He is studying Law there. The other one is in University of Maiduguri.... The other one is on Youth Service at Markurdi. Two have graduated (Mrs Bridget Ezebudike, personal communication, 4 June, 2013; translation mine).

***Table 5: Anambra State school enrolment: primary, junior and senior secondary schools by gender (2008)***

| S/N | Item | Total No. of Enrolment | Males | Females | No. of Males in % |
|---|---|---|---|---|---|
| 1 | Primary School | 771, 586 | 358, 381 | 413, 205 | 46.4 |
| 2 | Junior Sec. School. | 193, 319 | 90, 767 | 102, 552 | 47.0 |
| 3 | Senior Sec. School | 89, 062 | 37, 059 | 52, 003 | 41.6 |

*Source: Extracted from the report of National Bureau of Statistics (2008)*

Angel-Urdinola and Wodon (2010) suggest that within the household, the control of resources by gender has implications on the outcome of the family and impacts on the community in the final analysis. As indicated in Table 3, 100% of women research participants maintain that the income generated from the business is used for the payment of children's school fees, healthcare issues, and feeding. Also 83.3% of the participants claim they use the money for supporting their children in business, while 65% claim they use the money for the renovation/building of family house and the payment of community levies.

The involvement of women in household economic provisioning, more than ever, is leading to role overlap. Women's participation in the trade is shifting cultural boundaries and redefining the woman's identity as insinuated in such statements as, "the husband answers her 'sir'", masculinising the woman. For some men, there is subversion of power, as according to Mr Jeremiah Obiezue, an informant, "*Umunwanyi ka ooooo. Oo fa nwa n'enyezi anyi nni. Ha choro ime anyi* overthrow" meaning "Women are greater ooooo. They are the ones that now feed us. They want to overthrow us". Implied in this statement is fear, occasioned by a perceived threat to men's ego, and a power shift, which is reinforced in changing power relations at the family level as a result of the changing economic fortunes of these women. For some women, on the other hand, "It is no longer fashionable for a woman to stay idle and say, 'Let my husband take care of me and the family'. Not at all." Women seem to have taken control of their destiny, and possibly have succeeded in subverting men's power to their advantage, through the instrumentality of economic empowerment. According to an informant, as long as the woman 'maintains' the children and meets their needs, she enjoys the cooperation of the family members, including the children. The children also recognise that the mother has become the bread winner, and often say: "Mummy *n'aka eweputa ego*" meaning 'it is mummy that brings in more money". In circumstances where the woman is the near sole provider of the family income, the man may lose his relevance, and may be sidelined and lose consultative power. Masculinity as defined by the culture, at this point, is no longer man's preserve, as a woman can actually assume 'masculine' when she possesses the qualities of 'work', 'income' and 'financial independence'.

### *Challenges in Long-Distance Trading and Coping Strategies*

Certain challenges were identified in this research as militating against rural women's participation in long-distance trading. The next section looks at these challenges and strategies the traders adopted in coping with them.

#### *Home Front Challenge*

Participants in this research identified the management of the home front in their absence as one of the major challenges they have to cope with. Though husbands of such inter-state traders take up a supervisory role at home, to the women traders, household responsibilities still constitute a challenge. Findings indicate that women with very young children – where the oldest is under 10 years, for instance – tend to engage in inter-state business within neighbouring states, with the possibility of returning the same day. Such states include Delta, Edo, Ebonyi, and Enugu. Those with teenage children are also bothered about the security of these children in their absence. To cope with this challenge, the woman trader makes arrangements with her siblings, mother-in-law or members of the extended family for assistance when it is not possible to get a live-in helper while she is away.

#### *Weak Financial Base*

Lack of adequate capital base constitutes a major challenge confronting the women traders. Majority of the participants complained of limited capital at their disposal. Loans are not available for the traders. The larger chunk of money for the business comes from limited personal savings and/or assistance from friends. As a result of lack of adequate capital, the business hardly grows from small scale to large scale.

***Security Issues***

Security of life and property while on business trips is a major challenge confronting the women. Cases of bandits waylaying the women and stealing their money abound. To address this, the traders make private security arrangements to accompany them on their business trips, while their business partners make local security arrangements as they go about purchasing their goods. In this way, they are able to negotiate the difficult terrains of their trade. However, the onset of Boko Haram insurgency has compounded the women's security challenge as certain parts of the country like Borno State in the northeastern Nigeria, have become inaccessible. The introduction of electronic banking has drastically reduced the cases of armed bandits' attacks. The women avail themselves of this opportunity and reduce the amount of cash they carry while embarking on their journeys. Although they do not seem to enjoy the business, because of the possibility of generating the income that will improve the standard of life of members of the household and keep their children in school, more and more women are joining the trade with the intention of disengaging from the business when their children are of age to render some financial support to the family. Road accidents were also identified as part of the major challenges. Goods and passengers are loaded in the same truck. Oftentimes, the women squat on top of the loads of goods in very uncomfortable manners. And in cases of road mishaps, they easily fall victims and many have lost their lives in the process. Participants recounted the number of their colleagues they lost to motor accidents during their business trips.

***Suspicion of Infidelity***

The issue of husband's suspicion of a wife's infidelity was also identified as a challenge in the business. Some husbands may become suspicious of their wives' movements. When this happens, this may create frictions at the home front and becomes a challenge to such a woman's continued participation in the business. As an informant stated, "*I ma na nwoke gbara olu ebe nwanyi noo. O nwere ike n' asi nwunye ya jee, mana O ga na aguru ya ana onu*". This means, "you know that a man is weak when women's issues are concerned. He may support the wife's engagement in the business but will be 'counting steps' for her." In other words, such a husband closely monitors the wife's movements. Yet, some of these suspicions may be genuine as it is not impossible for some drivers to have paramour among their women passengers, or some women having same among their male business partners at their destinations.

### *Conclusion and Recommendations*

This study of rural Igbo women's participation in long-distance trading activities has highlighted how the harsh economic reality of contemporary times has contributed in the redefinition of the woman's identity in the rural community, with a positive change in their economic fortune. Men's participation in housekeeping and caregiving, assuming supervisory role at home front also reflects how the socio-cultural indices are changing in response to this development. Although the community is patriarchal, men's attitude towards women is changing as a result of the economic crunch that has made it difficult for men alone to provide for the household. The income from long-distance trading has therefore enabled women to shape their destiny and enhance their political position within the home, though without a corresponding shift in their political powers within the public space. It is then right to conclude that the changing and shifting identity of women in the rural Igbo society under study is a reflection of the need to ensure human survival and continuity as well as live a quality of life that is meaningful. The current reality has provided the impetus that engenders and invigorates women's sense of agency. Many widowed, unmarried and married poor rural women find economic solace in exploiting the opportunity this form of trading activity offers. While the man may still retain the headship of the household, the woman may in fact be the economic backbone of the household. The control of the household income by women increases their decision making power, and as Karl Marx and Engels (1977: 57) note, a people's socio-economic reality determines the people's consciousness.

### *Recommendations*

- The major recommendation emanating from this study is the need to make available to rural women access to low interest loans, which will enable them to contribute more meaningfully to their family income.
- Scholarship facilities for indigent students will go a long way in offering opportunities for children from low income households to have access to formal education. This will alleviate the financial burden women bear reduce the drop-out rate of children from school.
- Improvement on security can safeguard loss of lives and goods. Government at all levels need to give priority attention to the security challenge in the country.

### *References*

Adesina, J. O. Yao, G. and Olukoshi, A. (Eds.). *Africa and Development Challenges in the New Millennium*. Dakar: CODESRIA.

Afigbo, A. 2005. First published: 1972. Religion and economic enterprise in Traditional Igbo Society. In: *Igbo History and Society – The Essays of Adiele Afigbo*. Falola, T. (Ed.). New Jersey: African World Press, Inc. 297 – 306.

Afigbo, A. 2005. First published: 1972. Trade and Trade Routes in Nineteenth Century Nsukka. In: *Igbo History and Society – The Essays of Adiele Afigbo.* Falola, T. (Ed.). New Jersey: African World Press, Inc.: 533 – 548.

Amuyunzu-Nyamongo, M. and Paul, F. 2006. Collapsing Livelihoods and the Crisis of Masculinity in Rural Kenya. Men's Issues in Development: In: *The Other Half of Gender.* Bannon, I. and Maria C. C. (Eds) Washington DC: World Bank: 219 – 244.

Angel-Urdinola and Wodon. 2010. Income Generation and Intra-household Decision Making: A Gender Analysis for Nigeria. In: *Gender Disparities in Africa's Labor Market*. Arbache, J. S., Alexandre, K. and Ewa, F. (Eds.).Washington DC.: International Bank for Reconstruction and Development/World Bank: 381 - 406.

British Council. 2012. Gender in Nigeria Report 2012: Improving the Lives of Girls and Women in Nigeria – Issues, Policies, Action. A Publication of British Council, Nigeria.

Correia, M. C. and Ian, B. 2006. Gender and its Discontents: Moving to Men-streaming Development. In: *Men's Issues in Development: The Other Half of Gender*. Ian, B. and Correia, M.C. (Eds.).Washington DC.: World Bank. 245 – 260.

Kelly, C. 2008. White Men: An Exploration of Intersections of Masculinity, Whiteness and Colonialism and the Engagement of Counter-Hegemonic Projects. In: *Masculinities in Contemporary Africa*. Uchendu, E. (Ed.). Dakar: Council for the Social Science Research in Africa: 110-132.

Kolev, A. and Nicolas S. 2010. *Gender disparities in African labour markets: A Cross-Country Comparison Using Standardized Survey Data*. In: *Gender Disparities in Africa's Labor Market*. Arbache, J. S., Alexandre, K. and Ewa, F. (Eds.).World Bank: Washington: 23-53.

Laver, E. J. 2004. First printed 1980. Kanem and Bornu to 1808. In: *Groundwork of Nigerian History*. Ikime, O. (Ed.). Ibadan: Heinemann Educational Books: 187 – 209.

Marx, K. and Frederick, E. 1977. *Manifesto of the Communist Party*. Moscow: Progress Publishers.

National Bureau of Statistics. 2009. Social Statistics in Nigeria. Federal Republic of Nigeria, Abuja, Nigeria. http://www.nigerianstat.gov.ng or http:/www.scribd.com/doc/5334 5549/social-statistics-in-nigeria-2009

Onwughalu, O. J. 2012. Globalization, Education and Igbo Priorities in the Nigerian Polity: Kedu Ife N'echu Ndigbo Ula in This Era Of Globalization?' A Paper Presented at the 10th International Conference of Igbo Studies Association (ISA) with the theme, The Place of the Igbo in a Globalized World, held at E. Franklin Frazier Centre for Social Work Research, Law Campus, Howard University, Washington Dc, USA. April 11 – 14, 2012.

Some, B. 2013. Hot Money: Gender and the Politics of Negotiation and Control Over Income in West African Smallholder Households. *Africa,* Vol. 83 Issue 2:251 - 269

The Holy Bible. New King James Version.

Women's Commission for Refugee Women and Children, Conceptualizing Masculinity/conceptualizations of Masculinity, September, New York 2005.

Uchendu, E. 2008. Introduction: Are African Males Men? Sketching African Masculinities. In: *Masculinities in Contemporary Africa.* in Uchendu, E. (Ed.) Dakar: Council for the Social Science Research in Africa: 1-17

Ukpokolo, C. 2010. 'Academic Freedom and Dual Career Academic Couples: The Complexities of Being a Woman Academic in the University Space'. *Journal of Higher Education in Africa.* Vol. 8. No. 1: 49 – 71.

Ukpokolo, C. 2013. 'Sexual Harassment and the Violation of Academic Freedom'. In: *The Idea of a Nigerian University: A Revisit.* Oyeshile, O. and J. Kenny (Eds.). Washington D.C.: The Council for Research in Values and Philosophy (CRSVP): 149 – 169.

Weitz, R. 1998. A history of women's Bodies. In: weitz, R. ed. *The Politics of Women's Bodies: Sexuality, Appearance, and Behaviour.* New York: Oxford University Press: 3 - 11.

Willot, C. 2009. "'Get to the Bridge and I will Help you to Cross': Merit, Personal Connections, and Money as Routes to Success in Nigerian Higher Education". *Bath Papers in International Development.* No. 6, August 2009. Working Paper Series of the Centre for Development Studies at the University of Bath.

# *Chapter Seven*

## INDIGENOUS PALM OIL PRODUCTION IN ORILE-OWU, NIGERIA: A GENDERED TECHNICAL AND ECONOMIC PRACTICE

*Samuel Oluwole Ogundele*

### *Introduction*

The prime goal of this chapter is the development of an understanding and knowledge of palm-oil production or processing which constitutes a set of complex metaphors embracing such areas of life and living as materiality, sociality, spatiality and power relations among the people of Orile-Owu. Indeed, such artifacts or features as flotation and sludge pits represent the material signature of the people's complex gendered world. Orile-Owu is a prominent settlement in Ayedaade Local Government Council Area of Osun State in Nigeria. Research efforts to date in this community show that there are certain profound ideologies or structures (rules and regulations) that form the sturdy fabric of palm oil production as the locals chart the pathways of their gendered material world. Our methodology in this context is embedded in literary excavations, ethnography, oral traditions and mapping of some production sites (Kottak 2004; Ogundele and Ebonine 2010; Hall 1996).

Palm tree/oil palm botanically christened *Elaeis guineensis*, is of tropical African origin. This tree is commonly found growing wild in many parts of the West African sub-region and as far afield as the Congo Basin (Onwueme 1979). The stem which is normally very erect measures up to 10 metres or more in height. It (the stem) terminates with a crown of leaves and bunches of palm fruits at the top of the plant (see Figures 5 & 6).

*Fig. 5: Some palm trees at Orile-owu*

*Fig. 6: Palm fruits*

However, some new breeds of oil palm today are much shorter, making harvesting of fruits far easier than hitherto. Oil palm requires rainfall of 200cm or more annually, with a short dry season, while warm temperatures and abundant sunshine averaging five hours daily are needed.

Although newly developed breeds of oil palm are now available in plantation forms, all the palm trees being exploited for oil among other things in the study area are found growing wild. However, oil palm plantations are gradually increasing in number and importance. It is pertinent to note here, that oil palm is the most widely utilised economic tree in Orile-Owu like other parts of Nigeria where it grows. Thus for example, the leaves are a vital resource in indigenous architectural and building technology, where they serve as roofing material (Onwueme 1979). Aside from roofing houses, palm trees are used in the construction of sheds or for making fences. The midrib of the leaflet is popularly used for making brooms for different household purposes. In addition, wine (*emu ope*) is obtained from the palm tree. This is a popular local alcoholic beverage among the Owu same as other Nigerian people especially those in the southern region of the country.

### *Uses of Space for Oil Production Purposes*

The conceptualisation of space by the Owu people especially for palm oil production purposes in Orile-Owu is entangled with social relationships. In other words, palm oil production sites known as *ebu* are a physical manifestation of a set of ideologies (rules and regulations) normally recorded through the lenses of orality (Onwuejeogwu 1981; Kottak 2004). Palm oil processing sites constitute one important settlement feature of the people, understandably because it (palm oil production) is second only to farming as a livelihood in the community. Indeed, palm oil production partially straddles the domain of agriculture.

Ile-Ejemu, Omokuajo, Ile-Apena and Alagbede are some of the areas within the community where palm oil production sites have been located. The sites are usually located near sources of water like rivers and streams. Two prominent sources of water in this connection are Obalufon and Omu rivers. Palm oil processing sites are located at the edges or peripheries of the settlement. This occupation or indigenous knowledge system involves the use of a considerable amount of water. This underscores the reason why an ecological factor plays a crucial role in their (palm oil production sites) locations.

Aside from this ecological consideration, locating production sites at the edges of a settlement goes a long way in reducing accidents to the barest minimum within the processing zone. Palm oil and the by-products are extremely slippery when they unavoidably splash on the floor of a site. In other words, palm oil production sites (*ebu*) are usually wet and slippery. Children and adults alike are therefore not encouraged to move around them (sites) except when it is most inevitable to do so. In this regard, both ecological and social factors do influence the location of palm oil production sites. But nobody or group of persons can just establish/develop a palm oil production site without getting the elders' approval. This is because land belongs to the community, although at a closer level, each extended family grouping or lineage has its own area of jurisdiction. Trespassing on lineage family land is almost a taboo.

Family land is not exclusively for male members, since women can also gain access to it by virtue of their status either as wives or daughters. The distribution of parcels of land for house construction, farming and palm oil production purposes among members is solely in the hands of the elders of each of the extended family grouping or lineage. Although elderly women are not excluded, the male elders are the main drivers of this social engine complex that sustains their age-old land distribution and management behaviours.

Despite this arrangement, some winds of change have started to blow gradually across the Owu material world with particular reference to land holding patterns. It shows that land ownership system as a vibrant component of culture is not immune to change. As a result of this development, a man can decide to buy land for any of the above-mentioned activities from a lineage that he does not belong to. However, monetization of land holding in this way is yet to gain in popularity in Orile-Owu (Aderibigbe 2010, personal communication).

When a piece of land is allocated to a member, some items like palm oil, fowls, alcoholic beverages especially palm wine are given to the elders who represent the heart and soul of the lineage group. This spatial or land holding arrangement, is a mark of social legitimation with the capacity to foster better relations within the extended family grouping and the community at large. It is within this framework that extra-household socio-economic alliances are sustainably developed.

### *Understanding Gendered Technical Practice*

After a parcel of land has been allocated to a woman (usually a wife

*Fig. 7: A flotation pit*

of a member of a given lineage) or more women, then the next thing is to look for men to clear the site. Site clearing and construction of features of varying types for palm oil production are gendered technical practices almost exclusively in the domain of males. However, some women can also assist indirectly by providing food and drinks for the working party of men between 4 and 6 in number. Digging flotation and sludge pits is a male-gendered task basically because it is laborious. The diameters of flotation pits in the four investigated palm oil production sites (*ebu*) in Orile-Owu vary from 1.4 metres to 2 metres while the depths range from 80cm to 100cm (See Figure 7)

Most of these flotation pits (*eku*) were cemented with specially prepared clay by women. Women also do the resurfacing of floors and walls of pits when the need to do so arises. This aspect of the indigenous knowledge system is purely female-gendered. These women could be the owners of the production sites or engaging in this activity or task for a fee. However, using modern cement to plaster walls and floors of flotation pits, is by men – usually professional bricklayers. The size of a production site determines the number of flotation and sludge pits to be constructed. Thus, for example, palm oil production site at the Alagbede area of Orile-Owu (with a length of about 20 metres and width of approximately 18 metres) has 4 flotation pits. This is the largest palm oil production site in the study area. The one at Ile-Ejemu has 3 flotation pits, while those at Omokuajo and Ile-Apena have 2 each (Ogundele 2004; Ogundele and Ebonine 2010).

*Fig. 8: A sludge pit*

*Fig. 9: A machine for pressing boiled palm fruits*

The construction of sludge pits is less elaborate and without any plastering at all. The average diameter for these pits is 1 metre, while the depths vary from 70cm to 100cm. These pits are used for retaining industrial wastes called *afo*. Waste/sludge pits are usually located at the peripheries of a production site. But despite the simple character of sludge pits, they are certainly a good example of a male-gendered task. Six waste pits were mapped at the palm oil production site located in the Alagbede area of the settlement. Each site also has a machine shed where boiled palm fruits are pressed. (See Figures 8 & 9).

According to all our informants (professional palm oil makers and other members of the community), the use of machines was a relatively recent development in the locality. This is traceable to the late 1980s. In other words, prior to this time (the late 1980s), processing of boiled palm fruits was manually done. Women trod on them (boiled fruits) in wooden mortars or canoe-like structures of wood. The use of these locally fabricated machines for palm oil processing shows the extent to which the indigenous knowledge system – as a component of culture, is inseparable from the phenomenon of change. Indeed, machines are gradually replacing human labour in palm oil production. This aspect of the work is not totally gender-specific. Thus for example, some women occasionally operate these machines when men are not available to do the work. The Owu people are carefully pushing back the boundaries of human knowledge and understanding as they construct and re-construct their engendered material world.

Women construct hearths where palm fruits are boiled for between 1 and 1½ hours depending on the intensity of the fire. Each hearth is a tripod of stones. Ten hearths were seen at the Alagbede area, while the numbers were smaller (5 to 8) in other palm oil production sites studied by us. Women are responsible for maintaining these production sites except when there is need for a major repair of flotation pits or when additional ones (flotation pits) are to be built by men (Bray 2007; McClure 2007).

### *Direct Palm Oil Processing*

Oil palm or palm tree, botanically christened *Elaeis guineensis* is one of the economic plants native to West Africa. It usually grows wild in many parts of West Africa and as far afield as the Congo Basin (Onwueme 1979). Except in cases of genetic disorder, stems of palm trees are very erect and terminate in crowns of leaves. Oil palm needs at least 200cm of rainfall annually with a short dry season. This is in addition to warm temperatures as well as enormous sunshine reaching at least five hours a day. The transverse section of palm fruit is made up of mesocarp (thin layer), pericarp (fleshy layer), endocarp (nut) and epicarp (shell). It is the pericarp that contains palm oil to be extracted.

Given the above short biological and geographical analysis of palm tree, it is not a surprise that our study area (Orile-Owu) located in the forest

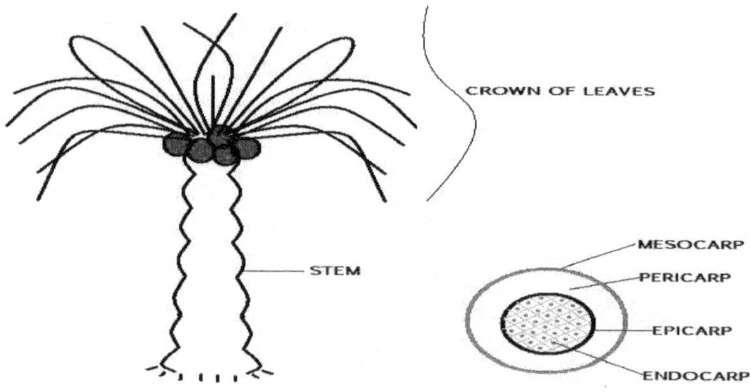


*Fig. 10a: A palm fruit structure*

*Fig. 10b: Palm kernels with epicarp and endocarp*

zone of Nigeria has an enormous amount of it. Indeed, oil palm is the most prominent economic tree in the locality and the people are exploiting it to the full in order to push back the frontiers of material and to a limited extent, social progress.

The first major step – harvesting of bunches of palm fruits after the production site has been built, is taken by a man. He does this by climbing the palm tree with the aid of strong but locally made ropes (*igba*) from the tough outer portion of the leaf rachis. The bunches of ripe palm fruits are cut with a short axe. After this, he descends from the tree top. Collection of these bunches is usually done by women and young children of working age. The material is then taken to the production site. As a matter of fact, palm fruits harvesting is a routine task for males while carrying the material home is almost exclusively for the female gender. In this regard, both materiality (the ideological basis for producing the Owu material world) and sociality or social life mesh at the crossroads of human knowledge and understanding.

The Owu palm oil producer heaps these fruit bunches for two or three days in one or two corners of the production site (*ebu*) in order to pave the way for fermentation. This helps in reducing the toxic content of the finished product (palm oil). In addition to this, heaping bunches of palm fruits for one or two days makes it relatively easier to separate or remove them (fruits). However, some palm oil producers still boil the fruits for about 20 to 30 minutes inside big drums (with a cylinder-like shape) to further loosen them (fruits), so that they can be removed with less pains. Suffice it to say that this process has the capacity to cause injuries to the hands of palm oil producers if great caution is not taken. his is because the bunches are very thorny.

After separating fruits from bunches, they (palm fruits) are put inside drums with water for main boiling. Dry wood inside tripods of stones provides the needed fire or temperature for this part of palm oil processing among the Orile-Owu women. Boiling palm fruits takes between 40 and 60 minutes. This is quickly followed by pounding to break up the oil-bearing tissues (pericarp), leaving the epicarp and endocarp for other purposes (see figures 10a & 10b). Today, machines are used instead of doing it manually.

Sexual division of labour and gender relations meet at this stage. Although men flex muscles in this connection, some strong women also operate these machines as observed by us during the research at the Omokuajo production site. In the past (before the 1980s), pounding boiled palm fruits was an exclusively female-gendered task involving the use of large wooden mortars and pestles (Oladeji 2010, Pers. Comm.). This is one good illustration of how gender roles change as the winds of modernity blow across a socio-cultural landscape. Mechanisms of socio-cultural change can be due to diffusion or borrowing of traits between cultures. They can also be explained against the background of independent invention/development arising from internal adjustments following comparable socio-historical and ecological challenges and problems by groups of humans in different climes and cultures. This scenario constitutes one reason for the existence of cultural generalities (Hall 1996).

The above situation explains the changing faces of Owu palm oil production system – a gendered work that must be understood within the framework of at least minimum fluidity. Thus for example, today a rich man or woman by local standards can buy a parcel of land and construct a palm oil production site, which he leases out to palm oil producers. The owner of this site does not necessarily have to be a professional palm oil producer. This is a relatively new economic mode of life that is yet to gain in popularity in Orile-Owu.

One or two women begin the process of separating kernels and impurities (with the aid of baskets) from the real oil. This is done inside the flotation pit. It is important to note that the macerated mass is a combination of kernels, oil, water and sludge among other types of impurities. A lot of water is poured into the flotation pit. The size of a flotation pit determines whether or not only one woman does the flotation work at a time. After harvesting of palm fruits from tree tops and pressing of boiled fruits with machines, men are not involved directly in palm oil production. Men are only involved in the task of digging flotation and sludge pits. However, this scenario does not reduce the amount of significance of men's roles in the production process.

Removing palm kernels and impurities is a necessary precondition for a successful flotation work. This exercise takes up to two or more hours to carry out. The fibres are made into balls (averaging 16cm in diameter). They are arranged in the sun for drying that may last between four and six days depending on weather conditions. Similarly, palm kernels are left in the open to dry gradually, so that the shell can separate easily from the nuts within a few days. This makes it possible to successfully obtain the real nut from the shell or epicarp. The balls of fibres called *iha* among the Yoruba resemble elephants' faeces and are a good source of domestic fires in Orile-Owu like other parts of both rural and urban Yorubaland (See Fig. 11).

Oily water and sludge remain after the fibres and kernels have been removed. This is followed by direct flotation technique, using a gourd to separate oil from water, while sludge goes to the bottom of the pit. Real oil goes to the edges of the pit and it is carefully removed with the aid of a calabash. The palm oil is put inside a container near the pit and flotation is repeated many times, until only water and sludge remain. This fresh palm oil is boiled inside a big drum for about 20 to 30 minutes in order to reduce to the barest minimum or eliminate living organisms (micro-organisms and other contaminants) that might have been directly or indirectly introduced

*Fig. 11: Iha-balls of fibres for domestic fires*

in the course of the processing (Ogundele 2011, Pers. Comm.). This is a local mechanism to ensure that the palm oil is safe for human consumption.

The following day, the water in the flotation pit is removed, leaving behind sludge (*afo*) which is taken and poured into special pits for that purpose. The sludge cannot last for more than 5 days in the pit before it gets bad or spoilt. The odour usually oozing out of spoilt sludge (*afo*) makes it most necessary to prepare it (sludge) as quickly as possible. This is a simple process. Handfuls of sludge are pasted on the walls of a building, one by one until the substance hardens. Hardening and drying may take up to 8 days or more depending on weather conditions (see Figure 12).

This is one by-product of palm oil production which serves as an item of

*Fig. 12: Oguso-handfulls of sludge pasted on a house wall for drying*

internal distributive trade. It is also a popular type of fuel for domestic fires and to a lesser degree, industrial purposes. Thus, for example, blacksmiths use it (*oguso*) for making fires during metallurgical operations, involving the use of furnaces and bellows.

*Oguso* is more favoured than *iha* (which was mentioned earlier) by many people in Orile-Owu as indeed, other parts of Yorubaland. This is because it (*oguso*) burns slowly and therefore lasts longer. *Oguso* and *iha* are important trade items that are commonly found in local markets and even urban centres across southwestern Nigeria – homeland of the Yoruba. Their (*oguso* and *iha*) centrality to life and living crosses status boundaries because even women with high Western education use them at least occasionally for large-scale cooking.

### *Spatial Organisation and Power Relations*

Palm oil production exercise in Orile-Owu straddles the spheres of material life and living as well as social essence. It is physical, social and psychological understandably because we are dealing with a complex human phenomenon. It is common knowledge that no appreciable material progress can be made among the palm oil producers, in the face of crises that are not immediately resolved within the framework of fairness. Social stability is a precondition for economic progress. The Owu palm oil producer is aware of this reality as a basis for sustainable development. One manifestation of this consciousness is the construction of certain internal mechanisms as a coping strategy (Scupin 2000).

This can be explained against the background of the construction of a social hierarchy, with the most senior member of the group as head. Seniority in this context is in terms of age and professional experience. However, in most cases the former criterion takes centre stage in the selection process. The head works very closely with every member within a production site. The next most senior person is automatically the deputy head. These two individuals are highly respected by the entire production team. An outsider can hardly notice his hierarchical leadership arrangement, given the enormous amount of genuine humility, approachability and sagacity of the executive members. Such a humble approach and unparalleled team spirit affect the ways responsibilities are shared and carried out within an

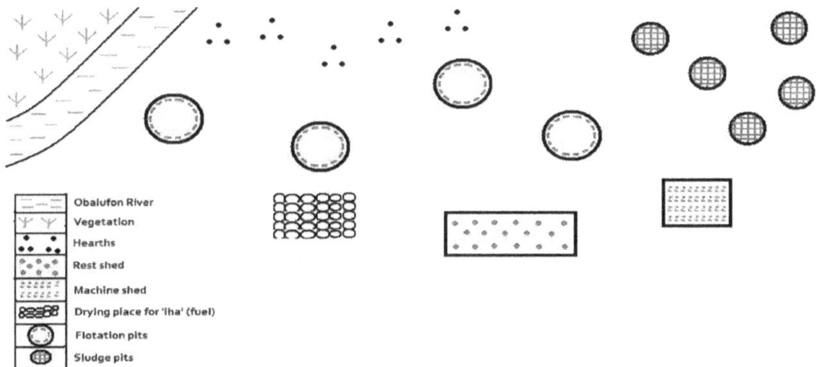


*Fig. 13: An ethnographic map of a production site at Ile-Ejemu*

industrial space.

As a food processing facet of the Owu economic structure, general hygiene and personal one occupy a conspicuous space in the vocabularies of their operation. The site must be cleaned every morning during the production period usually between November and May or early June. Cleaning is a collective exercise. At the end of each operation, flotation pits are thoroughly cleaned up in readiness for another round of processing of palm fruits. Defecation and/or bathing near the site are disallowed (see fig. 13).

Occasionally, when cases of poor hygienic behaviour of members occur, the head quickly calls the culprit to order. She does this with huge sagacity, so as to sustain the group and by extension, its livelihood. As noted above, leadership among the Orile-Owu palm oil producers, is about transparent honesty and/or self-discipline. Thus, for example, taxes and rents collected from palm oil producers who don't have their own permanent production sites, are kept by the head on behalf of her group. Such monies can be spent later to develop a daughter production site with a new head and a deputy. Sometimes, the users of this space pay in kind (usually some quantities of palm oil) to the owners.

Although seniority in terms of age is the main requirement to lead a group, democratic principles are not alien to these women. This underscores the reason why on rare occasions, a head may be removed if her behaviour smacks of bad leadership in all its ramifications. Palm oil producers also play active roles in the local politics, religion and social life of Orile-Owu through the lenses of their professional associations. The head is held in high esteem by the generality of the Owu people including the king (*Olowu*) – the heart and soul of the community. This recognition and respect derive from the fact that managing human resources, especially at a professional level, is not an easy task to accomplish. Thus, for example, during annual cultural festivals, particularly the Anlugbua one that holds on the first Saturday of every October, representatives of palm oil producers' associations across the kingdom also feature prominently in the scheme of things.

Even in modern-day politics, palm oil producers in the study area, are a force to reckon with. Their heads (in collaboration with other community leaders) work hand-in-hand with the *Kabiyesi* (the *Oba* or king) to chart the pathways of the community's political destiny. This is an exercise in indigenous gender and power relations, central to the production of the Owu material and to a limited degree, spiritual world.

Given all the above realities, we can legitimately claim that palm oil production in Orile-Owu, is a large capsule of scientific knowledge of the world in which the people live and the applications of it to the direct issue of human condition. By this token, the indigenous knowledge system (palm oil production) is a triumph of science over ignorance and material poverty. Certainly, there is need for more problem-oriented and thoroughgoing ethnoarchaeological and socio-anthropological investigations of the locality.

### *Conclusion*

Our investigations of indigenous palm oil production in Orile-Owu, a settlement that straddles the spheres of rurality and semi-urbanity in southwestern Nigeria provide an array of opportunities for developing an understanding of Owu materiality, sociality and spatiality. This is within the framework of sustainable development. Palm oil processing is a technical and economic practice that occupies a huge space in the Owu gendered material and to a lesser degree, social world. This underscores the reason why it (palm oil production) is a crossroads of human enterprises.

Both men and women are involved in different activities or tasks in the course of palm oil production. This is in sharp contrast to the popular notion that indigenous palm oil processing is exclusively female-gendered. Thus, for example, harvesting ripe palm fruits and constructing flotation and sludge pits, are tasks for men to accomplish. On the other hand, women do the direct flotation work among other things. The by-products *iha* (ball-like in shape) and *oguso* (flat and roughly circular) are sources of domestic and to a limited extent, industrial fires.

The importance of this material cuts across different social and economic strata in Yorubaland. As a matter of fact, both the context (that is the physical aspect of palm oil production) and the text which includes the people's ideologies and norms, are studied with a view to developing an appreciation and understanding of the symbolic meanings /values of this indigenous knowledge system in Orile-Owu.

## *References*

### *Interview References*

Aderibigbe, M.O. 2010, personal communication.

Ogundele, O.A. 2011, personal communication.

Oladeji, R. 2010, personal communication.

Bray, F. 2007. Gender and Technology. *Annual Review of Anthropology*. Vol. 36: 37-53.

Hall, M. 1996. *Archaeology of Africa*. London: James Currey. Cape Town: David Philip.

Kottak, C.P. 2004. *Anthropology – The Exploration of Human Diversity*. New York: McGraw-Hill.

McClure, S.B. 2007. Gender, Technology and Evolution: Cultural Inheritance Theory and Prehistoric Potters in Valencia, Spain. *American Antiquity*. 72(3): 485-508.

Ogundele, S.O. 2004. *Rethinking West African Archaeology*. Ibadan: John Archers (Publishers) Ltd.

Ogundele, S.O. and Ebonine, U.P. 2010. Owu History in an Ethnoarchaeological Perspective. *Nyame Akuma*. No. 74 (December): 12-24.

Onwuejeogwu, M.A. 1981. *The Social Anthropology of Africa*. Ibadan: Heinemann Educational Books Inc.

Onwueme, I.C. 1979. *Crop Science*. London: Cassell.

Scupin, R. 2000. *Cultural Anthropology: A Critical Perspective*. New Jersey: Prentice-Hall.

# *Chapter Eight*

## RELIGION AND THE PARTICIPATION OF WOMEN IN POLITICS IN ZIMBABWE: CHANGING IDENTITIES AND PERSPECTIVES (1960S - 2014)

*Tapiwa Praise Mapuranga*

### *Introduction*

The position of women in African politics depends from where one comes from, and on which particular practice is being referred to. Generally, the construction of who a woman is in African traditional religions depends on whether one is coming from a patrilineal or matrilineal context (Phiri 1997:32). It will really be unfair to label all African practices as oppressive and dominating to women and thereby inhibiting them from participation in politics. There are some liberative aspects that maybe found within these African customs and practices. This chapter examines the values of women in the political sphere in Zimbabwe. It argues that there has been a slow but increasing number of women politicians. However, in order to appreciate this changing significance of women, this study finds it worthwhile to mention that women generally suffer due to an oppressive background borne out of certain patriarchal and colonial attitudes within selected societies. Such colonial and patriarchal attitudes have in most cases been a stumbling block to the participation of women in the public spheres such as the political space. Despite such negative perceptions of women that existed, this study seeks to find the liberating dimension that has brought change to the lives of selected women in Zimbabwe today. This is achieved through the use of the theory called Africana Womanism. This a term coined by Hudson-Weems (1993: 24) for women who 'reject the status of victim, who consider themselves as victors and sisters in charge of their own destiny. Their primary obligation is to progress of their cultural way of life through the stability of family and commitment to community.' By application of this theory, this study argues that the patriarchal oppression of women, when and where it occurs, is not consistent with the values of Africana Womanism (see for example Hudson-Weems, 2000). This is because Africana Womanism acknowledges and celebrates the key position of women in Africa within cultures, families and other institutions. As such, this study celebrates the lives of selected women politicians in Zimbabwe, beginning the colonial period to the contemporary period (2014). These women have been a voice that exudes the significance and value of women in society. The next section examines the concept of Africana Womanism in relation to politics and religion in Zimbabwe.

### *An Africana Womanist Perspective: The Political Status of Women in Zimbabwe*

African Womanism is a term coined by Hudson-Weems (1993: 24) for women who 'reject to be considered powerless and victims'. This study argues that, the patriarchal oppression of women, especially when they are not given equal opportunities to participate in politics, when and where it occurs, is not consistent with the values of Africana Womanism (see for example Hudson-Weems, 2000). This is because Africana Womanism acknowledges and celebrates the key position of women in Africa within cultures, families and other institutions. Africana Womanism places emphasis on the significance of women and their complementarity with men (Muwati, Gambahaya and Gwekwere 2011). As such, the political sphere should be a space for both men and women so that they can complement one another.

Using Africana Womanism, one may note that Shona religion and culture emphasise on the significance of the mother through sayings and proverbs such as:

- *Musha mukadzi* (A home is because of a woman).
- *Kusina mai hakuendwe* (It is not as safe to go to a place where your mother is absent),

- *Nherera inoguta musi unofa mai* (The last day for an orphan to be fed well is the day the mother passes away).

The proliferation of such aphorisms in Shona culture drives the writer to incline her rational processes towards the fact that women are revered. Using these particular proverbs, one can only note that it is a culture that recognises women. What this means is that apart from embellishing discourse, proverbs pronounce what a people consider as their 'law'. Such sayings present some of the cases where Shona culture does not sanctify the oppression of women, but reveres them. This is also supported by Mangena and Muwati (Unpublished Paper) when they argue that "what this means is that, in most Africana contexts, the woman is a subject and not an object. She does not occupy the periphery where she is acted upon..."

It is from these arguments that this chapter argues that African traditional religions like Shona and the Chewa of Malawi have always recognised the leadership potential of women in their religio-political spheres. As Gaidzanwa records, with considerable numbers of women joining the liberation struggle in the late 1960s and 1970s, the image of the subservient and industrious mother or daughter came to be challenged by the female combatant (Gaidzanwa 1992: 110). A clear example is the legendary Mbuya Nehanda who played the role of a great leader by being both a spirit medium and a guide to the liberation struggle for the independence of Zimbabwe. Yvonne Vera (1993), one of the leading Zimbabwean women writers, devoted a book to the memory of Nehanda.

Apart from using African traditional religions to appreciate the status of women especially in politics, there are some biblical figures who also stand tall amidst patriarchal structures to participate in politics. Two significant women mentioned in the Bible include Deborah and Esther. Deborah served as a judge and served the word in power and fearlessly spoke God's word (Judges 5: 1-31). Esther stands as strong heroine who was later given the throne and became a queen in a patriarchal society (Esther 1-10).

It therefore sounds plausible to argue that religions such as Christianity and African traditional Religions in Zimbabwe have been highly influential to the participation of women in politics. This unveils, as will be explained later, a direct relationship between religion and politics in Zimbabwe.

However, one has to note that without an application of Africana Womanism, one would observe some loopholes within the religious traditions of Zimbabwe which considered women as weaker vessels and thus could not participate in politics. This was so evident especially during the colonial period where there was a fusion of such oppressive cultures with colonial mentality. According to As Ziyambi (1997: 7-9):

> Incidentally, these notions of the subservient and industrious woman found resonance within traditional African culture. As a result, the collusion of white and black patriarchy resulted in the formulation and codification of the legal system known today as Customary Law... Under Customary Law, a black woman remained a legal minor all her life under the custodianship of her father husband or eldest son as her life progressed from childhood, to marriage and widowhood or old age.

How then did such mentalities from the colonial period, compounded with negative cultural practices affect the position of women in politics?

### *Women in Politics in Zimbabwe: Before Independence*

The space of women in Zimbabwe pre Independence was very limited. Issues related to politics such as elections, campaigning and holding any political office were usually identified with the 'public' sphere of life and this is in turn related to masculinities. Therefore, what was 'normal' was to have a male as a politician and not vice versa. Women would rather form other 'feminine' groups and associations as long as they did not include them into the political realm. As highlighted by Gaidzanwa (2004:12), "women's associational lives centre on churches, burial societies and charitable and related organisations rather than on political parties". Religion and culture kept women in the kitchen, as they were deemed more helpful when it came to 'private' issues, or rather it was said that the woman's place is in the home. Such patriarchal attitudes made it very difficult for women to fully participate in politics. As argued by Munando (2010:123):

> Women in Zimbabwe have their place in the private domain (the home), while the duty of fending for the family has been assigned to men. Gender roles have been prescribed in a manner that has systematically marginalized women from p[olitical processes. For example, the prime duty of a wife

> is to cook and prepare food for the husband who will go and attend a political rally...It is through such processes that women are taken away from major events that influence national politics.

It is from such perceptions that Nhongo-Simbanegavi (2000) has also examined the participation of women in the Zimbabwe liberation war of the 1970s. She describes the marginalisation of women in the liberation army, the Zimbabwe African National Liberation Army (ZANLA). Generally, one can say that women's roles were not considered serious enough to fit into the political sphere, which was considered rough and tough and thus very masculine. There was discrimination in the guerrilla camps in that women were often headed into roles that involved cooking and caring for the sick and wounded.

Apart from such interpretations of patriarchy and religion, Munando (2010:122-125) identifies other factors that continue to make women absent from the political process. These include violent political environments, sexual abuse and harassment, lack of initiatives and assertiveness, the media, reproductive health issues and HIV and AIDS, and the lack of a culture of reading for women. Many studies have argued that religion and culture play a pivotal role on all these forms of oppression[1]. This chapter challenges this view as a limited interpretation of religion by examining the contribution of religion on the changing pattern of the participation of women in politics in Zimbabwe.

### *More Names and More Voices: Women in Politics in Zimbabwe*

Despite, on the one hand, the interpretation of religion as oppressive and patriarchal for the subordination of women in politics amongst other spheres, it is interesting, on the other hand, to note that the period after 1980 (post independence), saw more women openly finding a place for themselves in the political realm. Munando (2010:120) examines three ways in which women participate in politics. She identifies participation

[1] See for example, publications by the Circle of Concerned African Women Theologians, especially on HIV and AIDS. However, these women writers have of late started to appreciate the liberative dimension of African traditional religions and culture.

at grassroots level: this is where the majority of women's participation lies. Women also participate in politics through voting. The last level identified by Munando is the participation of women at leadership levels when they take up positions. Despite the low numbers of women participating in politics at the level, the study appreciates the increase in their numbers especially partly due to changes in gender ideology, coupled with the government's efforts in making women part of the process. Notable figures who have risen to this level of taking up leadership roles include Joice Mujuru, Oppah Muchinguri, Sabina Mugabe, Shuvai Mahofa (all ZANU PF), Priscilla Misihairambwi-Mushonga, Thokozani Khupe (Movement for Democratic Change (MDC), and Margaret Dongo (Zimbabwe Union of Democrats (ZUD). The coalition government of Zimbabwe that was formed in 1999 saw more women finding space as members of the cabinet. These include:

- Theresa Makoni (MDC-T): Co-Minister of Home affairs
- Tracy Mutinhiri (ZANU PF): Co- Minister of Labour and Social Welfare
- Paurina Gwanyanya (MDC- T): Co- Minister of Labour and Social Welfare
- Priscilla Misihairambwi- Mushonga (MDC-M):Minister of Regional Integration and International Co-operation
- Sithembiso Nyoni (ZANU PF): Minister of Small and Medium Enterprises and Co-operative Development.
- Jesse Majome (MDC-T): Deputy Minister of Women's Affairs, Gender and Community Development
- Flora Buka (ZANU PF): Minister of State in Vice President Nkomo's Office
- Sekai Holland (MDC-T): Minister of State in the Prime Minister's Office (Healing Organ)

The few selected are cabinet ministers who, among other female politicians, have stood against all odds to make politics a place for women too. Even in the last held elections of 2013, 124 women were sworn-in on 3 September as new Members of Parliament (MPs) in the 8th Parliament of the Republic of Zimbabwe. Following these last elections, women now comprise 124 of the 350 MPs in Zimbabwe's new Parliament, including 86 women in the National Assembly – 60 in the reserved seats and 26 elected directly to the 210 constituency seats.

According to the website[2]:

> Women's representation in Parliament more than doubled from 17 per cent following the 2008 general elections, to 35 per cent in the elections on 31 July 2013. Zimbabwe now joins the ranks of the more than 30 countries worldwide that have used a special electoral quota system to increase women's representation in Parliament to at least 30 per cent, which is considered the minimum for collective action.

However, for the purpose of this study, this chapter will particularly examine the political roles of two of women: Joice Mujuru and Olivia Muchena.

***Joice Teurai Ropa Mujuru***

She was born Runaida Mugari on April 15, 1955 in Mt Darwin. She got married to Solomom Mujuru in 1977 who passed away in 2011. She was also known as Teurai Ropa (spill blood) during the war which followed her performance during the struggle. Joice Mujuru is the first ever female to rise up to the rank of vice president in Zimbabwe. Amongst other roles in the government, Joice Mujuru has served with the following portfolios:

- Minister of Community Development and Women's Affairs (1980- 1985).
- Minister of State in the Prime Minister's Office (1985-1988).
- Minister of Community Development, Cooperatives and Women's Affairs (1988-1992).
- Resident Minister and Governer of Mashonaland Central (1992-1996).
- Minister of Information, Post and Telecommunication (1996-1997).
- Minister of Rural Resources and Water Development (1997-2004).
- Vice President of the Republic of Zimbabwe (2004 - 2014).

All these political roles, amongst others, serve as significant pointers to her abilities and capabilities as a woman politician. They also serve to illustrate

---

[2] (www.unwomen.org/en/news/stories/2013/9/zimbabwe-women-mps-sworn-in)

the length at which the government of Zimbabwe is willing to go in terms of allowing women to participate in politics. This is also illustrated by the works of another distinguished woman, Olivia Muchena. The next section gives a brief overview of her political career.

### *Olivia Muchena*

Her full name is Olivia Nyembezi Muchena. She was born on born 18 August 1946. She studied for a PhD in Agriculture Extension Education with minors in Technology and Social Change at Iowa State University in the United States of America. She served quite a lot in the academia in a number of tertiary institutions. Amongst other roles, she has also served in various positions in the Zimbabwe government, including the following:

- Deputy Minister of Lands and Agriculture (1995-2001).
- Minister of Science and Technology (until 2009)
- Minister of Women affairs, Gender and community development (2009 - 2014)

This study notes a striking significance of these 2 selected women in terms of their political careers and the religious lifestyle. Joice Mujuru is a devout member of the Salvation Army and Olivia Muchena is a staunch member of the United Methodist Church. It is from this resemblance that we shift our discussion to the relationship between religion and politics to the lives of these women, amongst other politicians.

### *The Significance of Religion: Women in politics*

At times religion restricts the participation of women in politics, as we have highlighted earlier. There are such instances where religion prescribes for women to be 'respectable and responsible' (see Hinfelaar 2001); as women who do not delve in masculine responsibilities such as politics. However, it is interesting to note a positive effect of the significance of religion in the lives of the women politicians selected in this study.

Joice Mujuru is a member of the Salvation Army. Olivia Muchena is a member of the Methodist Church. Both of these members are 'uniformed women'. Wearing a uniform in such churches as theirs carries a lot of value and spiritual significance. These uniforms are a source of pride and identity for the women who wear them. They mark a stage in the spiritual life of one who is allowed to wear it by the church authorities.

Such religious identity as which these women have maybe one way with which they gather support and a huge following for themselves. Of note is the role played by the Salvation Army in promoting Amai Mujuru's (as she is known by her fans) status. Because of her participation in the church, Christianity surely provides a roadmap for her political endeavours. Her religious colleagues can easily identify with her (especially when they dress in the churches uniform). It is highly probable that her fellow 'sisters' can easily be manipulated to be her political supporters. The same applies to Olivia Muchena. She can participate and mingle with *madzimai eru-wadzano* (women's guild) in her church's uniform, as is often shown by the media. As illustrated, their identity with the church helps them in a way to maintain balance as politicians despite patriarchal attitudes surrounding them. According to Mapuranga (2013):

> From the above references, one can conclude that both Mujuru and Muchena become significant figures both as churchwomen and as politicians. In the light of the quest for political legitimacy, the church becomes a stepping stone and gives them a strong support base from both their fellow church colleagues and society at large. A person with credibility from the church, for the society, becomes someone worthwhile to support and follow. Thus, being churchwomen gives Mujuru and Muchena credibility and legitimacy in their political endeavors. These women politicians use their image as religious functionaries to promote their political agendas. There are advantages associated with posing as a "religious woman" in politics. A Christian woman is seen as loyal, loving, subservient, truthful, and above all, God fearing, and thus, she fares exceptionally well against a woman from the gender/civil society/women's movement. Even from the male members of the society, a female politician is more acceptable. Christian "women politicians" are thus regarded as less threatening and more acceptable in a patriarchal culture such as Zimbabwe's.

In this study (2013) Mapuranga critically examines the relationship between women's groups in both political and religious circles. She argues that:

> The women's membership of political parties is more or less similar to membership in the Mothers' Unions. The same faces of women active in politics are the same faces of women in church. An example can be derived from the ZANU-PF Women's League/MDC's Women's Assembly. There is more or less the same membership. How one transforms from *mai vesangano*('mother' of the women's church assembly) to *mai vemusangano* ('mother of the women's league) in the political party is intriguing. What simply changes is the regalia: the women's church uniform differs from the political party's women church uniform. This is why some of the songs sung in church have been adapted for political campaigns.

Apart from the role played by religion in the political careers of these women, this chapter argues that the government of Zimbabwe has also done much in support of women in politics. The next section examines the contribution of the government for the existing change on increased participation of women in politics.

### *Why more women: An Examination of Selected Reforms by the Government of Zimbabwe.*

Gadzanwa calls for action that improves the participation of women in politics in Zimbabwe. She (2008: 48) suggests that:

> While women can do well in the general society in Zimbabwe, in politics, the structures and processes tend to be especially exclusionary, favouring men over women and creating barriers that women have to surmount in order to participate. A multiple approach is therefore important in generating reforms within political parties, creating support systems for women outside and within the parties and sensitising the general populace about the need for a better electoral system that creates and maintains equal opportunities for both men and women to participate in electoral politics in Zimbabwe.

Perhaps it is in line with such calls that the government is making effort to adjust its laws on the participation of women. Consequently, more women's names are cropping up where politics is concerned. Some of these laws, as indicated by the Ministry of Women Affairs, Gender and Community Development[3] include:

- The Electoral Act (1990): This allows women to participate in general and by elections for the Presidency or in Parliamentary and local elections as voters or candidates without any discrimination.
- General Law Amendment Act (Section 12 Chapter 8:07): This states that women in Zimbabwe are legally entitled to take up political and public offices such as those that can be held by men.
- SADC Protocol in Gender and Development: This was ratified on 22 October 2009. Among other things, it advocates for gender parity (50/50) in politics and other decision making bodies.

Basing on these selected laws, one may conclude that there have been remarkable changes in the electoral system in Zimbabwe. Since 1980, the government of Zimbabwe has been adopting some laws that empower women after a realisation that women can and should contribute something if the nation was to progress in all spheres. Also among these adoptions are the recommendations by the Committee on the Elimination of Discrimination on women (CEDAW). Article 7 (UNIFEM 2001: 31) declares that:

> …State Parties to take all appropriate measures to eliminate discrimination against women in public and political life …State parties are directed to ensure to women on equal terms with men are those relating to the formulation and implementation of government policy, holding public office and performing public functions at all levels of government…

As such, more women are being groomed for politics in post independent Zimbabwe due to increase in electoral reforms and the general political literacy in women themselves. Good examples are found in the last senatorial elections (2007-2008) where women were supported in their campaigns. Women had to be considered in elections and the government of Zimbabwe resolved to have at least one woman in every three positions, hence Joice Mujuru became the first ever female vice President of Zimbabwe. Scholars

---

[3] Ministry of Women Affairs, Gender and Community Development, "Laws that enhance the Status of Women in Zimbabwe: 1980-2010". This is a pamphlet that highlights in brief the laws that have been used to support women's empowerment from independence to date.

have generally questioned her appointment. Was it really because the government wanted to include women in politics, or it was a mere ploy to win the votes of women who comprise more of the electorate? Despite other 'noble' reasons that may be forwarded for the appointment of women politicians such as Mujuru's ascendency to Vice President, other scholars such as Okoiti (2008: 75) denounce such a standpoint, where 'affirmative action becomes a means of developing winning strategies'. She says, "affirmative action is not a slogan for politics; it is a strategy for development. Hence, affirmative action must stop being a bumper sticker and become a plan of action." On the other hand, some have support this cause as noble. Mbaya (2005: 54) suggests that:

> ...The persistent marginalisation of women was therefore not in the interest of the ruling party as the 2005 elections approached. This might well have been one of the motivating factors in the appointment on the eve of the elections of Joice Mujuru as Zimbabwe's first female vice President. The fact that the ZANU leadership proceeded with this move in spite of internal opposition from much of the 'old guard' indicates the value it attached to the female vote. With the female electorate appeased, a ZANU win became increasingly likely...

The implementation of such decisions by the government of Zimbabwe and individual political parties is definitely a crucial starting point on the need to open more avenues for women in politics. Without doubt, these have precipitated the changing status of women in politics especially in the period after independence. However, such ideas and rules would not be very helpful without other changes that are identified by Burn (2005). She examines other general reasons that she gives for the increase of women in political participation.

Burn (2005: 257) suggests a number of reasons for increased women's political participation which include changes in gender ideology. Politics is no longer viewed strictly as a 'male thing'. The importance of women in the political set up as political leaders was usually shunned by men. Men saw themselves as the only sex fit for, and endowed with political capabilities.

However, despite these improvements by the government of Zimbabwe, it is interesting to note that scholars such as Zungura and Nyemba

(2013:210) feel that such policies as discussed remain disempowering to women, unless the system is always implemented. According to them,

> Constitutional quota system is the panacea to women increased involvement in politics. Countries which have quota systems have reached the 30 percent. Researches have indicated that there is no direct relationship between increased women participation in politics and democracy, since countries which are viewed as examples of democracies like the United States of America have not implemented the quota system. Zimbabwe lags behind in terms of women participation in politics as the country has been a signatory of diverse conventions empowering women but never to be adopted as law in the country. The only solution for Zimbabwean woman is constitutional quotas as well as behaviour change on the party of male politicians who are on record chanting vulgar songs and languages when women are presenting or contributing in parliament. Women who have been privileged to join politics through quotas have not been respected they are viewed as joining not through merit, there is a relationship between quota system and increased women involvement in politics but no direct relationship between quota system and gender equality in terms of political resources.

Despite the fact that there is an increasing number of women participating in politics now in the country after independence as compared to prior 1980, it goes without saying that these women face quite a number of challenges. The forthcoming section unveils some of these.

### *Not Without Struggle: Challenges for Women in Politics in Zimbabwe*

The journey in politics for women has not been so smooth sailing without any hurdles. Amongst other challenges that are faced by women in politics, Gaidzanwa (2004: 19-20) identifies such challenges as lack of funding for female candidates and hostility from men in society. In her conclusion on the study of women and politics in Zimbabwe (2004:48), she writes:

> Thus, fears of sexual and personal violation, lack of funding, confidence,

> exposure and experience in bargaining and cutting deals makes women less able to compete in electoral politics. Political parties remain the most important sites of contestation and reform that make the difference between success and failure in men's and women's electoral careers. While women can do well in the general society in Zimbabwe, in politics, the structures and processes tend to be especially exclusionary, favouring men over women and creating barriers that women have to surmount in order to participate.

In another article on a Kenyan perspective, Okoiti (2008: 58) blames culture as impeding the full participation of women in politics. She says, there are:

> Retrogressive cultural and traditional practices that tend to sideline women, subjugating them to male domination from the cradle to the grave. These range from son preference ideology, lack of beliefs in the importance of educating girls, forced marriages, female genital mutilation…

Despite the reference to Kenya, what Okoiti describes is a whole list of the effects of traditional religious beliefs and culture on the African woman in general. One could therefore argue that religion and culture (both Christianity and African Traditional Religion) have not been all supporting for female candidates in politics. A critical reflection on other challenges for women in politics such as lack of funding and hostility from men (Gaidzanwa 2004: 19) shows that religion and culture play a dominant role. It is religion that informs men that they cannot be led by women (1 Cor 11:3) due to some masculinities it brings about. It is religion that keeps women in the kitchen and therefore they cannot get funding for any public roles, even in politics. Women, as patriarchy dictates, can never do anything worthwhile, particularly in politics. Whilst men are said to rational and make important decisions, women are portrayed as emotional and they can only be good in singing and ululating on issues they do not even understand. Bennet (1999: 5) says:

> Such is the power of patriarchy that female activities are almost always judged inferior to men's: while men deliberate and judge, women intrigue,

> men exchange information, women gossip, men intercede with the supernatural force, and women are witches...

This is supported by Chiroro (2005: 91) who observes that,

> Patriarchy still remains entrenched in political institutions and political parties. A culture that uncritically accepts the need for women as political leaders does not exist. The under representation of women in Zimbabwe has been so stark since 1980 that the injustice seems beyond question when women occupy a mere 16 per cent of the seats in parliament. It should be clear that there is something unsatisfactory in the current political arrangements...

Patriarchy is embedded in most religious traditions. Therefore, as long as religion influences society in all spheres of life, then women will always be seen as minors. Gaidzanwa sees politics as one dimension of human life that is hardest hit by patriarchy. She says, (2000:48):

> ...while women can do well in the general society in Zimbabwe, in politics, the structures and processes tend to be especially exclusionary favouring men over women and creating barriers that women have to surmount in order to participate.

Such patriarchies have clearly stifled women in political participation. Kamau (2008: 8) also acknowledges the presence of these challenges that women in politics face. She says:

> Despite this progress, serious and persistent obstacles still hinder the advancement of women and their participation in decision-making process. Some of the principal obstacles are related to persistent poverty, lack of equal access to health, education, training and employment, cultural barriers, [and] the impact of armed conflict and natural disasters that affect some of the countries in the region.

These have stirred sexist attitudes that render women as incapable. However, by showing the shift on the numbers of women taking part in politics in Zimbabwe today, this study has made an attempt to interpret women's capabilities using a more liberal and generous theory of Africana feminism. Though women are still few, they are increasingly participating in politics as they are allowed to do so through more broadminded interpretations of religion and culture in Zimbabwe.

## *Conclusion*

As illustrated in this study, there has been a relative increase in the number of women politicians in Zimbabwe from the period prior to independence to the contemporary period (2014). However, it is critical to note that their numbers are still low as compared to their male counterparts. Religion and culture stand as some of the major reasons responsible for this trend. On the one hand, tradition, culture and the colonial mentality have been in a way blamed for relegating women to the periphery of politics. On the other, a more positive interpretation of the same religion and culture has availed opportunities for women to take up political roles. Their identity is gradually changing as they are becoming more active in the politics of the country. As the society learns to live with the fact that women can be politicians too, then more women may continue to find space for themselves within politics in Zimbabwe. As such, this study concurs with the idea that, 'the participation of women has been very low but there is adequate room for improvement if women take up the initiatives and become aggressive toward their cause' (Munando 2010: 126).

## *References*

Bennet, T.W. 1999. *Human Rights and African Customary Law*. Western Cape: Juta and Co Ltd.

Burn, S.M. 1995. *Women Across Cultures: Global Perspective*. New York: Mc Graw Hill.

Chitando, A. 2008. Imagining a Peaceful society, a vision of Children's Literature in Post-conflict Zimbabwe. *Discussion paper 40*, The Nordic Africa Institute.

Chiroro, B. Persistent Inequalities: Women and Electoral Politics in the Zimbabwe Elections in 2005. *Journal of African Elections* 4(2), October 2005. 91-106.

Evans- Pritchard, E. 1965. *Theories of Primitive Religion*. Oxford: Clarendon Press.

Gaidzanwa, R. 2004. Gender, women and electoral politics in Zimbabwe. [PDF], *EISA Research Report* 8. Johannesburg: EISA.

Hinfelaar, M. 2001. *Respectable and Responsible Women: Methodist and Roman Catholic Women's Organisations in Harare, Zimbabwe (1919-1985)*, Zoetermeer: Boekencentrum.

Hudson Weems, C. 2000. Africana Womanism: An Overview in Out of the Revolution*: In: The Development of Africana Studies,*

Delores, A. and Lanham (Eds.). Lexington Books. 205-217.

Hudson Weems, C. 1993. *Africana Womanism: Reclaiming Ourselves*. Troy, Michigan:Bedford Publishing.

Kamau, N. 2008. The Value Proposition to Women's leadership: Perspectives of Kenyan Women Parliamentary and Civic Leaders (2003 to 2007). In: *Perspectives on gender discourse: Enhancing Women's Political Participation 6(08)*, Heinrich Boll Stiftung: East & Horn Africa Office. 7-36.

Mangena and Muhwati. *Kelland on Rape and Objectification: An Africana Womanist Response*. Forth-coming Publication.

Mapuranga, T.P. 2013. Religion, Politics and Gender: The Zimbabwean Experience with Special Reference to the Period 2000-2008'. *Prayers and Players:* In: *Religion and Politics in Zimbabwe.* Ezra, C. (Ed.). Harare: SAPES Books. 177- 188.

Mbaya, S. 2005. Securing the female electorate in "Zimbabwe's Land Politics and the 2005 Elections". *Journal of African Elections* 4(2): 54-55.

Munando, E. 2010. Women's Participation in Politics. In: *Political Participation in Zimbabwe.* David, K. (Ed.). Harare: African Forum for Social Teachings (AFCAST) 120-126.

Muwati, I., Gambahaya, Z. and Gwekwerere, T. 2011. Africana Womanism and African Proverbs: Theoretical Grounding of Mothering/Motherhood in Shona and Ndebele Cultural Discourse. *Western Journal of Black Studies* 35(1): 1-8.

Nhongo-Simbanegavi, J. 2000. *For Better or Worse? Women and ZANLA in Zimbabwe's Liberation Struggle.* Harare: Weaver Press.

Okoiti, O.M. 2008. The Affirmative Action Debate: Developing winning strategies, in *Perspectives on gender discourse: Enhancing Women's*

*Political Participation 6(08)* Heinrich Boll Stiftung: East &Horn Africa Office: 53-76.

Schmidt, E.1992. *Peasants, Traders and Wives: Shona Women in the History of Zimbabwe, 1870-1939.* Portsmouth: Heinemann.

White, L. 1984. Women in the Changing African Family. In: *African Women South of the Sahara.* Hays, M.J. and Stichter, S. ( Eds). London: Longman. 53-68.

Ziyambi, N.M. 1997. *The Battle of the Mind: International New Media Elements of the New Religious Political Right in Zimbabwe.* Oslo: University of Oslo.

Zungura, M. and Nyemba, E. 2013. The Implications of the Quota System in Promoting Gender Equality in Zimbabwean Politics. *International Journal of Humanities and Social Science*, 3(2): 203-212.

**Internet Sources**

www.unwomen.org/en/news/stories/2013/9/zimbabwe-women-mps-sworn-in. Accessed 8th July 2014.

# Chapter Nine

## CONTESTING THE MARGINS OF MODERNITY: NEW WOMEN, MIGRATION AND CONSUMPTION IN THE WESTERN GRASSFIELDS OF CAMEROON

*Walter Gam Nkwi*

### *Introduction*

Population movements, the world over and in Africa in particular are nothing new in the sense that human beings have remarkably been the most mobile in the animal kingdom. In Africa, during the era proceeding the colonial period, there were usually collective movements of families or groups of families. These movements were motivated by several reasons. Amongst these reasons were internal readjustments or security concerns. The movements were accelerated and sustained by internecine conflicts/ warfare and slave raids and the search for 'greener pastures' in the colonial and post-colonial periods. It would appear that individual migration was exceptional and a preserve of men 'but common for women because patrilocal residence predominated, thus young wives were dislocated, even uprooted although this usually took place within limited areas (Coquery-Vidrovitch, 1997: 73). Male migration has been the oldest and it came much earlier than that of the women folk because most men were breadwinners of the family. With the introduction of the colonial economy which was accompanied by industrial complexes, the need for taxes to grease the colonial economy, plantations, wage labour, and migration increased. These migrants were responsible for much of the social change in their various societies especially when they returned.

On their return, these migrants were also responsible for the introduction of new houses constructed with zinc and stone, new architectural design in their areas of origin, new dressing patterns and even new manners of speech. By their daily encounters with the wider world, they also returned home from 'abroad' with their outlook changed and formed new social strata and hierarchies in the society. Hence they enjoyed enhanced prestige and social status amongst their peers. This would have been their reward for having travelled, lived, worked and achieved outside their home. The roles of this social category of people, women, who we have focused on in this chapter, are at the heart of this discourse. Of crucial importance to this paper is the gender touch. Historically, in this region and in most parts of Africa, men were the precursors of migration while women stayed behind to watch over the livestock, keep guard over the compound and look after the children. With widened horizons of knowledge, these men returned with modern things like the talking gramophones, zinc, shoes, and dresses, just to name but a few. All these things gave them additional and enhanced prestige, and thus they became those who brought modernity in their villages. The migration of men did not go on *ad infinitum*. With the introduction of schools, churches and colonial/post- colonial administration, heroic travels ceased to be a monopoly of men. Women too entered the space of migration and were also responsible for the introduction of modern things in the sub-region.

In what follows in this chapter, the attempt is to examine the migration of women and modernity, which has received scant attention in the literature of migration in Africa in general and in Cameroon in particular. Crucial to this discussion is the demonstration of how, in the course of migration modernity has become contested between men and women in the Bamenda Grassfields of Cameroon.

### *Methodological Assumptions and Typology of History*

It will be important to declare upfront that the bulk of information presented here constitutes the perspective of the informants. In other words much space was given to the voices of the informants. These migrants constitute just 'common people'. In dealing with their type of history, we go nearer to the people without a public voice as opposed to those individuals who held the reins of power and were at one time at the centre of politics. This meant dealing with the 'voices of the voiceless' and what has been produced in this article has been given priority to the oral informants (Nkwi, 2010). Informants were allowed to talk for themselves and so in the article we will get their voices. Inspiration was also drawn from three scholars. First, Alain Touraine (2002) whose concept of historicity is the ability of the community to provide an orientation and transform itself in the process, as well as his model of talking about a people's history as they see it. Second Axel Harneiet Sievers *et al.*, (2002) maintain that the history of the voiceless is an attempt to write the history from the perspective of non-officials. Drawing inspiration from Abner Cohen (1966), it was felt that 'the informants should speak for themselves'. Finally, Ranger (1999), Illiffe (1988), and Feierman (1990) provide historians of Africa with a model of the kind of research that has to be done in Africa. They urge that in writing the history of the African continent it is important to use the sources actually found there, in particular oral tradition. Here, an attempt has been made not only to use these sources but also to write a history which accords with the people's own testimony. It is of more relevance to declare that the informants in this article are individuals who represent a process that was going on in the society.

### *Locating the Study Area*

The Western Grassfields of Cameroon also known as the Bamenda Western Grassfields is a plateau covered with savannah vegetation as opposed to the forest regions of Cameroon. This was the reason why the Germans colonial administration (1884-1916) called the region the Grassfields (Rudin, 1938; Warnier, 2012; Chilver 1961; Kaberry, 1967; Nkwi, 1982). Politics in this sub-region were organised around Fondoms, each led by a Fon (a sacred and semi-divine ruler who is believe by his people to be performing quasi-religious functions) and most of these Fondoms grew out of aggressive politics of inclusion and exclusion through warfare that led to the subjugation of weaker neighbours by more powerful ones. They were characterised by clear socio-political hierarchies derived not only from status but also from kinship relations or lineages. The existing studies of the region mainly focus on the formation of the Fondoms and the history of political hegemony and social organizations.

These Fondoms include: Nso, Kom, Bafut and Bali. The people who originate from this region are those anthropologists called 'Tikars'. The people have similar socio-political histories which are encapsulated in language, culture or a common history of origin. This is generally found in the literature of the area (Chilver and Kaberry, 1967). Some of the authors have written on labour migration to the littoral quadrant of Cameroon where most colonial plantations were established (Konings, 1988 and 2001; Ardener *et al,* 1960). Not quite surprisingly, they have not researched on the female dimension of migration. This is a gap which this chapter intends to fill.

### *Tradition versus Modernity in the Context of Migration*

According to Fo Angwafo (2009: 70), "we are actively modernising our tradition and traditionalising our modernity". These words seemed to best describe the concept of *kfaang, mukalla, ba'ara or* modernity. The historicity of modernity and modernisation seems to be entangled within the European experience which ignored Africa as part of the globe. Modernisation was rooted in Post-Enlightenment Europe and was defended on the grounds of its change of European society from an agrarian to an industrial one.

In all these, its apologists strongly held that such change did not occur in African societies because they were understood to be static and their people were primitive hunter gatherers. This was just another way of denying Africa's great indigenous achievements (Depelchin, 2005:19-28). Enough literature however exists to show that Africa, especially from the 19th century, was part of the global processes (Wallerstein, 1986 and 2005; Forde and Kaberry, 1967; Ranger, 1963; Vansina, 1966; Oliver and Mathew, 1963; Thornton, 1992; Eltis, 1993). As Ferguson (1999: 14) has argued "the modernisation myth was bad social science because it was restricted and even so based on misconceptions about modern African history". In other words, modernisation was not as it was claimed, because Africa was not considered as part of the global processes. Fundamental to the understanding of modernisation is the fact that for any meaningful change to take place in any society the movement of people, ideas and cultures is necessary and there should be social and political reorganisation of that society.

As the concept 'modernisation' was justified as a European and North American idea, modernity is seen as something that is uniquely European. It was borne overseas and imposed on Africans by the Europeans. Over the years scholars have written about modernity from different perspectives (Ferguson, 1999; Appadurai, 1986; Fardon et al., 1999; Geschier *et al.,* 2008; Havik, 2009; Brinkman *et al.,* 2009; Giddens, 1990; Macamo, 2005; Deutsch et al., 2002; Comaroff and Comaroff, 1993).The literature on modernity suggests that it is a problematic term and when seen through analytical "binoculars, it is quite slippery, ambiguous and vague" (Comaroff and Comaroff, 1993: xii), because it seems that different societies and communities have their own way of perceiving and understanding the concept which has been largely coloured by being too "closely connected to Western ideologies of universal development". In other words, modernity can best be understood if we contextualize it in different world societies because there are peculiar ways of understanding and perceiving it. What it means to one society might not necessary be what it means to another.

Two scholars whose use of the concept has partially inspired this work are Cooper (2005: 176-193) and Ferguson (2006: 176-193). According to Cooper, "the most ordinary meaning of modern *(ity)* is that which is new, that which is distinguishable from the past". This seems a better way of looking at the concept, but Cooper does not say anything about the contents of modernity or the socio-cultural and economic impact of that phenomenon on changing societies. While leaning on other scholars, Ferguson went further than Cooper. According to him, "…modern Africa is today understood as a place of bricolage and creative invention where bits and pieces of what used to be called Western modernity are picked up, combined with local resources and put back together". By implication, Ferguson meant that modernity was not a "one way traffic concept". It is applicable when it combines what is indigenous with what is foreign.

### *Consumption/Consumerism*

Modernity as reflected in what was gathered from the informants arguably means that it should be accepted, translated, interpreted, adapted and appropriated by the people. In this paper consumption and consumerism will refer to the appropriation of modernity gotten as a result of migration of women. Consequently, it has socio-economic and political impact on a society by changing existing social hierarchies and creating new ones. In the sub-region with many indigenous groups, consumption of modernity would have different names but invariably mean the same thing. For instance, the Kom people, the second largest group in the region, refer to modernity as *kfaang*. According to them, it was not uprooted elsewhere and transplanted into their society. Kom people only accepted *kfaang* because it had relevance to their society, and more importantly, it was acquired through their geographical and social mobility. The mobility of Kom people introduced *kfaang* to Kom. This was, in most cases, because the people were able to navigate and negotiate with their different global encounters abroad and at home.

As a result *kfaang* was not a zero-sum game, neither was it a 'winner takes all' one. Cross-culturalism and conviviality played a central role for *kfaang* to be understood and accepted in Kom. This meant that spaces were created in the process for the two cultural worlds to survive. *Kfaang* had to be relevant in context. The contents of *kfaang* are *ndzi kfaang* or new roads, *afuem a kfaang* carpenter bee of newness, which was the motor vehicle, the new school (*ndo ngwali kfaang),* the new church (*iwo fiyini fyie kfaang),* new trees (*ghii ka mghii kfaang),* new clothes (*dzisi kfaang),* new plates (*ghii kang- a- kfaang),* new spoons (*ghii tuass-ghi-kfaang),* to name only a few. Most of the bearers of *kfaang* were mobile people and those who accessed *kfaang* as a form of education became very 'mobile' and this changed their status (Nkwi, 2011). They went to school because schooling was relevant to their context.

## *Migration: A Re-reading.*

People in Africa have always been mobile and their mobility might be as old as humanity itself. Scholars have studied mobility from many perspectives. For instance, Amin (1974) shows that migrations are not new to Africa. According to him, modern migrations are related to labour problems and he classifies them as: rural-rural, rural-urban, urban-rural, internal and international migrations. Aderanti Adepoju (1977, 1988, 2008 and 2010) claims that 'Africa is a continent of considerable ... migrations and various movements in response to political, social, economic, religious and security situations have been recorded from earliest times'. The opening of schools and plantations in the coastal area of Cameroon was one of the things that attracted labour from this region. This is not a new phenomenon anyway. Labour migration inside Africa has been a topical issue for scholars for a long time. It is generally accepted that European colonial rule in the continent accelerated labour migration. Scholars have shown that one of the outstanding factors for migration since the beginnings of the colonial rule has been labour. For instance, Patrick Harris's (1994) work on the migrant labour from Mozambique to the sugarcane plantations, diamond and gold mines of South Africa; R.A. Davidson's (1954) work on migrant labour in the Gold Coast and Charles van Onselen's (1976) on Southern Africa show the relationship which existed between labour migration and different forms of communication and labour identity in Southern Rhodesia between 1900 and 1933. These studies have not paid adequate attention to returned labour migrants.

History is useful for a fuller understanding of present day change in societies, especially because it helps us to better understand and explain current events by relating them to the past. The lives of people in the Cameroon Western Grassfields is coloured with labour migration so does many parts of Africa. The labour migration of these people, as shown in the interviews, took them to various parts of Cameroon and some parts of Nigeria like Yola, Ibi, Onitsha and Calabar, and even to the United Kingdom. From 1961 when Cameroon gained independence, and with improvements in roads infrastructure coupled with the civil administration policies regarding the transfer of civil servants, they moved to many more parts of Cameroon. This has been so because the region has not benefitted much in the colonial and post- colonial projects in developmental terms. Today, most of the female migrants from this region are found in different parts of the world. This might not be different elsewhere in Africa and Asia but here it is the continuity of what has started since the colonial period and importantly shows how women too were precursors of modernity. These women after their sojourn returned to their areas of origin with a different identity as they have travelled widely and widened their horizons just like their male folk were able to do.

### *Female Migrants from the Margins to Contesting Modernity*

The gender dimension of migration is striking. Women also migrated. The difference lay in the fact that most of these women who migrated did follow their husbands. In this case, it was husbands who determined their mobility. Labour migration of women as stated in literature showed that it started much later than that of the men. For instance, Clifford (1992) observes that "Good travel (heroic, educational, scientific, adventurous, ennobling) is something men should do. Women are impeded from serious travel. *Some of them (women) go to distant places but largely as companions…*". In other words, women travelled with men. This does not, however, mean that scholars have not studied the labour mobility of women as independent agents in Africa. Teresa Barnes (2006) studied the migration of women in Southern Africa, especially between South Africa and Zimbabwe during the colonial period. She employed statistical, documentary and oral evidence to critique the dominant paradigm that women were silent observers of migration in colonial Southern African historiography. She stated that "when historians follow the dominant model and consider mobility, travel, and migration *a priori* as male preserves, African women are automatically consigned to mass immobility. They are barred from centre stage and frozen in perpetual economic childhood". The author concludes rather that a "limiting view of African women's socioeconomic immobility in Southern Africa should be fundamentally challenged by further research..." Caroline Wanjiku Kihato (2009) has also researched the migration of women from different parts of Southern Africa to Johannesburg. She concludes that these women used different methods to find themselves in different locations in Johannesburg. What is indeed striking here is that this paper will go to add to the budding literature.

A case in point that represents women who migrated was Elizabeth Ngebo Nayah. She told her story in the following words:

> I was born in 1932 in Njinikom and grew up with catechist Ngongbi who was my uncle. I never went to school because, in those days, school meant nothing to a woman. Very few women went to school. During catechumen doctrine I fell in love with my husband who was a houseboy of Rev. Fr. Ivo Stockman. When Father Stockman was transferred to Mamfe he took him

> along. While in Mamfe negotiation started for our traditional wedding. Before the wedding came to an end my husband Ngehbo, was already in Jos and so I had to go and meet him in Jos. He had left Mamfe because the white priest had annoyed him. So I got married in St. Augustine's parish in Jos, Nigeria. I was taken to Jos by the eldest brother of my husband. We went on foot. It took us more than three weeks and we were constantly staying in mission houses. In many missions that we got to, we were told that Godfrey had just left for another mission. We encountered in about four mission stations and the last one which we entered was the biggest one in Jos where we saw my husband. After staying for a very long time, I was working in a bakery in Jos, my husband left me there and went to Lagos. While in Lagos he was cooking for a whiteman. I was alone in Jos trying out at the bakery, till he settled down in Lagos and called for me. I left Jos for Lagos by train. That was my first time of travelling by train. I was with my little son. I gave birth to all my other children in Lagos, and one of them has remained in Lagos. The most interesting thing that happened when I was in Lagos was the visit of the Queen of England. I was lucky to see her at the stadium. We finally came home on retirement in October 1978, and while at home, I was one of the first women to run a bakery and a restaurant (Elizabeth Ngehbo, Personal Communication, 20 June 2012.).

Another woman who represents the labour mobility of women in this region is Benedicta Neng Young, the daughter of a businessman. We met Benedicta in her 'flat'. Constructed of stones, it contains four bedrooms, three toilets, a dinning section, a kitchen and well tiled floor. It's unusual for a woman in this region because of the traditional norms, but she was helped out by her father who gave her a parcel of land. She told her story in the following words:

> I was born in 1937. At a young age I went to St. Anthony's Primary School, Njinikom, and was one of the few girls there. When I got to standard four, the manager of the school, Rev. Fr. Groot, instructed that girls were to continue their education at the Convent School at Shisong, Nso, Cameroon some 140 km away from home. I therefore entered standard 5 in 1951 and in 1952 passed to standard 6 in Shisong. After completing my

> primary school in Shisong, I went to the Queen of Holy Rosary College, Onitsha, Nigeria. A school of Nursing and Midwifery was opened in Shisong and my parents wanted me to go to Shisong. I spent one year at Shisong and returned to Nigeria for one more year. I later graduated from Abakaliki Nursing School. After graduation, I got my first appointment in Cameroon with the Wum Rural Council in 1957. My next job was in Tiko, Southwest Region of Cameroon situated some 450 km from home with the Cameroon Development Cooperation (CDC) hospital. I worked there only for 8 months, applied and was admitted into the University Teaching College, Ibadan, Nigeria. I studied in Ibadan for three years and obtained a Diploma. After wards, I returned to Cameroon in 1962 and worked with the General Hospital in Bamenda (today the capital of Northwest Cameroon) and it was there that I bought a car and got married. After a while, I went to England for a two- year course. Upon completion of my studies in England I was employed by the Cameroon Public Service. I worked successively at Ngaoundere, Nkongsamba, Mbanga, Buea, Douala and Yaoundé, before being transferred to Fuanantui, Njinikom, where I spent ten years. I retired in 1998 and was the first woman to own a medicine store, Royal Diamond Chemist. I was also the first Kom woman to, own and drive a car, Renault 4 in 1964. During my retirement I constructed my own house which you can see for yourself (Bendicta Neng, Personal Communication, 12 August 2013).

Elizabeth and Benedicta are representatives of women who introduced new things into their societies even though they migrated to different places and for different purposes. Elizabeth migrated to Nigeria and, upon her return she opened an ultra-modern restaurant and a bakery. On the part of Benedicta, she constructed a modern house and was also a nurse. Above all, the two women, in terms of conspicuous consumption, introduced modernity in the region. Apart from the two women who represented an entire mould in the society, female teachers too became quite relevant to our discussion.

### *Women Teachers*

Hardly can the teachers and their role be put in proper perspective without putting their origin in the context of missionary/colonial agenda.

It is not the kernel of this work to do so but a few lines will elucidate who they were. Teachers were products of missionary schools first, before colonial government established government schools in Africa. Mission schools were regarded as the most important transformative forces in African societies (Barton, 1915; Hopkins, 1966; Latourette, 1962; Oliver, 1956, Calvancanti, 2005; Subramanian, 1977). In the Western Cameroon Grassfields, Njinikom became the area which had the first Standard Six school and from all over the sub-region pupils went there to attend classes (Booth, 1976 ). At the end of Standard Six, those who were successful had the Standard six certificates and the most fashionable job at time was teaching although some became clerks. A teacher was generally the center of attraction in the village. They were role models. They combined many functions from sanitary masters, letter writers, interpreters to petition writers. Teachers were pillars that symbolized skill and neatness. They were those who, more than anybody else, understood the Whiteman's language and could communicate with him (Ajayi, 1965; Beilderman, 1982). During the cause of this research, a good number of them were already in their villages, old and thinking only of their past labour itinerary.

In the Bamenda Grassfields, school enrolment was mostly limited to men. That was accepted in the culture of the people. But the women were sooner or later to act as cultural brokers. This showed that schooling was not limited to men only. Women also attended school in growing numbers. Their number rose from three in 1928 to eight in 1951 at St. Anthony's School as it is shown by the table below

***Table 6: The first eight Girls at St. Anthony's School, Njinikom***

| NAME | ADMISSION NUMBER | AGE |
|---|---|---|
| Victoria N. Chia | 941 | 14 |
| Paulina Ndum | 1059 | 13 |
| Benedicta Neng | 918 | 13 |
| Rufina N. Fujua | 1055 | 14 |
| Mary Tosam Yongabi | 1060 | 14 |

| | | |
|---|---|---|
| Francisca Chia | 1058 | 14 |
| Mary Diom | 1188 | 13 |
| Sophia Kain | 1327 | 15 |

*Source: Admission Register (St. Anthony Primary School Archives )*

The admission of girls to the school was something new in Kom culture. The founding of Kom in the early 19th century was mostly attributed to women because they comprised the last remnants who moved out of Babessi through Nkar, Noni, Akeh and reached Laikom. When the foundation of the Fondom was threatened by the invading Mejang, assumed to have come from a stronger Fondom, the women were those who repelled the aggressors because their husbands had gone hunting. That incident, according to the men folk showed that women were powerful. Still, the thinking was that women were best suited to be at home, following their mothers to the farm and taking care of the children. At the onset of Western education in Kom, some Kom men did not believe that school or Western education was for women. Some men felt strongly that the women should remain at home. The first eight women who went to school reversed that thinking.

Not all the women who 'consumed' *kfaang, mukalla or ba'ara* successfully completed the school course. Sometimes, because of nuptial matters, the girl child dropped out of school to marry whoever asked for her hand in marriage through her parents. That explains why many girls had to leave school before completing their studies. It was therefore more of the decision of a girl's father. One of those girls was Theresia Nange Njuakom. She was born at Muloin, another village in Kom, in 1933. Her father, Paul Njuakom, was a catechist. In 1948 she went to St. Anthony's School, Njinikom, and because of her intelligence, she was rapidly promoted to Standard Two. Later, she went to Standard Three and subsequently to Standard Four. There was no Standard Four for girls in Njinikom at the time. She continued her education in Shisong. At the end of Standard Four, she came home on long holidays with excellent results, which had promoted her to Standard Five. The news at home was that somebody had come to ask for her hand in marriage and in those days, as Theresia claims:

> Once your parents told you that news you were only condemned to accept. ... Because of that, my education came to an end in Standard four. That was in 1954 and in April 1955, I got wedded to Lawrence Wallang. Lawrence was a Catholic school teacher. After our wedding, my movement was dictated by my husband. Wherever he was transferred to work we went together. We worked in Tabenken, Oku, Mankon, Kumbo and several other places which I cannot quite remember (Theresia Nange Njuakom, Personal communication, 31 July, 2008).

The experience of Theresia was further confirmed by other women. For instance, Nyanga Clara and Mary Tosam Yongabi both confirmed that women were not allowed to continue schooling once they had a suitor, and a suitor in those days never met the girl directly but rather met the parents of the girl. Once the parents accepted, the girl could not refuse.[1] This was a similar situation amongst Ugandan women and men. In both situations the male folk gradually changed their attitudes.

Some schools were established to satisfy the needs of girls. In Uganda, the Gayaza Girls' Boarding School was founded although it was to educate the daughters of chiefs and clergy; while in Cameroon, a Girls Boarding primary school was founded in Shisong and later in Njinikom and Mankon. A Girls' Boarding Secondary School was founded at Okoyong, Mamfe in 1956 with 18 girls (Musisi, 1992). Abidogun (2007/8: 29-51) has observed that, with the introduction of colonial and missionary education, gender roles were considerably affected amongst the Igbo of Nigeria. Thus, similar cases were observable elsewhere in Africa.

Using the concept of 'navigation', Joanna Both has sought to understand girl and young women migrants in Ndjamena, Chad. The work aimed to contribute to a 'broader understanding of the positions of girls and

---

[1] Interview with Theresia Nange Njuakom, Bochain, Njinikom, 31 July 2008. The case of Theresia was further confirmed by many women whom I contacted in the field. For instance, Nyanga Clara, interviewed 14 December 2007 at Njinikom and Mary Tosam Yongabi interviewed 13 August 2008 at Bochain, Kom all confirmed that women were not allowed to continue schooling once they had a suitor and a suitor in those days never met the girl directly but rather met the parents of the girl. Once the parents accepted the girl could not refuse.

young women in Chad'. Both concludes among other things that 'the girls are not only being shaped by the urban structures, but partly shaped themselves...'(Both, 2008: 79). Kihato (2009) has also researched the migration of women in different parts of Southern Africa to Johannesburg. She concludes that these women used different methods to get themselves in different locations in Johannesburg. Thus, the movement of women to Shisong inasmuch as it paints a different picture also contributes to the literature on women as independent migrants who moved without being dictated to by men. The novelty of the picture is heightened because the women were not economic migrants. Their mobility was not informed by economic imperatives as the cases of Barnes and Both have shown.

It has, for some time now, been maintained erroneously that men migrate in search of money and women migrate because they want to follow their men. Simelane (2004) has argued that migration in Swaziland was dominated by men due to the existence of opportunities in the labour market, and he takes the economic factor as the primary issue which illustrated men's mobility in colonial Swaziland. According to the author, it is not correct to see the mobility of men in economic terms but rather more in the sedentary situation of women. The reason for the sedentarism of women is to be found at the level of homestead relations. Robertson (1984) went further to show that many Southern African countries including the Congo, had restrictions placed on the migration of women by the colonial government, and the idea was that only men could work in the mines.[2] This error has led to the paucity of material as far as women mobility in West Africa is concerned. Cordell *et al.* (1996: 39) accept the view that the history of mobility of women is limited except when situated in nuptial terms. While studying women in Burkina Faso, Cordell *et al.* contended that 'although a very large proportion of female migration is indeed related to marriage, the overall picture that emerges is more varied than might first be supposed' (see also Lambert, 2007: 129-148; Cockerton, 2002: 37-53; Ulicki and Crush, 2000: 64-79). Our case study in this paper therefore helps us to start seeing the autonomy of women in migration literature especially

---

[2] Owners of mines were against their labourers ever moving to the mine areas with their women so wives were constantly kept out of the reach of their mine.

in the Bamenda Grasslands.

In 1959, a girls' primary school was opened in Njinikom, St. Marie Gorretti's School, making the third girls school in the Bamenda Grassfields. The other two schools were founded in Nso and Mankon. The population steadily rose between 1959 and 1980 as shown below:

***Table 7: Number of girls at St. Marie Gorretti's Primary School between 1959 and 1980***

| Year | No. of Girls in Enrolment |
|---|---|
| 1959 | 25 |
| 1960 | 29 |
| 1961 | 32 |
| 1963 | 38 |
| 1965 | 45 |
| 1968 | 55 |
| 1970 | 98 |
| 1972 | 105 |
| 1973 | 115 |
| 1974 | 150 |
| 1975 | 189 |
| 1976 | 200 |
| 1977 | 210 |
| 1980 | 250 |

*Source: Compiled from St. Anthony's Primary School Archives, Njinikom.*

These figures suggest that the number of girls enrolled in schools increased progressively and by implication there would be a rippling effect of Western education on their attitude. Kom was transformed through their activities. Besides classroom teaching, a domestic science centre was opened in 1971, headed by a nun, Rev. Sr. Mary Theresia. The centre was to provide training for girls sewing, knitting, cooking, domestic activities like keeping the environment clean, basic hygiene, and womanhood, to name just a few.[3] A similar school was opened in East Africa (Thurnwald 1932: 175-184).

One result of education was the creation of a new social hierarchy consisting of female teachers. Some of these female teachers bought and owned things of conveniences like radios or talking gramophones and put on Western dresses, among other things. In a world where television sets never existed, having a radio made one a king in the perception of the people. Homes that had radios were centres of attraction for neighbours who came to listen, without understanding, except a few who went to school. As female teachers, their homes became venues where cases were settled and where people flocked to in order to emulate the latest fashions. One of the ladies whose going to school was directly linked to her migration like many others was Mary Tosam Yongabi.

Mary was born in 1935 at Isailah quarter, Njinikom. She went to St. Anthony's School in 1945. In that year many girls entered the same class, and so the authorities started thinking about opening a school for girls separately. In Standard Four she continued her education in Nso because girls had been separated from boys and there was no separate school for girls in Kom. In that year the Catholic Education Authorities had authorised the opening of a separate school for girls in Nso and another one in Kumba. So it became mandatory that all the girls that were in Standard Four were either to go to Nso or Kumba and parents were asked to come and collect certificates. It was then that she went to Nso and continued the second term there in 1950. After obtaining her Standard Six Certificate in 1955, she continued to St. Francis Teacher's Training College, Fiango, Kumba. Many Kom people believed in the tradition that women were good for the home and looking after the children. She claims that all girls performed very well because there was stiff competition in their class. After successfully completing her Standard Six and her course at Teachers' Training College, Fiango, she taught in Babanki from 1959 - 1961; Oku from 1961-1964 and Njnikom from 1965-1968; Fuanantui from 1968-1975; Tinifoinbi from 1979-1980 and Njinikom from 1980-1988.[4] The school first widened the

[3] File Ci (1967) 2 Economic and Social Reports, Menchum Division, 1967-1974 (NAB).

[4] Interview with Mary Yongabi, Bochain Quarter, 13 September 2012.

mental horizons of pupils who later became teachers. Secondly, it influenced their geographical and social mobility. The teachers also represented social hierarchies. They became the 'carriers' and transmitters of modernity *par excellence*. This type of modernity was based on *gwali* (the book) which was known as *ngwali kfaang* in Kom. The reasons many of the pupils became teachers after elementary school was because teaching was very fashionable and prestigious in the 1940s and 1950s, if the testimony of my informants is to be believed.

## *Conclusion*

The story of migration in pre-colonial and colonial Africa was largely an affair of men dictated by various dynamics such as trekking for long distances to conduct trading purposes. Labour migration has been a topical issue in labour history and has been largely responsible for the migration of men. It was through such migrations that modernity was encapsulated in modern things. They were the first people to become familiar with the 'singing' and 'talking boxes' namely gramophones and radios, as well as shoes, Western clothes and new cosmetics and would in time possess them, thus, further distinguishing themselves as people of newness and the new way. They were also responsible for the introduction of new houses constructed with zinc and stone, thus, they gained more prestige amongst their peers. Yet, as time progressed, in the mid-1930s and 40s their female folk also took to migration and were also responsible for the introduction of new things in the society. Modernity thus had become contested by the two genders. The gender dimension is further striking as this paper has illustrated that women as well as men could also play important role in the transformation of societies.

The women became the *kfaang, miikalla, bara* women in their own right. All these terminologies from the discussion so far connote newness – innovation and novelty in thinking and doing, and the material indicators and relationships that result from it. In many ways, the terminologies translated but were not limited to 'modernity' and 'modernization' in the Western sense. The most important characteristic of *kfaang, miikalla, bara* therefore is that which is 'new', and this might have come from without and something, which was not the characteristic way of seeing and doing things. People of the Western Grassfields accepted and appropriated it only when it was relevant to their needs, blended the old and new, thereby confirming the views of Sanjay Joshi (2001: 89) and Chatterjee (1997: 107) that "the forms of modernity will have to vary between different countries, depending upon specific circumstances and social practices."

***Bibliography***


Abidogun, J. 2007/08. Western Education's Impact on Northern Igbo gender Roles in Nsukka, Nigeria. *Africa Today*.54(1) :29-51.

Aderanti, A. 1988. Linkages between Internal and International Migration. *The African International Social Science Journal.* 50(157): 387-395

Aderanti, A. 2008. *Migration in Sub-Saharan Africa*. Uppsala: Nordic Inst.

Aderanti, A. 2010. *International Migration within, to and from Africa in a Globalized World*. Lagos: Sub-Saharan Pub and Traders.

Aderanti, A. 1977. Migration and Development in Tropical Africa: Some Research Priorities. *African Affairs*.76 (303): 210-225.

Ajayi, J. F. 1965. *Christian Missions in Nigeria: The making of New elites.* London: Longman.

Amin, S.1974. *Modern Migrations in Western Africa.* London: Oxford University Press.

Angwafor, F. 2009. *Royalty and Politics: The Story of My Life*. Mankon, Bamenda: Langaa Research and Publishing CIG.

Appadurai, A. 1996. *Modernity at Large: Cultural Dimensions of Globalization*. Minnesota: University of Minnesota Press.

Ardener, E. S. A. & Warmington, W.A. 1960, with a contribution by M.J Ruel, *Plantation and Village in the Cameroons: Some Economic and Social Studies* Oxford: Oxford University Press.

Axel, H. (Ed.) 2002. *Africa and South-Asia. A place in the world: New Local Historiographies from Africa and Asia.* Leiden: Brill.

Barnes, T. 2002. Virgin Territory? Travel and Migration by African Women in Twentieth-Century Southern Africa. In: *Women in African Colonial Histories*. Jean A. Susan, G. and Nakanyke, M.(Eds.). Indiana: Indiana University Press: 164-185.

Barton, J.L. 1915. The Modern Missionary". *The Harvard Theological Review*. 8(1): 1-17.

Beidelman, T. O. 1982. *Colonial Evangelism: A Socio-Historical Study of an East African Mission at the Grassroots*. Bloomington: Indiana University Press.

Booth, B. F. 1976. *The Mill Hill Fathers in West Cameroon: Education Health and Development, 1884-1970* Oxford: Oxford University Press

Both, J. 2008.Navigating the Urban Landscapes of Certainty Human Anchorage: Girl Migrants in N'Djamena. Mphil Thesis in African Studies Submitted to the African Studies Centre/ University of Leiden.

Brinkman, I. Mirjam, de B.B and Hisham, B. 2009.The Mobile Phone, Modernity and Change in Khartoum, Sudan. In: *Mobile Phones: The New Talking Drums of Everyday Africa*. Mirjam, de B. Francis, B. N. and Inge, B. (Eds.). Mankon, Bamenda: Langaa Research and RPCIG: 61-91.

Cavalcanti, H. B. 2005. Human Agency in Mission Work: Missionary Styles and their Political Consequences, *Sociology of Religion*. 66 (4): 381-398.

Chatterjee, P. 1997. *Our Modernity*. Dakar: CODESRIA.

Chilver, E. M. 1963. Native Administration in West Central Cameroons, 1902-1954. In: *Essays in Imperial Government*. K. Robinson & F. Madden. (Eds.) Oxford: Basil Blackwell:100-108.

Chilver, E. M. 1966. Zintgraff's Exploration in Bamenda, Adamawa and the Benue Lands,1889-1892 Buea, Cameroon: Ministry of Primary Education and Social Welfare and West Cameroon Antiquities Commission.

Chilver, E. M. 1967. The Kingdom of Kom in West Cameroon. In: *West African Kingdoms in the Nineteenth Century*. Daryll, F. & Kaberry, P.M. (Eds.). Oxford: Oxford University Press: 123-315.

Chilver, E.M. 1970. Chronology of the Bamenda Grassfields. *The Journal of African History*, 2 ( 2): 249-257.

Chilver, E. M. 1971. Chronological Synthesis: The Western Region, Comprising the Western Grassfields, Bamum, the Bamileke Chiefdoms and the Central Mbam. In: *The Contribution of Ethnological Research to the History of Cameroon Cultures*. Clau de,Tardits. (Ed.). Paris: Editions du Centre National de la Recherché Scientifique: 453-475

Chilver, E.M. and Phyllis M. Kaberry 1970. *Traditional Bamenda: The*

*Pre-colonial History and Ethnography of the Bamenda Grassfields. Buea*: Government Printers.

Chilver, E. M.1961. Nineteenth Century Trade in the Bamenda Grassfields. *Afrika und Uerbersee.* 14(4): 233-258.

Clifford, J.1992. Travelling Cultures. In: *Cultural Studies.* Lawrence, G. Cary, N. and Paula, T. (Eds) New York: Routledge: 97-98.

Cockerton, C. 2002.Slipping Through their Fingers: Women's igration and Tswana patriarchy. *Botswana Notes and Records.*34:37-53.

Cohen, A. 1966. Politics of the Kola Trade: Some Processes of Tribal Community Formation among Migrants in West African Towns. *Africa: International African Institute.* 36 (1): 18-36.

Comaroff, J. L. & Jean, C.(Eds.). 1993. *Modernity and its malcontents: Ritual and Power in Postcolonial Africa.* Chicago and London: The University of Chicago Press.

Cooper, F. 2005. *Colonialism in Question: Theory, Knowledge, History.* Berkeley/Los Angeles/ London: University of California Press.

Coquery-Vidrovitch, C. 1997. *African Women: A Modern History.* Boulder, Colorado: Westview Press.

Cordell, D. D. Joel W. G. and Victor P.1996. *Hoe and Wage: A Social History of a Circular Migration System in West Africa.* Boulder, Colorado: Westview.

Davidson, R.B. 1954. *Migrant Labour in the Gold Coast.* Published by the Department of Economics, University College of the Gold Coast, Achimota.

Delpechin, J. 2005. *Silences in African History: Between the Syndromes of Discovery and Abolition.* Dar ES Salaam: Mkuki na Nyota Publishers.

Deutsch, J. Peter P. and Heike S. 2002. *African Modernities: Entangled Meanings in Current Debates.* Oxford: James Currey.

Eltis, D.1993. Labour and coercion in the English Atlantic World from the Seventeenth to the Early Twentieth Century. In: *The Wages of Slavery: From Chattel Slavery to Wage Labour in Africa, the Caribbean and England.* Michael, T. (Ed.). London: Oxford University Press: 207-226.

Fardon, R.; Wim Van, B. & Ryke V. (Eds.).1999. *Modernity on a Shoestring: Dimensions of Globalisation, Consumptions and Development in Africa and Beyond.* Leiden: Brill

Feierman, S. 1990. *Peasant Intellectuals: Anthropology and History in*

*Tanzania*. Madison: University of Wisconsin Press.

Ferguson, J. 1999. *Expectations of Modernity: Myths and Meanings of Urban Life on the Zambian Copperbelt*. Berkely: University of California Press.

Ferguson, J. 2006. *Global Shadows: Africa in the Neoliberal World Order*. Durham and London: Duke University Press.

Forde, D. and Phyllis, K. (Eds.) 1967. *West African Kingdoms in the Nineteenth Century* London: Oxford University Press.

Geschiere, P. Birgit, M. & Peter, P. (Eds.). 2008. *Readings in modernity in Africa*. Oxford: James Currey.

Giddens, A. 1990. *The Consequences of Modernity*. Stanford, Calif.: Stanford University Press.

Harniet-Sievers, A. (Ed.). 2002. *Africa and South-Asia. A place in the World: New Local Historiographies from Africa and Asia.* Leiden: Brill.

Harris, P. 1994. *Work, Culture and Identity: Migrant Laborers in Mozambique and South Africa, c.1860-1910: Social History of Africa*. London: James Currey.

Havik, P.J. 2009. Motor Cars and Modernity: Pinning for Progress in Portuguese Guinea, 1915-1945. In: *The Speed of Change: Motor Vehicles and People in Africa, 1890-2000.* Jan- Bart, G. Sabine, L. and Klaas, van W. (Eds.). Leiden: Brill: 48-74

Hopkins, R. 1966. Christianity and Sociopolitical Change in Sub-Saharan Africa. *Social Forces,* Vol. 44, No. 4: 555-562.

Iliffe, J.1988. *The African Poor: A History*.Cambridge: Cambridge University Press.

Iliffe, J. 1995. *Africans: The History of a Continent*. Cambridge: Cambridge University Press.

Joshi, S. 2001. *Fractured Modernity: Making of a Middle Class in Colonial North India* London: Oxford University Press.

Kihato, C. W. 2009. *Migration, Gender and Urbanisation in Johannesburg*. PhD Thesis Submitted to the Department of Sociology, University of South Africa.

Konings, Piet. 1988. *Uniliver Estates in Crisis and the Power of Organisations in Cameroon* Hamburg: LIT Verlag.

Konings, P. 2001. Mobility and Exclusion: Conflicts Between Autochthons and Allochtons During Political Liberalization in Cameroon. In: *Mobile Africa: Changing Patterns of Movement in Africa and Beyond.* de Bruijn, M. Van Dijk, R. & Foeken, D. (Eds.). Leiden: Brill: 169-194.

Lambert, Michael 2007. "Politics, Patriarchy, and New Tradition: Understanding Female Migration among the Jola (Senegal, West Africa)" In: *Cultures of Migration: African Perspectives.* Hans, P.H. and Georg K. (Eds.). New Brunswick: Transaction Publishers: 129-148. Latourette,

Kenneth Scot. 1962. *Christianity in a Revolutionary Age: The twentieth century outside Europe.* Vol.5.New York: Harper and Bros. Macamo, E. S. (Ed.). 2005. *Negotiating Modernity: Africa's Ambivalent Experience.* London: Zed Press.

Musisi, N. B. 1992. Colonial and Missionary Education: Women and Domesticity in Uganda, 1900-1945. In: *African Encounters with Domesticity.* Karen, T. H. (Ed..) Brunswick N.J.: Rutgers University Press: 172-194.

Nkwi, P.N. 1982 *Traditional Diplomacy: A Study of Inter-Chiefdom Relations in Western Grassfields Northwest Province of Cameroon.* Yaoundé, Cameroon: Department of Sociology, University of Yaounde.

Nkwi, W. G. 2010. *Voicing the Voiceless:Contributions to Closing Gaps in Cameroon History, 1958-2009.* Mankon, Bamenda: Langaa. RPCIG.

Nkwi, W. G. 2011. *Kfaang and its Technologies: Towards a Social History of Mobility in Kom (Cameroon). 1928-1998.* Leiden. The Netherlands: ASC Publications.

Oliver, R. & Gervase, M.(Eds). 1963. *History of East Africa* vol.1.Oxford: Clarendon Press.

Oliver, R. A. 1956. *How Christian is Africa?* London: Longmans Green and Co.

Ranger, T. O. 1999.*Voices from the Rocks: Nature, Culture and History in the Matopos Hills of Zimbabwe.* Oxford: James Currey.

Robertson, C. C.1984. *Women in the Urban Economy.* Margaret, J.H. and Sharon, S. eds.*African Women South of the Sahara.* London and New York: Longman: 205-225.

Rowlands, M. 1978. Local and Long-Distance Trade and Incipient State Formation in the Bamenda Plateau in the Late 19th century. *Paideuma,* No. 25: 1-19.

Rudin, Harry. 1938. The Germans in Cameroon: A Case Study in

Modern Imperialism. Yale: Yale University Press.
Simelane, H. S. 2004. "The State, Chiefs and Control of Female Migration in Colonial Swaziland, c.1930s-1950s," Journal of African History. Vol.45, No.1:103-124.
Steven, F. 1990. *Peasant Intellectuals: Anthropology and History in Tanzania*. Madison: University of Wisconsin Press.
Subramaniam,V. 1977. Consequences of Christian Missionary Education. Third World Quarterly. Vol.1, No.3: 129-131.
Thornton, J. 1992. *Africa and Africans in the Making of the Atlantic World, 1400-1680* Cambridge: Cambridge University Press.
Thurnwald, R. 1932. SocialTransformations in East Africa" *The American Journal of Sociology.* Vol.38, No.2: 175-184.
Touraine, A. 1974. *Pour la Sociologie* Paris: Editions du Seuil.
Ulicki, T. & Jonathan, S.C. 2000.Gender, Farm Work and Women's Migration from Lesotho to the new South Africa. *Canadian Journal of African Studies*. Vol.34, No.1: 64-79.
Vansina, J. 1966. *Kingdoms of the Savanna* Madison: University of Wisconsin Press.
Wallerstein, I. 1986. *Africa and the Modern World* Trenton, New Jersey: Africa World Press.
Wallerstein, I. 2005. *Africa: The Politics of Independence and Unity* Lincoln and London: University of Nebraska Press
Warnier, J.P. 2012. *Cameroon Grassfields Civilisation* Mankon, Bamenda: Langaa RPCIG .

# *Chapter Ten*

## SAINTS AND SINNERS: AFRICAN HOLOCAUST, "CLANDESTINE COUNTERMEMORIES" AND LGBT VISIBILITY POLITICS IN POSTCOLONIAL AFRICA

*Kwame Edwin Otu*

*Between 1885 and 1887, within ten years of the first knowledge of the Catholic faith, twenty-boys and men of Uganda laid down their lives for their religion. The story of their conversion from paganism, of their battle for Christian virtue and of their sacrifice of life itself...but as all were victims of Mwanga the Kabaka, or king, of Buganda and majority were natives of that country, some description of its social and political structure is needed in order that the reader may appreciate fully the remarkable charge wrought in the souls of these young men through the action of grace and the teachings of Christ John F. Faupel.*

The deluge of LGBTI human rights politics and the growing political homophobia in parts of sub-Saharan Africa continue to be undertheorised and underhistoricised. In recent years, the study of sexuality and gender in Africa has attracted scholarly attention. These have resulted in the production of compelling studies that have justifiably questioned the claim that homosexuality is un-African (Murray and Roscoe 1997; Aarmo 1999; Kendall 1999; Epprecht 2004 & 2008). In doing so, these studies have equally revealed that the misconception that homosexuality was imported to Africa remains the product of a vexed historical moment. (Aarmo 1999; Hoad 2007; Epprecht 2008; Reid 2012).

LGBT human rights organizations such as Aidspan, The Global Fund, among others, have not wholly engaged with the findings generated from critical LGBT studies. Some the outcomes of this studies, for instance, suggest that LGBT human rights interventions heighten the predicaments of sexual minorities. (Hoad 1999; Epprecht 2008). I argue here that very few studies have been critical of how the formation of the nation-state, an outcome of colonial rule, in Africa erased particular practices and ideas regarding gender and sexuality. (Hoad 1997& 2007; McFadden 2005; Epprecht 2008). By positioning itself as the moral custodian and agent of sexual citizenship and belonging, the postcolonial nation-state reinforced the colonial logic that dislocated the gender and sexual trajectories of the multiple sociocultural groups inhabiting its boundaries. These were polymorphous, ranging from what Ifi Amadiume calls "male daughters and female husbands" to Stephen Murray and Will Roscoe's trenchant observation of the presence of "boy wives" on the continent. Thus, while it is by now common knowledge that both colonial and Christian influences shaped the contours of sexuality, gender, and belonging in postcolonial Africa (Murray and Roscoe 1997; Hoad 2007; Epprecht 2008; Dankwa 2009; Kaoma 2010&2012), the paradoxical erasure of these very formations in the debates incited by sexual politics remains problematic. In this chapter, I illuminate how the elision of particular historical episodes in sexual politics might clarify how both LGBT human rights organization and the nation-state become complicit actors in the production of Africa as the 'heart of homophobic darkness.'

Closely examining two incidents, one historical and the other contemporary, I elucidate the extent to which the 'neoliberal and neocolonial collusion,' to use Patricia McFadden's (2011) apt formulation, hones the matrix in which LGBT human rights reason and heteronationalist ideologies get articulated. The first incident is set in precolonial Uganda at the turn of the twentieth century. Then known as Buganda, it was a kingdom that had an established political organisation under the absolute rule of the Kabaka—the king—before the onset of missionisation and colonisation. I analyze J. F. Faupel's African Holocaust (1962) and the infamous attempt by the Ugandan Parliament to pass the "kill gay gays bill" in 2009 to trouble the fraught rhetoric of "heterosexual Africa" and "African homophobia."

***The Contested and Fraught Scenes of Sexual, Gender, and Racial Transformations.***

The proliferation of Christianity and colonisation in precolonial Uganda transformed this region into a "contact zone," to use Mary Louise Pratt's formulation (1991, 2). Here, the inhabitants of Buganda, by virtue of their interactions with white missionaries from both Catholic and Protestant denominations, transformed the latter as much as they were transformed by them. This epoch represented a watershed moment for Christianity in precolonial Uganda.

In this contact zone, understandings about sexuality and gender underwent tectonic shifts, as Christian notions of gender and sexuality replaced existing logics underlying being masculine and feminine. I argue in a latter segment of this essay that the intercourse between coloniality and Christianity would result in the conception of rigid understandings of gender and sexuality in dominant public spheres (Epprecht 2004 and 2009). This era was also marked by the Catholic and Protestant missions' radical proselytizing projects, which, not only reached out to and converted several inhabitants in the kingdom to Christianity, but also appointed the new converts as conduits for the spread Christianity. Some of the converts were royal pages, whose status, contingent on their homoerotic relationship with Kabaka Mwanga, afforded them some royal privileges.

Following their conversion to Christianity, the royal pages aborted their homoerotic relationships with the king. In the regime of Christianity, homoeroticism was construed as antithetical with doctrinal teachings of the Church (Faupel 1962). Against this backdrop, Christianity emerged as the barometer for measuring experience for the converts. The pages' conversion to Christianity also symbolically marked the supersession of the king's absolute power over them by the missionaries, as the latter's ability to convert the pages from 'paganism' to Christianity challenged the resolute authority of Mwanga. Realizing that his leadership as king was under threat and in question, Mwanga gave an order for the pages' execution between 1885 and 1887.

The attempt by the Ugandan parliament in 2009 to legislate the "kill the gays' bill" throws us back into history. While certainly a testament of what Ann Stoler (2008, 1) calls "imperial debris," the content of the bill resonated with the execution of pages at the turn of the century eerily. Unleashing global outcry, the incident positioned Uganda on the global map of sexual undemocracy. Unsurprisingly, the country was discursively framed as homophobic and intolerant in both Western media and human rights discourses. The experiences of sexual minorities in Uganda become synecdochic of sexual minorities' experiences in Africa as a result. In this rather tenuous representation, sexual minorities in Africa were portrayed as hapless victims of predatory homophobic governments on the continent.

The construction of LGBT experiences in human rights discourses following this incident was bereft of any attention to the complexities of class, race, ethnicity and religious orientation—such as the growing influence of the Christian Right—economic vampirism, neocolonialism, the consequences of colonialism, to outline but a partial list. In this light, homophobia became less a subject of history and more an issue of the contemporary moment, with the continent framed as lacking the wherewithal to succumb to the transformations wrought by neoliberal globalisation. By describing Africa as intolerant and homophobic, these discourses recapitulated Africa with epithets drawn extensively from existing racist repertory (Epprecht 2008). Hence, again and again, the continent, imagined as the 'heart of darkness,' (Conrad 1990) was re-forged in the foundry of negativity as a space awaiting redemption and the incandescence of Euro-America. As the anthropologists Clarke and Thomas note, "historically embedded patterns of racialization play out in contemporary transformations of daily practice" (2006, 10) in the age of globalization. Here the tendencies of racialization became prominent; inclinations that ignored the complexes animating homophobia in Africa.

The resonances that bring together the execution of the royal pages and "the kill the gays bill" illuminate the complexity of being and becoming a sexual citizen and a sexual dissident in the postcolonial situation. Despite their articulation in radically different historical conjunctures, the events hold the promise of exposing how particular ideas about the construction of sexual propriety and impropriety were contingent on changing power formations and historical circumstances.

As Michel Foucault argues, the dispersion of power across time and space has different implications in different contexts and for different subjectivities (2012). Examining the silenced voices in the history of Africa's sexual politics, I unpack the "clandestine counter-memories" overwritten by hegemonic colonial, Christian, and national histories. [1]To do this, I pose the following questions: Does the execution of the royal pages figure in how LGBT human rights politics is articulated today? Are LGBT movements and discourses in Africa ahistorical? Might the nation-state have *unimagined alliances*, to use Roderick Ferguson's (2004:10) felicitous term, with LGBT liberatory movements in Africa such as their repression of the historical episodes that radically transformed understandings about gender, sexuality, and citizenship in Africa?

### *On Historical Ruptures and Sutures: J.F Faupel's African Holocaust, a Clandestine Memory?*

J.F. Faupel's exceptional chronicling of the execution of the royal pages between 1885 and 1887 in the kingdom of Buganda titled African Holocaust teems with examples of the transformations understandings about gender and sexuality in Africa. Transposing the execution on the recent attempt in Uganda to implement the kill the gays' bill in 2009, I examine how the latter event resonates with the order by the king of Buganda, Kabaka Mwanga, that his royal pages be executed. These two events, while remarkably denoting that one cannot step in the same culture twice, as the anthropologist Marshall Sahlins (2002) argues, re-vindicates the power of "palimpsestic time," á la Jacqui Alexander (2005) and Ella Shohat (2001). Like the palimpsest, which retains the residue of previous inscriptions, the two incidents remarkably re-inscribe events from the past into the present and perhaps the future (Shohat 2001; Gopinath 2005; McFadden 2011).

*African Holocaust* celebrates the Catholic Church, ignoring the unpalatable impacts it had on Uganda. The book stages the 'dramatic interenactment,' to use Fred Moten's (2003:3) apt description, of sacrifice and persecution. Not only opening up points from which to critique the tides of colonialism and Christianity in Africa, the historiography presents insights into the solidification of gender and sexuality as peremptory sites of heteronormative

---

[1] I am interested in the power of the archive and the extent to which hegemonic archival works can paradoxically function as sites that produce counter-hegemonic memories.

desire. Defending Catholic Christianity, Faupel's account paradoxically contains the seeds of the clandestine counter-memories that contest the parochial construction of sexual citizenship in Africa in our present dispensation. In LGBT human rights discourse and practice, the historical impulses that punctuated the sexual landscapes of the African continent have yet to extensively modify the very ideologies about sexuality inherited from colonial times. The omission of massive historical episodes in the politics to liberate sexual minorities and the nation-state's repression of that very project produces what Amar Wahab (2012:1) calls a "homophobic state of reason."

The main characters in Faupel's narrative are the kabakas, Mutesa and Mwanga, and some members of the royal court. The Catholic and Protestant missionaries and some colonial officials play significant roles in the narrative too. The crux of the narrative centers on the lives of twenty-royal pages, and how the circumstances surrounding their conversion to Christianity compelled their execution on Namugongo Hill.

### *The Coincidence of Christianity and Coloniality and the Execution of the Royal Pages*

Before the arrival of the Christian missionaries, Arab traders had long had a presence in Buganda, bringing with them Islamic ideologies and practices. The first Arab to be received in Buganda was the Sheik Ahmed-bin-Ibrahim (Faupel 1962). The Sheik's visit conceived commercial trading ties between Arabs on the East African Coast and in Zanzibar and the kingdom of Buganda. These networks will politically enhance Arab presence, as they occupied political positions in the court of the kabakas. It is argued that Mutesa, the Kabaka before Mwanga, practiced Islam long before the arrival of the English Mission in the nineteenth century and Christianity. The arrival of the first missionaries was, however, preceded by some English explorers. According to Faupel:

> The early explorers Speke and Grant, and later Stanley, after experiencing the chaos and confusion prevailing elsewhere, were so impressed by the appearance of law and order they found in Buganda that in their accounts they tended to glamourize the country and its ruler and to overlook the

> fundamental evil that was so closely bound up with that much was good (Faupel 1962, 1).

The onset of Christianity was undoubtedly preceded by the traces left by the explorers Speke, Grant, and later Stanley. The introduction transformed the cultural, economic, moral, sexual, social, and political trajectories of the kingdom. For instance, in a letter published in the *Daily Telegraph* in 1875, Stanley shows how Mutesa, who previously disposed to Islamism, expressed "astonishing enthusiasm" [Faupel's words] towards Christianity. Not only will this appeal open the flood gates for "Christendom to evangelize in Buganda," but as Faupel maintains, "within three days of its publication, the Church Missionary Society received from an anonymous benefactor an offer of five thousand pounds for a mission to the Great Lake" (1962, 12).

The English missionaries, notable and influential among them, Alexander Mackay, Shergold Smith, and Rev. C.T. Wilson, were among the first caravan to arrive. These missionaries set in motion a strong whiff of Christian sentiment among the inhabitants of the kingdom. With magnanimous support from the Christian Missionary Society (CMS), the newly arrived missionaries tilled the ground for the cultivation of protestant Christianity. Not long after the cultivation of Protestant Christianity, the French Catholic Missionaries entered the kingdom with the goal to evangelise to its inhabitants.

The arrival of the Catholic missionaries coincided unprecedentedly with the expansion of French overseas territories in Africa. This connection between colonial expansion and Christianity is silenced and masked in Faupel's narrative. Still, it can be claimed that the tensions between the Protestants and the Catholics reflected the political conflicts and ambitions for overseas territories between England and France. Describing the antecedents of the tensions between the Protestants and Catholics, Faupel writes:

> The coming of the White Fathers to the Court of Mutesa aroused great resentment in Protestant missionary circles, in which it was generally assumed that, by sending them, the Catholic Church 'deliberately set herself to oppose Protestantism rather heathenism and, with eyes open with solemn protests sounding in her ears, commenced that career aggression which was to bar such bitter fruity in the days to come' (1962, 14).

However, it is still difficult to determine whether the wedges animating both Christianities were the outcome of geopolitical economic differences, as Faupel does not foreground this possibility in *African Holocaust.* Rather, he insists that the cause of the division was more religious than political. A shorter account on pre-colonial Uganda at the turn of the twentieth century by the British Lieutenant A. F. Mockler-Ferryman's titled *Christianity in Uganda* presents a different perspective. In this short essay, Mockler-Ferryman (1903, 3) describes how the colonizing mission influenced or was influenced by growing missionary activities in the colonies. Observing the events wrought by Christianity in Uganda as having political intentions, he suggests that by going to foreign lands without protection from their nations, missionaries tended to put themselves in harmful and uncertain situations (Mockler-Ferryman 1903, 3). Such dangerous situations, he asserts, delayed the project of colonisation. Making this observation in the first decade of the twentieth century, Mockler-Ferryman presents a historical version of the contemporary contradictions that characterise human rights activists' goals and the Western nations that they represent. Like the missionary projects that preceded them politically, human rights are an exemplar of modern day missionary attempts.

The redemptive attempts of these human rights movements fall in line with what Patricia McFadden, à la Uma Narayan, calls the "politics of rescue" (2010, 10). The articulation of salvage politics, while disguising the actual intentions of Western interventions in supposedly oppressed spaces, contributes, fortifies what McFadden (2011, 3) calls the "hegemonic waves of colluding amnesia." Thus, the extent to which the English and French Missionaries, despite their theological orientations, pursued objectives that overlapped with those of their respective nations—nations that craved colonial expansion—should not be overlooked. Hence, the Christianity/Coloniality nexus just like the neocolonial and the neoliberal collusion becomes evident in the articulation of Christianity in pre-colonial Uganda. It marks the source of the tensions that arose between the kabakas and Christianity—a tension that will eventually beget the execution of twenty-royal pages between 1885 and 1887—on the orders of Kabaka Mwanga and his leading officials.

According to Faupel:

> Of the twenty-two Uganda Martyrs declared "Blessed" in 1920 by Pope Benedict XV, twenty died between 26 May and 3 June 1886. The other two were Joseph Mukasa Balikuddembe and Jean-Marie Muzeyi. The former was put death in November of the previous year, and the latter in January of the year following, in 1887. Thirteen of the Catholics who died during the nine days of 1886 were royal pages; four were royal bandsmen or guards; and three belonged to the entourage of the county chief of Ssingo (1962, 132).

If Faupel's estimate is accurate, then twenty two royal pages were executed between 1885 and 1887. The pages' execution was centrally defined by their refusal to have homoerotic intimacy with Mwanga, which was the corollary of their rejection of the Kiganda tradition. However, Mwanga's decision for the execution was propelled by other factors too. For instance, Faupel notes that:

> It was the pages who bore the brunt of Kabaka Mwanga's fury. Indeed it seems possible that, but for the intervention of the Chancellor Mukasa, the pages and the royal retainers alone might have suffered. Mwanga himself was not moved by any strong or enduring hatred for Christianity itself but by anger against those who, instead of being the abject slaves that both he and Kiganda tradition expected them to be, dared, under the influence of Christianity, to call their souls their own, and refused to comply with demands they considered sinful (1962, 132).

Faupel's claim seems to be empathetic to the king, suggesting the extent to which Mwanga himself wavered between Christianity and pagan beliefs and the possibility of his reluctance to execute the royal pages. It points to Mwanga's indecision and discomfort, not with the pages, but also, the very institutions and vicissitudes set in motion by the proliferation of Christianity. Furthermore, the narrative suggests that Mwanga may have been less furious had the Chancellor Mukasa and other indigenous leaders who staunchly resisted the Christian missionaries not instigated him. For instance, he writes: "The principal instigator, the chancellor Mukasa, was certainly moved by hatred of Christianity" (1962, 74). This position seems to be suggesting that the king might have been less severe in the punishment wielded on the bodies of the pages—death by execution on Namugongo hill.

### *Racialising African Sexualities*

Celebrating the pages' conversion to Christianity, Faupel demonizes the Kabakas, their retinue, and the Islamic traders with whom they had socio-economic exchanges. The twenty-two royal pages and the missionaries are projected as the protagonists in this precolonial drama and the Kabakas and their supporters emerge as antagonists. While this bifurcation is prominent in the narrative, figures such as the Kabakas disrupt this seeming binary by utilizing the internecine conflicts between the Protestant and Catholic missionaries to their advantage. The arrival of the first missionaries in Buganda was an event that placed the kingdom on the map of European ambitions. The transformations wrought during this encounter and succeeding ones included the displacement of sexual fluidity by sexual binarity, the dislocation of paganist practices by Christianity, and the eventual usurpation of the sociopolitical structure of Buganda by the colonial structure instituted by British imperialism. Here, the contours of British coloniality together with missionary Christianity conceived not only a colony but also a trammeled erotic framework of desire (Stoler 1994; McClintock 1995; Hoad 2007; Epprecht 2008).

Within this structure, both civilisation and Christianity gained superiority over 'savagery' and 'paganism.' The collision of erotic cultures was, therefore, fundamental, in a large measure, to the project of colonization, missionary Christianity, and the consolidation of white sexual superiority. (Hoad 2007; Epprecht 2008). It was in this contact zone that heteronormativity emerged as a compulsory and an immanent feature of [being] and [becoming] "civilised" and "human."

IIf Michel Foucault observed in his *History of Sexuality* (1976) that there emerged in Europe and "authorized vocabulary" for broaching the discursive limits of sex (Butler 1993), then in the colonial context that vocabulary ultimately entwined with racial discourses circulated by missionaries, colonial officials, and racist scientists. (Stoler 1994; McClintock 1995). In this context, sexual practices and ideologies were articulated through the prism of racial difference, or "colonial difference," to use Walter Mignolo's felicitous terminology (2002, 1). It is this colonial difference, which is sutured to the "coloniality of power," as Anibal Quijano (2000) asserts, that triggered the displacement and dislocation that informed the wider sexual landscape in which the new imaginaries about proper and improper sexualities were constituted. It must be acknowledged then that Foucault's pointed observations, while influential, were inattentive to how the histories of colonisation and the coloniality of power transformed the course of the sexual order of things in colonial contexts. Against this backdrop, anything, other than the European *order of things* seemed to have been rendered invisible in Foucault's account (2012).

The trajectories of sexuality in Africa, while contingent on the shifts induced by colonisation and Christianity, were also the corollary of capitalist processes and modernity on the continent. (McClintock 1995; Stoler 1995; Mignolo 2002). Constituted by the racialisation of Africans, these projects both enabled and solidified colonisation. In this regard, colonised territories faced the quadruple behemoths of colonialism, Christianity, capitalism, and modernity, all of which were configured and sustained by European racialist imaginations and ideologies.

Inarguably, the latter were the turbines that propelled the engines of capitalist modernity (Mignolo 2002; Quijano 2000), whereas imperial capitalism, together with the proliferation of Christianity of Protestant and Catholic orientations, fashioned new and hegemonic modulations of the erotic—most of which were white, Christian, and heteronormative. The colonial difference that animated the contact zones described above, then, constituted the milieu in which the execution of the twenty-two royal pages occurred in the kingdom of Buganda. With the royal pages' conversion to Christianity inciting the execution, their deaths will generate uproar in the Christian and colonial worlds, leading to the eventual annexation of Buganda by England under the leadership of Frederick Lugard (Faupel 1962; Mockler-Ferryman 1903).

Faupel describes Kabaka Mwanga as a flippant king who embraced Christianity, Islam, and paganism. He is also noted for being an unpopular Kabaka because of his intense predilection for homoerotic acts—acts that some historical accounts claim were inherited from his Mohammedan contacts in Eastern and Southern Africa (Faupel 1962). Deriving homoerotic satisfaction from the royal pages, Mwanga sustained his indomitable authority as king.[2] The pages' eventual rejection of homoerotic intimacy with the Kabaka vicariously questioned the Mwanga's supposed resolute leadership, compelling him to give orders for their execution. Hence, for Faupel, "to gloss over the unpleasant vice to which Mwanga was addicted would be to disregard the decisive factor in the story of persecution" (1962, 82). In a later iteration, he adds that "there can be no doubt that Mwanga turned against the adherents of the faith to which he was naturally attracted mainly because of the firm resistance offered by these young Christian pages who, according to *Kiganda* tradition, should have no desire but to obey their Kabaka's slightest wish" (1962, 82). In the moral imagination of Catholic Christianity, this tradition was constructed as the shackle that ensnared the king and his loyal followers from embracing Christianity. It was a pathological vestige of Buganda culture.

In view of the above, Faupel's account on the executions both spectacularises and exaggerates the execution of the royal pages, determining their martyrdom and eventual beatification. For example, the execution is presented in a manner that runs parallel to Christ's crucifixion. Thus, characterised by historical depth and narrative power, *African Holocaust* is an historical example of how violence gets "aestheticized" (Bruder 1995, 23). In his very graphic description, which may also well be described as a historic thick description (Geertz 1973), he offers a graphic portrayal of the events leading to and surrounding the execution of the pages. The narrative teems with the penchant to create beauty out of violence—in other words, it stylises violence. In the background to the execution, Faupel presents evidence of conflicts and tensions between Christian missionaries,

---

[2] I do not want to suggest here that homoeroticism, or homosexuality, was widespread in precolonial Uganda at the time. Available historical documents on the kingdom of Buganda suggest that the Kabaka before Kabaka Mwanga did not engage in homoerotic acts. Mwanga's desire for homoerotic sex is, therefore, often seen as an exception and the outcome of his relationships with Islamic diplomats and traders who had a presence in the royal court. While these are the accounts that are accessible, the fact that they are produced not only by Catholic and Protestant missionaries, but also by colonial officials like Speke, Stanley and Lord Lugard warrants further interrogation. Also, we do not know yet why Mwanga, unlike his father, Kabaka Mukasa, engaged in homosexual sex. Whether this was a public secret or public knowledge before the onset of colonization and missionization continues to be unknown.

Islamic leaders and traders, as well as practitioners of paganism. Of crucial significance, too, is the conflict among Christian missionaries, tensions that created divisions among converts to Christianity.

The brouhaha generated by the attempt by legislators in Uganda to legislate a "kill the gays bill," which was presided by David Bahati, a Member of Parliament (MP), with support from the Christian Right in the United States, is an event that opens colonial wounds. Eerily similar to the support received by the missionaries from the Christian Missionary Society at the turn of the century, it shows how the colonial continues to rivet postcolonial situations. The President of Uganda, Yoweri Museveni, like Kabaka Mwanga, played a marginal role in the process, leaving the MPs to decide on the fate of sexual minorities. Thus, Chancellor Mukasa and MP David Bahati share an uncanny affinity that is reflected in their call for the execution of the converted royal pages and gays in Uganda respectively. This strange alliance reproduces a narrative of saints and sinners, which is manifested in contemporary same-sex visibility and invisibility politics as the alliance between the nation-state and LGBT movements.

### *Becoming Saints and Sinners: Exposing the Unimagined Alliances between Christianity, LGBTQ Movements and the Nation State*

Here I examine the extent to which the circumstances leading to execution of the royal pages by Kabaka and his retinue resonates with the 2009 appeal by a section of the Ugandan parliament to legislate the "kill the gays' bill." In doing so, I show how David Kato's murder, occurring after the victory of Sexual Minorities Uganda against the State and some media houses, crystallised the image of Uganda as homophobic. The construction of Kato's death, much like the royal pages a century earlier, which was represented in the persecution narratives, led to the posthumous beatification of David Kato in neoliberal LGBT human rights politics as a "Saint."

Kato's persecution and death synecdochically represented sexual minorities' lives in Africa as animated by oppression and hatred, a construction that disregarded experiences the impacts of class, ethnicity, religion, and gender. So, if the execution of the royal pages and their consequent beautification symbolically and materially represented the redemptive character of Catholic Christianity and Christianity in general, Kato's murder and the reactions expressed by neoliberal LGBT human rights movements were repackaged as redemptive gestures in the same guise.[3] Hence, if for Faupel, the Christian pages' death was a corollary of "their conversion from paganism, of their battle for Christian virtue and of their sacrifice of life itself" (1962, 1), then Kato's death, while not homophobically related, was read by LGBT human rights advocates as a sacrifice for the liberalization LGBT human rights politics in Uganda in particular and Africa in general.

In both narratives, there is a ghostly re-presentation of the West as the source of incandescence for Africa. In LGBT human rights discourses, for example, Africa continues to be marked negatively as intolerant to homosexuality, ignoring, as it were, the immense historical, sociopolitical and cultural complexities. Hence, not only is the heart of darkness narrative, to reprise the Conradian dictum, reinforced, but the homogenisation of LGBT experiences in Africa as uniform despite the likelihood that some sexual minorities may not even subscribe to LGBT nomenclature goes unrecognized (Murray and Roscoe 1998; Elder 2003; Epprecht 2008; Dankwa 2009; Gaudio 2009).

Unlike the royal pages, whose death reflected the persecution meted out to Christian converts, Kato's death, in queer liberal imaginaries, therefore, represents the contemporary plight of sexual minorities in Africa, as well as the unflinching efforts by Western neoliberal human rights organizations to overcome the harsh conditions in which they subsist. Kato's beatification by the international LGBT human rights community is akin to the beatification of his precursors—the royal pages—by the international Catholic and Christian community. The pages' ability to embrace Christianity, a move that magnified the West as the paragon of religious, racial, and sexual supremacy, rested on the rejection and the pathologisation of paganism and homoerotic relationships with Kabaka Mwanga. Similarly, Kato's martyrdom is enabled by his ability to embrace LGBT nomenclature and engage in queer liberal projects in postcolonial Uganda.

The stature of this vociferous activist makes him the poster child of the persecution sexual minorities in Sub-Saharan Africa. Therefore, if Kato was

---

[3] Here I am referring to Joseph Conrad's infamous construction of Africa as the "heart of darkness," a trope that continues to be ruminated in a variety of ways not only in LGBT human rights discourses but in human rights discourse and activism in general.

murdered because he was a self-identified gay man in a space that on the surface vehemently disavowed public homosexual practice and identity—although so-called investigations conducted by Ugandan law enforcement proves the contrary—then his death, as rearticulated in Western LGBT human rights discourse, foregrounds his humanity with the experiences of LGBT in the West. Such a view dangerously neglects the historical ruptures and sutures conditioned around and by the colonial difference, and the transformations set in motion by Christianity.

In her trenchant analysis of the sensationalisation of the execution of the two young boys in Iran accused for engaging in homosexual acts in 2005 in the Western media, Mitra Rastegar writes that "a story of homophobic persecution casts these victims as an example not only of commonality, in the form of a universal LGBT experience, but also of difference, in the form of an essentialised "civilisational" (i.e., cultural and religious) divide between a violently intolerant "Islam" and a progressively more tolerant "West" (2013, 2). Thus, Kato's beautification, in the domain of LGBT human rights activism does not only elide the crucifixion of the royal pages by the Kabaka, who is construed as blood-thirsty paedophilic. In fact, it also erases the powerful influences wrought by coloniality and Christianity, and how such influences did contribute to the pages' execution. By mobilizing and advancing the common connections between sexual minorities such as Kato and LGBTs all over the world, especially in Western contexts, LGBT human rights reactions toward his death assume the role of the missionaries in precolonial Uganda.

The beatification of the royal pages by the Pope in the sixties and David Kato's martyrdom solidify Western neoliberalism as the redemptive quintessence of freedom. While, in fact, neoliberal humanitarianism may have foregrounded the anticlimactic milieus in which sexual minorities' lives were nestled, such exposures calculatingly and uncalculatingly were erasures and distortions in of themselves. In view of this complexity, an exploration of the trajectories of Christianity's relationship with coloniality and sexuality in Africa and the nation-state's appropriation of Christian values is much needed.

In the conclusion to this chapter, I show that the recalibration of Christianity in Africa today and the ascension of LGBTQ visibility politics, reveals the contradictions in both the colonial and postcolonial management of sexualities in being and becoming a citizen. The religious, social, economic, and political reengineering engendered during the colonial era can be read as providing new grounds for the articulation of heterosexuality and homophobia.[4] These articulations were elided in the demands by nations like Britain and the United States that LGBT human rights be legalized in Sub-Saharan Africa. While they continue to obscure the neoliberal and neocolonial collusions of our time,[5] they further contribute to what Reverend Kapya Kaoma has recently described of LGBT politics and the influences of the Christian Right in Africa as the "cultural wars" (2010, 7). Although Kaoma pays attention to the role that Christianity plays, he does so rather limitedly. His argument disarticulates the Christian Right's forays today from those projects instituted by colonial Christianity, and is inattentive to the historicisation of the colonial/Christianity nexus.

Extending Kaoma's perspective, I point to the extent to which the cultural wars of today are themselves very historical, colonial and Christian, and the degree to which they will continue to be so for some time. Here, LGBT human rights organization's battle for same-sex visibility and the nation-state's resistance to that move must be recognised as the products of a particular historical moment. Understanding these as the complicated echoes of the past may reveal how the colonial difference leaves a lot of questions unanswered in the articulation of LGBT human rights politics.

Faupel's account on the internecine clashes among Christian missionaries and the Kabaka and his retinue anticipates the cultural wars we observe. Therefore, to fathom the resoluteness of the Ugandan government on the issue of executing gays, one must seriously take into account the historical formations that provided the backdrop against which these cultural wars

---

[4] Ann Stoler's rather eloquent analysis on *Race and the Education of Desire and Carnal Knowledge and Imperial Power* teem with examples of the corollaries of the displacements instituted by colonialism in non-European worlds.

[5] Following David Kato's death in 2011, David Cameron, Hillary Clinton and Ban Ki Moon, sent strong statements to nations that criminalized homosexuality—most of which were in developing countries—to decriminalize it. Using aid as bait, these leaders were quick to remind these nations about their state in the world as poor countries whose assistance depended heavily on their countries. The contexts in which these demands were made also reflect a particular collusion between these leaders and the leaders of the nations at which the warnings at directed.

continue to be waged. The "kill the gays' bill" instigated by the Ugandan Member of Parliament David Bahati disconcertingly runs parallel to Kabaka Mwanga's fury evidenced in his decision to kill the royal pages. These historical episodes express the unimagined alliances that LGBT organizations have with the nation-state and religious organisations like churches in Africa. These alliances contribute to the erasure, both covert and overt, of historical echoes.

### *Conclusion*

I conclude that the racialization of Africa as the heart of homophobic darkness in LGBT human rights discourses needs to be situated in the longue durée of colonial and missionary displacements, which effects continue to be seen in the present context. By paying limited attention to how gender and sexuality came into being and also became, therefore, requires a critical interrogation of such representations as a "homophobic Africa" and a "heterosexual Africa." Such negligence, while seemingly abstract, also has real life and embodied consequences for sexual minorities, whose lives are the turf on which the cultural wars between the nation-state and LGBT human rights organizations are waged. The African proverb that "when two elephants fight it is the grass that gets trampled" clearly captures the ruptures and the sutures wrought in sexual minorities' lives in the postcolonial conjuncture.

Exploring how homosexuality and homoeroticism came to assume un-African and un-Christian identities, therefore, requires a critical consideration of the shifts propelled by coloniality and Christianity. So if coloniality and Christianity made both saints and sinners out of the twenty-two royal pages executed by the Kabaka, then it can be argued that the activities of the neocolonial state and neoliberal LGBT human rights organizations 'secularly' transfigure David Kato into a saint and a sinner concurrently. The murder of Kato under the whims and caprice of the heteronormative nation-state is similar to the execution of the royal pages. In both instances, both subjects were "willful" to use Sara Ahmed's (2010, 10) insightful description. It is this common thread that also links Kato's martyrdom to Matthew Shepard's, the young gay man who was beaten and left to die hanging on a fence in Wyoming. Shepard's martyrdom, which would lead to his elevation to 'secular' sainthood, is celebrated by the passage of the Matthew Shepard and James Byrd Hate Crimes Prevention Act in 2009 by President Barack Obama (Reddy 2011).

Ironically, by shoring up the portrayal of the United States as sexually superior and inclusive, the bill reproduces "other" countries as homophobic—and this is the case with Uganda, where the Christian Right articulates inflammatory discourses. Such a construction differentiates Kato's martyrdom from Shepard. In Kato's case, Africa (Uganda), which is portrayed as heterosexually exclusive and also caricatured as leaning towards degeneration, is demonized. In this representation, too, the fact that South Africa is one of the first countries to decriminalize homosexuality in the world is entirely eclipsed. Thus, it appears that within this neoliberal modularity, the exceptionalism of South Africa is even found wanting.[6]

Viewed from a different conceptual angle, Kato's death, including the fact that he fought against homophobia, is repackaged in LGBT human rights discourse as a shared 'universal' LGBTQ experience. This universality positions David Kato as perhaps Africa's first queer saint, joining the likes of Matthew Shepard. Such a beatification all too often misses the colonial difference, suggesting the erasure and amnesia that currently animate the articulation of same-sex visibility politics in Africa. Therefore, if homosexuals in the kingdom of Buganda, such as Kabaka Mwanga, were labeled as sinners, it was the sinfulness of the latter that created the possibilities of sainthood for the royal pages.

Similarly, Kato's murder perpetuates the demonisation of the African continent. Against this backdrop, Kato's martyrdom, together with his ascent to sainthood under the auspices of neoliberal LGBT human rights organisations and some Western governments, are nourished by the representation of Africa as intolerant and a place where homosexuals are persecuted. A close examination of the aforementioned events reveals the intermingling of 'pasts' and 'presents.' Hence, in both the execution of the royal pages and the murder of David Kato, a dominant narrative of saints and sinners

---

[6] I am interested in further investigating the place of South Africa in the portrayal of Africa as homophobic. The entire packaging of Africa as homophobic, in my opinion, questions the contested and questionable view that Neville Alexander calls South African Exceptionalism.

emerge as a useful optic from which to assess the LGBT visibility politics today and the nation-states' gravitation towards suppressing that visibility.

***References***

Aarmo, M. 1999. "How Homosexuality became un-African." In: *Female Desires*. Blackwood, E. and Wieringa, S. (Eds). New York: Columbia University Press.

Ahmed, S. 2010. Feminist Killjoys (And Other Willful Subjects). In: *Polyphonic Feminisms: Acting in Concert*. Issue 8.3: 1-10

Alexander, M. J. 2005. *Pedagogies of Crossing: Meditations on Feminism, Sexual Politics, Memory, and the Sacred.* Durham: Duke University Press.

Bruder, M. E. 1995. Aestheticization of Violence, or How to do Things with Style. Accessed at http://www.gradnet.de/papers/pomo98.papers/mtbruder98.htm

Butler Judith. 1993. Bodies that Matter. In*: On the Discursive Limits of Sex*. New York: Routledge.

Clarke, Kamari. M and Deborah Thomas. 2006. "Introduction." In: *Globalization and Race: Transformations in the Cultural Productions of Blackness*. Clarke, M. K. and Thomas, D. (Eds.). Durham: Duke University Press: 1-36.

Conrad, Joseph. 1990. *The Heart of Darkness*. New York: Dover Publications.

Dankwa, Serena. O. 2009. It's a Silent Trade: *Female Same-Sex Intimacies in Post-Colonial Ghana. NORA.* Vol. 17, No. 3, 192–205.

Elder, Glen. 2003. Hostiles, Sexuality and the Apartheid Legacy*: Malevolent Geographies*. Athens: Ohio University Press.

Epprecht, Marc. 2004. *H*ungochani*: The History of a Dissident Sexuality in Southern Africa.* Montreal: McGill-Queen's University Press.

Epprecht, Marc. 2008. "Bisexuality and the Politics of Normal in African Ethnography." In: *Anthropologica* .48: 187-201.

Epprecht, Marc. 2008. Heterosexual Africa? In: *The History of an Idea from the Age of Exploration to the Age of AIDS*. Athens. Ohio University Press and Scottsville: University of KwaZulu-Natal Press.

Faupel, John F. 1962. *African Holocaust*. New Jersey: P.J. Kennedy and

Sons.
Ferguson, Roderick. 2003. Aberrations in Black*: Towards a Queer of Color Critique*. Minneapolis: University Minnesota Press.
Foucault, M. 2012. *Order of Things*. New York: Routledge.
Gaudio, Rudolf. P. 1998. "Male Lesbians and Other Queer Notions in Hausa." In: *Boy-Wives and Female Husbands: Studies of African Homosexualities*. Stephen M. and Will, R. (Eds.). St. Martin's Press: 115-128.
Gaudio, R. P. 2009. Allah Made Us*: Sexual Outlaws in an Islamic African City*. New York: Wiley-Blackwell.
Geertz, C. 1973. *The Interpretation of Cultures*. New York: Basic Books.
Gopinath, G. 2005. Impossible Desires*: Queer Diasporas and South Asian Public Cultures*. Duke University Press.
Herdt, Gilbert. 1997. *Same Sex, Different Cultures: Exploring Gay and Lesbian Lives*. Boulder: West View Press.
Hoad, N. 2007. *African Intimacies: Race, Homosexuality, and Globalization*. Minneapolis: University of Minnesota Press.
Kaoma, K. 2012. *Colonizing African Values: How the US Christian Right is Transforming Sexual Politics in Africa*. Political Research Associates.
McClintock, A. 1995. Imperial Leather *.In: Race, Gender and Sexuality in the Colonial Contest.* New York: Routledge.
McFadden, P. 2011. Resisting Neo-Colonial/Neoliberal Collusion: *Reclaiming our Lives, our Futures*. Lecture delivered at the Africa Gender Institute. University of Western Cape.
Mignolo, W. 2002. The Geopolitics of Knowledge and the Colonial Difference. In: *The South Atlantic Quarterly*. 101.1: 57-96.
Mockler Ferryman, A.F. 1903. Christianity in Uganda. In: *African Affairs* 2 (vii) :276-291. Moten, F. 2003. In the Break*: The Aesthetics of the Black Radical Tradition. Minneapolis: University* of Minnesota Press.
Murray, S. and Will, R. 1997. Introduction. *Boy-wives and Female-husbands. In:: Studies in African Homosexualities*, Stephen M. and Will R. (Eds.). New York: St. Martin's Press.
Pratt, M. L. 1991. Arts of the Contact Zone. In: *Profession*: 33-40.
Quijano, A. 2000. Coloniality of Power, Eurocentrism, and Latin America. In: *Nepantla: Views from the South* 1.3: 533-580.
Rastegar, M. 2013. Emotional Attachments and Secular Imaginings. In:

*GLQ*. Vol. 19. No. 1: 1-29.

Reddy, C. 2011. *Freedom with Violence: Race, Sexuality and the US State.* Durham. Duke University Press.

Reid, G. 2011. How to Be a Real Gay. In*: Gay Identities in Small Town South Africa.*Natal: University of KwaZulu Natal Press.

Sahlins, M. 2002. *Waiting for Foucault, Still.* Chicago. Prickly Paradigm Press.

Shohat, E. H. 2001. Introduction. In: *Talking Visions: Multicultural Feminism in a Transnational Age.* Ella S. (Eds.). Boston. The MIT Press.

Stoler, L. A. 1996. *Race and the Education of Desire: Foucault's "History of Sexuality" and the Colonial Order of Things.* Durham: Duke University Press.

Stoler, A. 2002. Carnal Knowledge and Imperial Power. In: *Race and the Intimate of Colonial Rule.* Berkeley: University of California Press.

Stoler, A. L. 2008. Imperial Debris: Reflection on Ruins and Ruination. In: Cultural Anthropology. Vol. 23(2):191–219.

# *Chapter Eleven*

## 'BEING AND BECOMING': RETHINKING MOMENTS OF ENCOUNTER

*Anwesha Das*

### *Introduction: When Stories Encounter .*

> Our historical differences actually make a difference. This happens because no human society is a *tabula rasa*. The universal concepts of political modernity encounter pre-existing concepts, categories, institutions, and practices through which they get translated and configured differently. - Dipesh Chakrabarty[1]

Histories shape and reshape the contours of a place, people, and cultures. It holds true of any place, "including, of course, Europe or, broadly, the West," (Chakrabarty xii) as well as of the countries in Africa. Every place has its own histories, its own stories which carve out its unique identity, and which deny being uprooted by the imposition of stories alien to it. No society is a *tabula rasa*, as Chakrabarty highlights. Every cultural group—be it in England, or Nigeria, or India—has its own stories which build up a distinct structure of thoughts, traditions and practices, which are linked to the place, and cannot be supplanted by stories from other cultures. Chakrabarty raises a rhetorical question: "Can thought transcend places of their origin?" (xiii)

---

[1] See Chakrabarty, xii.

hinting at the significance of the intertwined relation between one's place of origin and its predominant role in determining one's thoughts. Diverse stories owing to the diversity of cultures in diverse places, give birth to diverse perspectives, diverse ways of reading cultures, reading people, reading each other within a culture. Stories differ, perspectives vary. The question arises: What happens when these disparate thoughts meet each other, standing face to face? Do they attempt to understand the difference among them, or is there a propensity to be judgmental of the other? What happens at that *moment of encounter*? Histories of civilizations have witnessed long periods of violence, of stories of domination, of discord giving rise to bitter encounters. Why does every civilization actively participate in the celebration of this practice to deny each other a space, a space of co-existence, a space of mutual respect?

This chapter attempts to rethink these questions, these disturbing concerns, in highlighting some of the major issues in the Nigerian writer Thomas Obinkaram Echewa's novel *I Saw the Sky Catch Fire*. The issues make one think again and again, posing the question: How do divergent stories of people with differing thoughts, define and redefine them as beings "being and becoming," retaining and reconstituting their identities, in the process of their interaction with each other? This chapter takes into account stories of women from two generations, to uncover questions underlying cross-cultural as well as cross-gender encounters. Focusing initially on the encounter between Igbo women and a Western woman anthropologist, the chapter then proceeds to bring out the story of Stella and Ajuzia, in Echewa's novel *I Saw the Sky Catch Fire*.

### *The Western Anthropologist and the Colonial Gaze*

"The anthropologist . . . does not *find* things; s/he *makes* them. And makes them up," writes Trinh T. Minh-ha. The Western anthropologist, in writing up a culture, *constructs* the culture s/he goes to *study*, and thereby claims to produce—what s/he calls—a *scientific* reading of the culture, its customs, and even the folklores.[2] In doing so, s/he is deliberately conscious

---

[2] Talal Asad highlights that:

of the fact that the text has to conform to the conventions of thoughts of her/his own people. The anthropologist's *study* is therefore, strictly a result of the dominant structures of thought governing the Western society, during the colonial era. This tendency to approach diverse cultures, with a preconceived notion of superiority of the Western culture, has led to the inferiorization of other cultures during colonial rule.[3] Clifford Geertz talks about the propensity of Western anthropologists and ethnographers to judge other cultures according to certain cultural traits considered *universal* pertaining to the culture of the West:

> The notion of a *consensus gentium* (a consensus of all mankind)—the notion that there are some things that all men will be found to agree upon as right, real, just, or attractive and that these things are, therefore, in fact right, real, just, or attractive—was present in the Enlightenment and probably has been present in some form or another in all ages and climes. . . . [This approach] demands (1) that the universals proposed be substantial ones . . . (2) that they be specifically grounded in biological, psychological, or sociological processes . . . (3) that they [are] . . . core elements in a definition of humanity . . . (38-39)

Therefore, the *consensus gentium* approach denies to take into account the cultural particularities of disparate cultures in the world. The diverse cultures of the colonized have thus been subjugated by Western anthropologists during the colonial period. They have failed to understand the divergent stories and cultural norms of other cultures, and takes up a Western ethnocentric perspective to *scientifically examine* them.

---

> They [ethnographers/anthropologists] even construct folk memories. . . . In the long run, therefore, it is not the personal authority of the ethnographer, but the social authority of his ethnography that matters. And that authority is inscribed in the institutionalized forces of industrial capitalist society . . . which are constantly tending to push the meaning of various Third World societies in a single direction. This is not to say that there are no resistances to this tendency. But "resistance" in itself indicates the presence of a dominant force. (163)

[3] What I say about Western anthropologists here is not a generalization of the works of all anthropologists in the West. I take into consideration majority of anthropological writings during and immediately after colonization in Nigeria, related to a subjugated portrayal of the cultures of different ethnic groups in Africa, especially in Nigeria.

Ngũgĩ wa Thiong'o points out how anthropology in the eighteenth century has had its impact on the Enlightenment; and proceeds to highlight that: "Enlightenment, after all, assumes darkness as its other. And the darker the other, the more visible and luminous the light from the European stars" (32).[4] The anthropologist therefore *constructs* the culture under *study* with an objectifying gaze, *observing* and *theorizing* about the traditions and cultural mores of a group of people. This propensity to label cultures and languages with a hierarchy frustrates a "globalectic" view of the world to develop.[5] Ngũgĩ calls this "linguistic feudalism," which "leads to aesthetic feudalism within and between nations" (60-61). He therefore argues for the need to break down the hierarchy, and questions the absence of a space for dialogue. Fred Dallmayr very aptly argues that: "Cultural interaction does not always occur in the 'space of dialogue'" ("Dialogue Community"). In Echewa's novel, *I Saw the Sky Catch Fire*, there is a questioning of this loss of dialogue, and a challenging of Western ethnocentric perspective by Igbo women.

### *"Woman to Woman"*

*I Saw the Sky Catch Fire* is a sequel to Echewa's novel *The Crippled Dancer*. It brings into perspective incidents from two different periods: Nne-nne's narrative in 1959, and an account of the Aba Women's War in 1929. Ajuzia gives an account of Nne-nne's narrative regarding the Aba War and other issues before he leaves for the United States to study, followed by his return

---

[4] See Thiong'o, 32-33

[5] Ngũgĩ questions the absence of an equal space for cultures to engage in dialogue, and puts forth his notion of "globalectics":

> . . . Globalectics combines the global and the dialectical to describe a mutually affecting dialogue, or multi-logue, in the phenomena of nature and nurture in a global space that's rapidly transcending that of the artificially bounded, as nation and region. The global is that which humans in spaceships or on the international space station see: the dialectical is the internal dynamics that they do not see. Globalectics embraces wholeness, interconnectedness, equality of potentiality of parts, tension, and motion. It is a way of thinking and relating to the world, particularly in the era of globalism and globalization. (8)

from the States after five years, when Nne-nne unleashes another set of stories related to Igbo women. Ajuzia who had left for the States leaving his wife Stella and their newly born daughter W'Orima behind, returns to find Stella pregnant by another man, and refuses to accept her as his wife. Nne-nne turns a critical gaze towards Ajuzia in questioning his lack of responsibility towards Stella, and unveils the dilemmas a woman encounter in the absence of her husband.

This chapter focuses on Nne-nne's narrative revealing the moments of encounter of village women with a Western woman anthropologist, Ashby-Jones; and thereafter takes up the episode of Stella and Ajuzia, highlighting the resistance Igbo women pose against male domination. The novel underlines how the Western ethnographic lens of objectification of African men and women is challenged when a White woman anthropologist, Elizabeth Ashby-Jones, interrogates Igbo women, and she herself is questioned in turn by them, about European ways of life. Rajender Kaur highlights this aspect, and argues that: "The text subverts the ethnocentric perspective by turning the critical gaze back on western women in having the Igbo women who are being questioned ask Elizabeth Ashby-Jones questions in return. Thus, they constantly resist being objectified . . ." (2).

In *I Saw the Sky Catch Fire*, the objectifying gaze of Ashby-Jones is challenged. However, the manner in which Igbo women question her, does not objectify her or the White culture. The character of Ashby-Jones draws one's attention to the incomprehensibility of White women towards African women: ". . . the novel's intriguing chapter on ethnography entitled 'Woman to Woman: Ugbala and Elizabeth Ashby-Jones' focuses on the race-gender divide as it figures in colonial relations, disrupting the effects of the 'female universal' (*Ndom*) . . ." (Brodzki 213). Nne-nne's account reveals how *Ndom* works as an agency to question back the White woman, and later revolt against British tax imposition. Nne-nne engages in an intergenerational transmission of the histories related to Igbo society, as an attempt to preserve stories from being wiped out, to Ajuzia, the only descendant of their family.[6] She reveals how Ashby-Jones was embraced by Igbo women as a "Fellow Woman": "They were especially pleased, the address

[6] See Brodzki, 209-211.

said, that a fellow woman had come to visit them, that they could address her as '*Nwanyi Ibem,*' or Fellow Woman, and that she could understand their *grief*' (91). But Ashby-Jones, with her lens of eurocentrism, declines to understand their culture; and develops a condescending attitude towards them, as is well evident in the notes in her diary:

> ... Generally flat, with a short, wide nose without bridge; flared nostrils; thick Negroid lips, with no noticeable hue. . . . They stare at you with a bored, droll, almost sheepish and unintelligent look, except that they appear studious and knowing. What one senses is not unintelligence or drollness but detachment and indifference. . . . they may be afflicted by a peculiar type of tribal strabismus, which seems to enable them to see more than one of whatever that are looking at, and perhaps like those reptiles which can rotate each eye independently, they may see you from more than one perspective, each picture on a different screen of their dark minds.. . (104-105).

Despite being embraced as "*Nwanyi Ibem*" or "Fellow Woman," Ashby-Jones maintains her authority as a colonizer, and fails to comprehend Igbo customs. Her encounter with the village women is more of a *study*, than of understanding and respect towards them. She is typical of a Western anthropologist who "experiences the indigenous environment and lifeways for oneself ... But the professional text to result from such an encounter is supposed to conform to the norms of a scientific discourse whose authority resides in the absolute effacement of the speaking and experiencing subject" (Pratt 32).

Echewa here provides an anthropological account of Igbo life from the insider's point-of-view through Nne-nne, alongside the ethnographic notes of Ashby-Jones in her diary. Her account is oral. It is an oral narration to Ajuzia, revealing the afflictions faced by Igbo women at the time of the Aba War. It is an oral history, filled with proverbs, stories, bringing out the significance of *Ndom*: "By recounting her story to Ajuzia ... Nne-nne, who had always tended to be silent and fierce, is speaking on behalf of herself, her gender and her culture" (Brodzki 210). It is not a *scientific study* but a *deeper understanding* of customs, of circumstances under which Igbo women took Ashby-Jones as hostage during the War. Faced with the insult of being "counted" by the British government and with the decision of the imposition of tax, the women revolted against the British government.[7] Nne-nne's narration, however, does not objectify the White woman.

Ashby-Jones's inability to understand Igbo culture and her actions to flouts their customs, lead to a misinterpretation of her motives by Igbo women, which results in taking her as hostage. The episode of her imposing presence at the time of child-birth, brings out her disrespect towards the beliefs of Igbo people which restrict strangers to Igbo society to be present during child-births. Taking into account such dominating nature of Western anthropologists, Minh-ha writes:

> The anthropologist-nativist who seeks to perforate meaning by forcing his entry into the Other's personal realm undertakes the desperate task of filling in all the fissures that would reveal the emptiness of knowledge.... this knowledgeable man spends his time spying on the natives, in fear of missing any of these precious moments where the latter would be caught unaware, therefore still living. The more indiscreet the research, the greater the value of its revelation (68).

Ashby-Jones's repeated interrogation of Igbo women regarding their ways of life is devoid of an intention to appreciate the rich variety of language, to recognize the nature of governance among them where hierarchy is not maintained. Her study is based on a *misreading* of Igbo customs. The novel subverts the discourse of the White anthropologist, through Nne-nne's lens of portrayal of the White anthropologist. Ashby-Jones caricatures Igbo women, portraying their culture with a lens of condescension; but Nne-nne provides a portrait of Ashby-Jones without an attempt to demean her culture. Ajuzia recalls Nne-nne's account:

> ..."She asked questions and more questions and wrote everything in her notebook. The story by everyone who met her was that she was so busy writing in her notebook that she had no chance to hear what was said

---

[7] Igbo people consider counting them as an insult to them, since they are not animals to be numbered.

> to her..."
>
> Nne-nne then began sketching a caricature of Mrs. Ashby-Jones in the act of writing, sitting square and erect on a backchair, a notebook open on her lap, a slowly waving Oriental fan in her left hand, her right hand moving furiously across the pages of her notebook... (89-90).

Nne-nne's portraiture brings out the disinterested approach of the anthropologist towards

Igbo culture. Everyone was struck by the way and speed with which she wrote, and "they bemoaned how little she listened to them when they tried to convey to her 'the burden of life' that was falling too heavily on them" (Brodzki 214). She is questioned back by Igbo women, but one finds that there is no tendency to objectify her culture:

> ... they [Igbo women] began to ask her questions:
>
> Did women in her country take titles? ...
>
> Again they wanted to know why she had really come to them, whether she was a spy from the Government, sent out to probe their feelings....
>
> Was it true that White men liked to suck their wives' lips? ... Was it true that White women had no milk in their breasts and that was why they fed their babies cow's milk? ... What was the grief of her life—the things she suffered as a woman and a wife? Did other women look down on her because she did not have a child? (94-95).

There is a strong Igbo worldview when village women question Ashby-Jones, but no tendency to—as Ashby-Jones does—study her "in a *systematic* and *scientific* way" (95). They do not have a condescending attitude towards her culture and ways of life. On the contrary, Ashby-Jones's notes in her diary stand as an epitome of the incomprehension of a Western anthropologist.

Western anthropology and feminist studies[8] relate issues concerning gender applicable to their society, to other parts of the world as well, claiming them as "universal," thereby denying the culture-specific differences; as Oyewumi (2011) points out:

> Gender is first, and foremost, a cultural construct. As such, it is intelligible only in a cultural frame; any theory of gender, therefore, must be attentive to the fact that there are many cultures in the world and Western culture is only one of them. Thus any claim made on the basis of studies in one culture cannot necessarily hold true for other cultures and should not be universalized (Oyewumi, 2011: 1050).

Therefore, diverse cultures with their varied societal patterns must be taken into account to develop *theories* of gender. Echewa questions the discourse which issues from Ashby-Jones' notes, thereby challenging Western anthropological discourse which denies to open up a space for the cultural specificities of divergent cultures. Kaur highlights the fact that: "By problematizing the ethnographic gaze, the text [*I Saw the Sky Catch Fire*] initiates a reconciliatory dialogue between the skepticism and distrust of 'Third World' women and the condescension and incomprehension of the western feminist" (2).

There is a reversal of power dynamics when Ashby-Jones is taken hostage, and is dressed like Igbo women, to keep her in disguise. Ashby-Jones is subjected to repeated questioning by Okwere-ke-diya. Echewa reveals how "Okwere-ke-diya questions the 'selfless' pursuit of knowledge that Ashby-Jones espouses and instead suggests that closer attention needs to be paid to the cultural practices and problems in the home country than those of far flung peoples or places, thus undermining ethnography's Enlightenment idealism" (Kaur 8). Her diary containing ethnographic notes is torn

---

[8] I do not speak of all feminist studies originated in the West here, but it is with respect to a major body of feminist studies in nineteenth and twentieth centuries written in the West about "Third World" women. As Kaur writes: "While it is true that in recent years feminist studies in the west have become more sensitive in engaging in a meaningful dialogue with 'third world' women, their overriding perspective and attitude still tends to be largely patronizing and condescending" (2).

apart, which symbolizes "the destruction of a whole discursive tool, a colonial discourse aimed at normalizing inequitable power relations between the West and its colonized subjects" (Kaur 7). However, she is not caused any harm, for Igbo women embrace her as woman. Their strong belief in *Ndom* stops them from causing her harm; as Ugbala says: "Anyway, she is a woman. And that tangles her around our necks, arms, and waists. We have no choice except to let her go. But we must drink the wine of union with her. We must swear with her" (216). The act of drinking the "wine of union" and swearing with her—a woman from a society different to their own—questions the supercilious attitude of Ashby-Jones, as is highlighted in their oaths:

> 'Let her feel our grief!'
> 'Let her feel Woman's Grief!'
> 'If she writes, let her write the truth about us!'
> 'If she speaks, let her speak the truth about us!' . . . (217)

This encounter with the Western anthropologist in the novel brings out Echewa's "quality of sheer imaginative penetration, the capacity to fathom the inner subjective lives of persons of another age, sex or race . . ." (Wright, "T. O. Echewa" 263). He opens out questions which rethink histories to question issues in the present: "Why can't people from different cultures treat each other with respect? Why is it always a necessity to consider some cultures as superior and others inferior?" (Interview).[9]

### *Woman to Man*

The second part of the novel focuses on Stella, the grand daughter-in-law of Nne-nne, and questions some of the patriarchal notions nurtured by men. Ajuzia faces the critical questions posed by Stella and Nne-nne, challenging his patriarchal veil of authority. Here, one finds that the subjugation of women has not only been highlighted by Western theorists of

---

[9] The comment has been made by the author in a personal interview, which is yet to be published.

gender but is also witnessed in the once-colonized parts of the world. It is important in this context, to point out that: "The fact that Western gender categories are presented as inherent in nature (of bodies) and operate on a dichotomous, binarily opposed male/female, man/woman duality in which the male is assumed to be superior and therefore the defining category, is particularly alien to many African cultures" (Oyewumi, "Conceptualizing Gender" 4).

With regard to the condition of women in the diverse cultures of Africa, most of the gender theorists in Africa have highlighted the fact that distinctions among the categories of male/female, men/women, have been made during and after the rule of the Empire. They have highlighted the dualism inherent in Igbo cosmology, which opens out equal space for men as well as women; and attribute the import of patriarchal societal structure from that of the colonizers. Chinyere Ukpokolo highlights how the kolanut (*oji*) ritual emphasizes a philosophy of life where men and women gain an equal state of importance: ". . . the invocation of the Earth goddess in the ritual creates space for female participation and involvement. Her position, role and the fact that she must, of necessity, be included, ensures a voice for the Igbo woman in peacemaking. . . . The kolanut aims at perpetuating peace, love, and unity" (172). Also, in the use of *ofo*[10] while performing rituals, she brings out the necessity to invoke the Earth goddess, which is symbolic of "the female representation," and "[i]n this interconnectedness, man and woman engage in mutual participation in peace building processes" (178).

Sabine Jell-Bahlsen has talked about the Igbo belief in the supreme authority of the Mother, as expressed in the Igbo word *Nneka*: "One of Igbo civilization's core values was expressed in the name, *Nneka*, Mother is Supreme. . . . illuminates the Igbo respect for motherhood. Furthermore, the importance of female kinship links is expressed in Igbo proverbs such as, 'when in trouble, run to your mother's home' . . ." ("*Nneka*" 202). Oyewumi

---

[10] "Ofo . . . an instrument of traditional peacebuilding among the Nanka Igbo, is made of a stick or pieces of sticks of Detarium senegalense tree tied together. . . . The ofo stick or staff is employed in serious discussions and in taking serious family or community decisions that are especially intended to be binding on every member of the family or community. Thus, it becomes a seal to an agreement when it is used to invoke the spirit of the ancestors and the Earth goddess. This is called the isu ofo mechanism" (Ukpokolo 176).

also brings out the non-gendered nature of Yoruba families, unlike the gendered nuclear families in Western countries.[11] The intrusion of colonial culture with an aim to disrupt the culture of the colonized, has led to "imposed class and sex stratification," which has denied space to "group solidarity," and "shared political authority," hardly leaving out space for women (Allen 75). Oyewumi's words in this regard are extremely significant to consider:

> . . . the colonial state was also a male-dominant state; colonial racism and colonial sexism were intertwined in complex ways. The European colonizers not only had favorite races and "tribes"; they also had a favorite gender. . . . Africa's colonization by Europeans in a sense was a gift to white people, and a boon for both white and African men, albeit in varying degrees. For the colonizers and their inheritors, it is a gift that keeps on giving. However, for African men, it is a toxic gift. And alas, those who would transform Africa are also the class and gender beneficiaries of the colonial state. This is at the core of why male dominance continues to gain footholds and to expand in our current dispensation. . . . ("Decolonizing the Intellectual" 29-30)

She emphasizes the internalization of a dominating patriarchal worldview of the West by African cultures and societies, which needs to be done away with. Even, the African cultural traditions and proverbs turn out to be gendered when translated into English, resulting in a misinterpretation of the traditions.[12]

Ukpokolo points out that the Igbo kolanut ritual has been patriarchalized after colonial intervention, due to the "omission of the Earth goddess," signifying "the denial of the female position and voice . . ." (175). Jell-Bahlsen too has questioned the Christian construction of Igbo culture, and underlines how the Church has played an important role in disgracing women healers by calling them witches. It is the implementation of the societal structure of the Victorian England in Igbo society, which has been

[11] See Oyewumi, "Conceptualizing Gender."

[12] See Oyewumi, "Decolonizing the Intellectual," 19-21.

responsible for the loss of space for women outside the domestic sphere (Allen 80). Questioning such tendencies to inferiorize women, giving rise to an unequal gender structure in society, Jell-Bahlsen repeatedly highlights the Igbo worldview which "calls for mutual tolerance ... social equilibrium and mutual respect" ("*Nneka*" 217).

In fact, very interestingly, T. Akachi Ezeigbo, propounds her theory of "Snail Sense Womanism," pertaining to the specific condition of Igbo society after colonization, and calls for mutual cooperation and collaboration between men and women. Ezeigbo writes: "My own gender theory, Snail Sense Womanism, is 'a strategy that allows women to collaborate and cooperate with men to bring about social change, even as a snail 'collabrates' and 'cooperates' with rocks, boulders and thorns in its journey to accomplish its destiny in life.' ..." (198). Echewa in his novel *I Saw the Catch Fire* too, questions the dominating tendency of men which results in misunderstanding and misreading of each other in husband-wife relationship.

His novel opens with the first person narrative of the eve of Ajuzia's departure to America to get a university degree, followed by his homecoming, when he returns to find Nne-nne in death-bed, and his wife Stella pregnant by another man. When he refuses to accept Stella as his wife anymore, Nne-nne unveils the predicament of a woman in the absence of her husband for a long period of five years immediately after marriage, and thereafter questions his indifference even to write letters regularly. Echewa brings forth the wars which Stella continually needs to fight against Ajuzia, at the brink of Nigeria's independence, in 1959. Even after their marriage and the birth of their daughter W'Orima, Ajuzia initially fails to understand the dilemmas of Stella. The incomprehensibility of a man to comprehend a woman's dilemmas, is highlighted by Stella: "Man come and man go. As you and I sit here and now, I believe you mean everything you say, but what about tomorrow? ..." (251). Ajuzia, at certain moment, does discern the bindings which are forced on a woman, bindings disguised under the veneer of responsibility as mother and wife; while it is a man who is always free to leave:

> ... The man was always free to come and go as he chose, and nothing limited him except his own willingness to stay. A woman did not have the same choices. A woman never left. Could I imagine, for example, that

> she, Stella, would leave me and W'Orima while she went overseas? No, if parenthood was a funeral, then a man was only a guest mourner. . . . (256)

But he refuses to accept her as his wife anymore on finding her pregnant. Nne-nne and Stella's mother challenges the tendency of a man to question women's activities without taking a critical look into those of his own. Nne-nne's words to Ajuzia actually question his chauvinistic attitude towards Stella:

> ". . . Together we all wondered what had become of you, why you did not make a way for her [Stella] to join you, as you had promised . . . Did you forget her? Did you forget all of us? . . ."
>
> ". . . for five years a young woman like her endured life without a husband. The child she was nursing when you left home became weaned. . . . If her affection for you was not deep, she would have been long gone by now." (274)

She points out how men are entitled to enter into relationship with many women, but the same fails to happen for women.

The novel constantly turns back the gaze on Ajuzia as a husband and his disregard of Stella's dilemmas. In a moment of conversation with Stella's mother, Ajuza is questioned about his inability to perform the duties of a husband towards his wife, and is blamed for failing to take up the responsibility of his wife and daughter. When Ajuzia cross-questions her if she justifies Stella's pregnancy, she speaks up against the sham veil of authority which a man seems to put up, claiming his innocence, and inflicting blame on his wife: ". . . what she did was not the only wrong thing that has been done. I cannot sit here and indulge your wounded innocence or discuss with you how much Stella has offended you and therefore how angry you have a right to be. No. . . ." (297). Stella's attempted suicide, her loss of pregnancy, and Nne-nne's words of wisdom, imbibe within him a sense of realization of Stella's perspectives, and her sufferings. Stella highlights the fact that his taking up a lover in the United States would never have been a trouble, since "it is different for a man to have a woman on the side than it is for a woman to have man" (300).

Later, when Ajuzia decides to return back to the United States, and insists on Stella accompanying him, she refuses to abandon her roots, recalling the histories woven together by Nne-nne, making Stella very much a part of the histories of the village, of the family: ". . . I feel a part of the history of your family because Nne-nne filled me full of it, and made me a member of it, and showed me where W'Orima and I were joined to it. . . . I cannot simply stumble along behind you . . ." (318). Brodzki upholds that: " Female ingenuity, courage, autonomy, and survival in the face of male impotence and unreliability are the dominant strands of this particular discourse [by Nne-nne]" (210). Her decision to stay back echoes the spirit of Nne-nne who has always declined to leave her compound, also "persuading her husband Aju, not to turn an ethnographic gaze upon his own culture" (Kaur 17).

The novel, by bringing out the predicament of two women from generations apart, by bringing out encounters between Igbo women and a Western anthropologist, and that between a wife and a husband, does not merely highlight women's resistance to Western incomprehensibility or male dominance, but *questions the very moment of encounter* between people with divergent perspectives and ideologies.

## *Conclusion: When Stories Reshape Identities*

The question—asked in the first section of this chapter—keeps haunting: What happens when disparate thoughts and stories meet each other, standing face to face? What happens at those *moments of encounter*? Looking back at Chakrabarty's exposition regarding the inter-relation among "thought" and "place," one can very well say that one's thoughts and stories, relating to the histories of one's place of origin, shape one's self, as well as shape one's perspective regarding the existence of other divergent places and cultures with multifarious histories. When people from such diverse cultures, or those from the same culture with contrasting views meet, it is that *very moment of encounter* which *reshapes* the selves, identities, at the same time, questioning the politics of such perplexed encounters, which forces one to engage in a critical reading of one's own self along with that of the other. The perpetual process of "being and becoming," of preserving one's self yet transforming one's self, entails a healthy engagement in dialogue with each other, a means of bridging discordant views of each other, questioning the absence of mutual respect and understanding.

To conclude with Chinua Achebe, talking about the differences between human beings and cultures throughout the world, and highlighting the need to rethink the space one needs to open out for another fellow human being:

> . . . the Bantu declaration "Umuntu ngumuntu ngabantu" represents an African communal aspiration: "A human is human because of other humans." Our humanity is contingent on the humanity of our fellows. No person or group can be human alone. . . . If we learned that lesson even this late in the day, we would have taken a truly millennial step forward (166).

### *References*

Achebe, C. 2009. *Africa is People: The Education of a British-Protected Child*. London: Penguin Classics: 155-166.

Allen, J. Van. 1976. 'Aba Riots' or Igbo 'Women's War'?: Ideology, Stratification, and the Invisibility of Women." *Women in Africa*. In: *Studies in Social and Economic Change*.

Hafkin, N. J. and Bay, E. G. (Eds). Stanford: Stanford University Press: 59-86.

Asad, T. 1990. The Concept of Cultural Translation in British Social Anthropology. *Writing Culture. In: The Poetics and Politics of Ethnography*. James C. and Marcus, G. E. (Eds). Delhi: Oxford University Press: 141-164.

Brodzki, B. 1999. History, Cultural Memory, and the Tasks of Translation in I Saw the Sky Catch Fire. PMLA 114.2 (1999): 207-220. Jstor. Web. 12 Dec. 2010.

Chakrabarty, Dipesh. Preface to the 2007 Edition. Provincializing Europe: Postcolonial Thought and Historical Difference. New Delhi: Oxford University Press.

Dallmyr, Fred. 2010.Dialogue Community as a Promising Path to Global Justice. WPF Dialogue of Civilizations. 22 October 2010. Web. 14 Dec. 2011. <http://Anwesha Das 233| www.wpfdc.org/index.php?option=com_content&view=article&id=281%3Adialo gue-community-as-a-promising-path-to-global-justice&catid=40%3Aanalytical- materials&Itemid=100&lang=en>

Echewa, T.Obinkaram. I Saw the Sky Catch Fire. New York: Dutton, 1992.

Ezeigbo, T. A. 2011. Gender Sensitivity and the Role of Umuada in Conflict Resolution. *Against All Odds. In: The Igbo Experience in Postcolonial Nigeria*. Nwauwa, A. O. and Okorieh, C. J. (Eds.). New Jersey: Goldine and Jacobs Publishing. 189-200.

Geertz, Clifford. 2000. *The Interpretation of Cultures*. New York: Basic Books.

Jell-Bahlsen, S. 2011. Nneka: Is Mother Still Supreme in Igboland? Reflections on the Biography of Eze Mmiri, Madame Martha Mberekpe of Orsu-Obodo, Oguta, 1934-2007. *Against All Odds*. In: *The Igbo Experience in Postcolonial Nigeria*. Nwauwa, A. O. and Okorieh, C. J. (Eds.). New Jersey: Goldine and Jacobs Publishing: 201-224.

Kaur, R. Challenging the Ethnographic Gaze of Western Feminism: Colonial Discourse and the Politics of Representation. In: *I Saw the Sky Catch Fire*. 1-22. Unpublished manuscript by courtesy of the author.

Minh-ha, T. T. 1989. *Woman, Native, Other: Writing Postcoloniality and Feminism*. Bloomington: Indiana University Press.

Oyewumi, O. 2004. Conceptualizing Gender: The Eurocentric Foundations of Feminist Concepts and the Challenge of African Epistemologies. *African Gender Scholarship: Concepts, Methodologies and Paradigms*. Vol.1. Dakar: CODESRIA: 1-8. Knowledge4empowerment.wordpress.com. Web. 14 Jan. 2012.

_______1998. "De-Confounding Gender: Feminist Theorizing and Western Culture: A Comment on Hawkesworth's 'Confounding Gender.' *Signs* 23.4 (1998): 1049 - 1062. Jstor. Web. 24 Nov. 2011.

________ 2011. "Decolonizing the Intellectual and the Quotidian: Yorubá Scholars(hip) and Male Dominance." *Gender Epistemologies in Africa: Gendering Traditions, Spaces, Social Institutions, and Identities*. Oyewumi, O. (Ed.). New York: Palgrave Macmillan: 9-33.

Pratt, Mary Louise.1990. Fieldwork in Common Places. Writing Culture: In:The Poetics andPolitics of Ethnography. Clifford, J. and Marcus, G. E. (Eds.). Delhi: Oxford University Press: 27-50.

Thiong'o, Ngũgĩ wa. 2012. *Globalectics*. New York: Columbia University Press.

Ukpokolo, C. 2011. Gender, Symbols and Traditional Peacemaking among the Nanka-Igbo of South-Eastern Nigeria. *Human Affairs* 21: 163-183.

Wright, D. 1997. T. O. Echewa: A Neglected Novelist. In: *Contemporary African Fiction*.

Wright, D. (Ed.). Bayreuth: Bayreuth African Studies Breitinger. 254-263.

# Chapter Twelve

## GENDER ADVOCACY IN AFRICA: INSIGHTS FROM IFÁ LITERARY CORPUS

*Omotade Adegbindin*

### *Introduction*

The question of the status of women in Africa has attracted the attention of scholars from different academic persuasions. The reason for this can be drawn against the background of the intensifying demands and struggles for gender equality in the society. Again, the place of women in Africa has become one of the most disputatious issues in recent times partly because of the keen struggle between the old African values and the new European values. Regrettably, a review of the literature of the West on feminism and several publications on the place of women in Africa all point to a mis-representation of the status of the African woman. A good reading of the most radical Western feminist critics, especially, reveals the contentious view that the African man is directly responsible for the problems of the African woman and, therefore, "women and men in contemporary African society are at war with one another" (Frank, 1987: 24). This paper jettisons this notion of African authenticity that guarantees male authority and exploitation of the African woman by the African man; the paper shows that African pre-colonial understanding of the relationship between men and women is nothing short of gender complementarity. Though African societies are frequently essentialised as communal and incompatible with gender equality or individual rights, it is our contention here that pre-colonial Yorùbá (African) culture had clear visions of gender relations that marginalized women, there also existed clear visions of gender relations that challenge the promotion of "the notion that men and women are different and unequal, with men being innately superior and, thus, in positions of authority" (Wyrod, 2008: 806). The paper draws from the *Ifá* literary corpus to recommend a complementarist agenda rather than separatist approach in gender advocacy in Africa.

### *Gender Issues in Africa*

The term "gender" is not a given at birth; it refers to the "non-physiological aspects of sex, a group of attributes and or behavior, shaped by society and culture, that are defined as appropriate for the male sex or the female sex" (Nfah-Abbenyi, 2005: 258). Gender identity intervenes through the development of the individual sexes. It must be noted that several issues have been subsumed under the discourse of gender both in the West and in African thought systems. Some feminists have argued that gender issues are concerns about the disparity between male and female sexuality; some others have identified the importance of mothering and family relations. Some feminists argue that gender is a social and/or cultural process involving a complex set of relations that inevitably interlock with other relations of age, race, class, ethnicity, ideology, and so on (Ibid.: 259).

It is argued that African women assume roles or duties similar to that of men or at the same level with men in Africa. It has also been contended that "biological categories are misleading in studying sex and gender since either sex can assume socially viable roles as male or female" (Steady, 2004:49). Another position on gender issues by some African writers is the rejection of the notion of gender in African thought. Oyeronke Oyewumi, among others, argues that gender must not be taken at face value. This is because feminism or gender issues are articulated based on Eurocentric form of stratification of the nuclear family set up. Using linguistic criteria of the Yorùbá, she argues that this does not conform with the social reality in Africa for the African society is not gender-classed (Oyewumi 1997:30).

To a very large extent, as scholars such as Acholonu (1995) have noted, most of the problems facing the African woman resulted from the intrusion of Western ideologies and socio-political systems in the colonized African societies. Nevertheless, in spite of the existed and existing complementarities between the two gender divides in Africa, gender stratification and discrimination have certain relative reality in our present society and therefore cannot be outrightly waved as being singularly a Western or colonial agenda which does not require concrete attention. This notwithstanding, it is significant to note here also that radical definition of feminism with the agenda of liberating women for women only, shows an attitude that does not conform to the African society.

The idea of feminism in African thought connotes a social transformation agenda that encompasses women's self-consciousness, self-expression or conditions of struggle. It addresses the needs of present African women in relation to their indigenous culture, which realizes their social well-being. Gender issues, especially those in relation to woman advancement campaign, have remained a global concern since the 1923 Santiago League of Nations. The codification of women affairs in the United Nations' founding documents in 1946 contributed also to increased world consciousness and sensitivity to issues affecting women. In this regard, gender-related problems encountered by females in Africa include oppression, alienation and invincibility both in historical records and in the society. These necessitate the need to emphasize their relevance, self-esteem and freedom within the African cultural context. This does not, however, imply an agenda to usurp the relevance of the males in the society nor their exploitation to the advantage of the African females. The need for a discourse on gender issues arises out of concern about certain unethical and inhumane acts against the female based largely on their femininity. These actions have been tagged gender-based violence. The word "violence" can be associated with acts of oppression, injustice and domination (Akintunde, 1999:122). Violence against women is in different ways and includes: assault – which means injury or fear of injury; kidnapping- unlawful removal or confinement; false imprisonment; sexual assault (rape)… (Ibid.:123). These can be grouped into physical and psychological actions.

The discriminatory acts against females are in diverse forms and, despite published works and presentations, they are still predominant in our society. In relation to education, it must be mentioned that this problem has been succumbed relatively in major urban areas in Nigeria. For instance, despite the educational opportunities available, career choices for females are not without gender coloration. Also, in rural areas, the level of convictions for female child education is still at low ebbs. This calls for proper dissemination of information, awareness of the importance of literacy to all irrespective of gender difference, which would in turn have its impact on the society. This calls for a revisit and reconsideration of the age-long barrier based on responsibility for the home because nurturing and literacy activities are not mutually exclusive.

In the recent times, sex related crimes perpetrated against females have witnessed geometrical increase that even those as young as below a year old are not left out and these crimes are not necessarily carried out by strangers. In addition to this is that thousands of women are coerced or otherwise abducted into prostitution or sold through other forms of trafficking, especially children between ages 10 – 14 years. These are in turn victims of assaults, slavery and violent attacks (Mwaura and Kimani, 2009:28). The spate of these crimes calls for total embrace of principles of solidarity, relatedness, survival, creative responsibility, resistance and transformation through which the females' dignity can be restored and preserved.

The Western based political and economic structures have grossly underrepresented women in the public space, with men holding majority of official positions of power and authority. This is because of the ideology of subordination of female to male authority and superiority/status system where women showed deference to men. However, events, ideologies and codes of etiquette in pre-colonial era have shown that the present realities do not represent the initial situations of women in Africa because there are societies where women wielded considerable influence and authority like a dual-sex political systems among the Igbo of southeastern Nigeria. The consequence of this is the need for challenge of the present ideologies though not with the intent of pursuing a win-lose agenda between women and men but to make room for females' participation, to a reasonable extent, in various spheres of life.

The socio-political alienation of women, as in the above, is in contrast to what was obtainable in the past in most African societies such as the Yorùbá, Igbo, Hausa, among others. For instance, in the pre-colonial Yorùbá society, there existed societies where women were very visible as several of them ruled either directly or indirectly as *oba*s or queen mother and wielded authority and respect. These were informed by women's innate abilities rather than gender ideologies, and their relevance was in all spheres of the community: political, economic, social and religious. Even in our present society, several women have contributed immensely to the development of their society both through individual efforts as well as cooperation with others in the society. However, this does not imply that this paper intends to portray women as being superhumans as this would mean that the position of gender advocates affirms what it intends to deny.

In his discussion of women's rights in urban Uganda, Wyrod identifies gender inequality as reactionary. According to him, reactionary discourses on gender "reflect an established hegemonic masculinity and are premised on maintaining patriarchal power relations that frame men's power over women as natural and inevitable" Wyrod (2008: 809)." It must be stated, however, that the reactionary discourses on gender are assailable when one considers historical records which point to the contrary. Here, the figures of such culture heroes as Queen Idia of Benin, Queen Amina of Zaria, Moremi of Ile-Ife, to mention a few, come to mind.

The mother of Esigie, an Oba of Benin in the 16th century, Queen Idia of Benin flourished in pre-colonial Africa. History has it that she played a significant role in the rise and reign of her son. When Oba Ozolua died, he left behind two powerful heirs to the throne, Arhuaran and Esigie. Arhuaran's attempt to assassinate Esigie failed because Queen Idia mobilized an army in defence of Esigie and courageously saw her son to the throne of the Oba of Benin. Her heroic deeds did not just stop with this; a resourseful military strategist and shrewd politician, she further aided the king in defending the kingdom against the Igala invaders. These feats earned her the title of the first *Iyoba* (Queen mother) of Benin. Queen Amina was the daughter of Bakwa of Turunku, the founder of the Zazzau Kingdom in 1536. Following the death of Bakwa in 1566, the crown of Zazzau passed to Amina's brother, Karama. Their sister, Zariaya, fled the region and little was known about her. While Karama was ruling the kingdom, the young Queen Amina was busy making a great mark within the military and, in no time, rose from a mere warrior of the Zazzau military to the leader of the Zazzau cavalry. When her brother died of illness, Queen Amina assumed the reign of the kingdom. During her reign, she led several military campaigns and the kingdom expanded with several vassal states under her control. Her 34 years of reign witnessed a great military exploits, as the lands of great

Katsina and also Kano were forced to hand over levies to her. On her part, Moremi, during the development of the ancient Yorùbá city of Ile-Ife, used her ingenuity to free her people from an oppressive neighbouring community, known as the Ugbo. This attests to the fact that politics of survival in pre-colonial African societies was gender blind.

In spite of the rich African values that promoted gender balance, certain ideologies embedded in some African mythologies, proverbs, and folk tales contribute to gender discrimination experienced, and the negative images ascribed to females in the society. For instance, certain Yorùbá sayings portray females as unreliable and inconsistent:

> *Obìnrin l'ọ̀dàlẹ̀, obìnrin l'èké*: The female is a traitor, the female is a false person.
>
> *Obìnrin ò se é finú hàn*: The female cannot be trusted to keep secrets

Such identity is obviously an undue generalization about females and its truth is questionable. However, it has the importunate effect on the society for it excludes the females from holding salient positions as well as creating a limited self-perception of the females, thereby reducing the level of reliance that can be placed on them. Due to this problem, there is the need to give the proper representation of the African females. Hence the need to embark on a reorder and not a debased one; to embark on a reorder to disabuse the minds of the people in the society on the unjustified sentiment on which the African female identity is hinged and change the conscious perception of females from such cultural stance.

Furthermore, certain traditional practices and beliefs are central to the discussion of gender issues in Africa. A notable problem is the plight of widows in Africa where widows are made to carry out certain dehumanizing acts. In some quarters in Africa, a widow is allowed to possess what belonged to her husband only if she agrees to marry within the family of the deceased, a form of forced marriage. Apart from this, there is the belief that a woman who has female children only either has no assurance of the home or inheritance for her children since these are not heirs who would retain the names of the family. Despite these problems, African women still pride motherhood and womanhood and concerns about family value.

One other customary practice consists of the woman's wife status in her husband's household, which is primarily dependent on her ability to bear children to continue his patrilineage. This makes the woman to depend solely on bearing children as that is what qualifies her as a wife or woman and ensures her sustainability in the matrimonial home. This is against the backdrop that there are instances whereby a woman is blamed for not having children even though the husband may be responsible for her inability to have children due to his impotency. Also, when a child is born and the child turns out "bad" such child is said to belong to the mother while the "good" or "worthwhile" child is the father's. Added to these issues is the relegation of the female child as she is not seen as continuing the lineage; as such, a woman who has no male child is not guaranteed inheritance or sustainability in the home since she has failed to produce an heir to the family. Hence, what is required is not campaign against home-building or woman emancipation through homosexuality; rather, what is required, in line with Ndibe's thought, is that:

> The burden of the African feminist is in part to re-humanize the struggle, to suffuse old concepts with new, never before considered meanings,…to ultimately move us towards the creation, neither of a man's world nor a woman's but of a human world (Ndibe 1991:3).

The above position, therefore, calls for a genuine and all-embracing gender advocacy and non-separatist agenda. In this, feminism in the African context is a call for humane recognition for women and freedom and opportunity which requires the concerted efforts of all – male and female alike. Hence it should be noted that it is not an agenda of separation from others in the society or seen as a cry for individualism or self-centeredness, but the spirit of collective consciousness, mutual reciprocity and role sharing. This calls for emphasis on the capability, and recognition of the innate human personality of the female. Importantly also, it is necessary to incorporate the idea of concerns about males as well in gender advocacy. This would strengthen the argument against the separatist agenda that has bedevilled the feminist thoughts and also unify the gender thought system as being of concern about human and not woman.

Gender outcry about women as discussed here incorporates not a mere emphasis on acceptability in the 'public sphere' politically, but also the importance of the family and the moral responsibility of individuals in the society are germane to social development in Africa. The problems of African females can be subsumed under the wider struggle by Africans irrespective of gender to liberate themselves from domination of diverse forms. Hence, issues of feminism or gender advocacy should not be seen as an agenda to deify a gender above the other or subsuming one below the other. This has been seen in some writings whereby arguments are posed to demonstrate seeming strengths of females over and above their male counterparts. For instance, it is argued in some quarters that women possess higher psychological, metaphysical and even material powers; their beauty is power and their component can unbalance the seeming domination of men. Another of such claims is that of Iheanacho who argues that certain acts like wailing at ancestral shrine; persuasion and nagging of the husband; protest march and decree; and mass exodus of women are devices which women use to influence men thereby making the men succumb to these feminine potency and device (Iheanacho 2009: 224 – 227).

### *Ifá Literary Corpus and the Complementarist Agenda*

Today's world has also taught the falsity of the notion of naturalized male superiority. In all fields of human endeavor – medicine, arts, science, philosophy, and so on – women have recorded prodigious feats. The exigencies of today's world have also revealed that women, just as feminist critics say of men, are capable of oppressing, exploiting and even subjugating the men folk. We have, for instance, women who are breadwinners of their different families and who have used their status to gain power, not different from hegemonic masculinity or patriarchal power. *Ifá* literary corpus provides us with a canto which substantiates the foregoing. In Ìrosùn Àwòyè, *Ifá* reveals:

*Àì sọ́kùnrin lobìnrin n jogún àdá*
*A dífá fún Láyínká Òròlú, omo Ògbóyè*
*Bí ò sí ti Láyínká Òròlú, omo Ògbóyè*

*Gbogbo òsòrò ni ò bá ti run...*[1]

Meaning:

When men are not available, women inherit the cutlass
Thus, divination was undertaken for Layinka Orolu, son of Ogboye If not for
Layinka Orolu, son of Ogboye
All sacred groves would have become desolate...

The above verse relates the oppression that the men of Ògbóyè community suffered in the hands of their women. In this ancient community, women grew so strong that they occupied all the important positions in the community as farmers, smiths, hunters, warriors, heads of clans, and so on. They desecrated the shrines and forced the men to serve them as slaves. Láyínká Òròlú fought his way out of the community to a distant land where a diviner counseled him to offer certain sacrifices in order to free his people from the grips of female dominance. He did as counselled and later returned to Ògbóyè where, to his amazement, peace had returned to the land and the natives could now worship freely and engage in their various activities.

On the surface, the narrative above seems to elevate the status of masculinity and valorize its social worth, but, more importantly, it shows that men are not innately superior to women. A Yorùbá adage says that "*fọ̀tún wòsì, fòsì wọ̀tún lọwọ́ fi n mọ́*", meaning that all hands need be on deck to ensure desired results or, literally, that "both hands are to scrub one another to achieve proper cleaning". This is germane to any discourse of human relationship in ensuring a healthy society. The cry of African women advocates as avowed earlier in this paper is, indeed, an important call for justice, fairness and equity in recognizing the deplorable state of the female in the contemporary society. It is worth noting that some progress has been realized in the African society in gender advocacy and recognition. Yet, in the bid to portray the humanness of the female, there is need to de-emphasize the uniqueness of femininity. An emphasis on the uniqueness of femininity would be misinterpreted to imply a separatist technique which does not comply with the African perspective to societal relationship.

---

[1]Sourced from Mr Olusegun Ogundele, a practising Ifa Priest..

In reiterating the femininity of women, the focus need not be to forestall the woman as overly important; rather, the motif should be to demonstrate that each person has a role to play in society and no role is more important than the other. This would ensure that the role of the woman in the society will not be denigrated. The relevance of gender advocacy is not to create an idea of females who can 'do better' what men can do, but it should be to educate the society of the qualities of the female which can be harnessed without exploitation to the benefit of the society; to disabuse the minds of both genders on the assumed frailty of the female, which causes her disrespect and mistreatment in the society.

Beyond the emphasis on the concerns about the females, there is need that, in the spirit of collective consciousness of Africa, no gender should be considered as self-sufficient. Thus, gender advocacy need not be a cry for the exploitation of the masculine gender to the advantage of the female, but should be the dissemination of the abilities of the female, its distinction from certain activities that would of necessity be carried out by the males, an attitude of role sharing and mutual reciprocity. This is in line with the position of the Third World group, "Development Alternatives with Women for a New Era" (DAWN) that:

> We want a world where inequality based on class, gender and race is absent from every country ... where basic needs become basic rights ... where all institutions are open to participatory democratic processes, where women share in determining priorities and making decisions (Sen and Grown 1987: 80 – 81).

The foregoing is supported by a verse of *Ọ̀fún Méjì* in *Ifá* literary corpus:

*Ẹ w'etí adẹ́tẹ̀*
*Ẹ w'etí ọ̀dúndún;*
*Ẹ w'etípásẹ̀ ahun*
*Ẹ w'àran ọ̀pẹ*
*Gẹ́gẹ́ ni wọ́n ń kora wọn*
*Ohun tó jọ'hun laa fi ń wé'hun*
*Èpo ẹ̀pà jọ pósí ẹ̀líírí*
*A diá fún Ọ̀rúnmìlà*

*Tí lọ rèé báwọn gb'Ọ̀rọ̀-mọ̀gìmọ̀gì ni'ìyàwó*[2]

Meaning:

See the leper's ear
And the *ọ̀dúndún*, a leaf like a shapeless ear;
See the tortoise's legs
And the flowery part of the palm tree
They look convincingly similar
Similar things should go together:
The groundnut pod resembles the coffin of the smallest rat
Divination was undertaken for Ọ̀rúnmìlà
Who chose a gnome as his wife…

Once, Ọ̀rúnmìlà, because of his peculiar status in his community, decided to take Ọ̀rọ̀-mọ̀gìmọ̀gì (a gnome) as his second wife without the approval of his first wife, Ọ̀sunlẹ́yọ̀. He approached the gnome and the latter agreed to be his wife under the conditions that (i) she would not share her room with anyone; (ii) no other human being other than Ọ̀rúnmìlà would be seeing her in her room. Ọ̀rúnmìlà agreed to all her terms. Ọ̀rọ̀-mọ̀gìmọ̀gì then promised to use her divine gift to assist Ọ̀rúnmìlà in his quest to become famous if only he could stick to the terms. She soon became Ọ̀rúnmìlà's wife and Ọ̀rúnmìlà had to warn Ọ̀sunlẹ́yọ̀ seriously not to enter Ọ̀rọ̀-mọ̀gìmọ̀gì's room. At first, things were going on well and Ọ̀rúnmìlà became so famous that he divined for Alárá and Ajerò, both great kings of his time.

One day, Ọ̀rúnmìlà decided to go on another journey to divine for Ọ̀ràngún Ilé-Àga (another great king of his time). Like before, he called Ọ̀sunlẹ́yọ̀ and told her to stick to the terms; she should fetch water and keep it at Ọ̀rọ̀-mọ̀gìmọ̀gì's doorstop anytime she needed to take her bath, place her food at the doorstep whenever she wanted to eat, and so on. At a point, Ọ̀sunlẹ́yọ̀ could not bear to be a "servant" to a junior wife any longer and so she decided to flout Ọ̀rúnmìlà's warning and confront Ọ̀rọ̀-mọ̀gìmọ̀gì. One morning, Ọ̀sunlẹ́yọ̀ came to the gnome's doorstep with the impression

[2] Sourced from Mr Olusegun Ogundele, a practising Ifa Priest.

that Ọ̀rúnmìlà had arrived from his journey. She knocked the gnome's door the way and manner that Ọ̀rúnmìlà used to do. Believing it was Ọ̀rúnmìlà who was by the door, Ọ̀rọ̀-mọ̀gìmọ̀gì opened the door and was confronted by Ọ̀sunlẹ́yọ̀ who, out of anger, began to mete out a stream of invective to the displeasure of the gnome who was indeed an "ugly" creature.

A while later, however, things started going awry: Ọ̀sunlẹ́yọ̀ and her children fell sick; Ọ̀rúnmìlà's clients no longer appreciated his system of divination and even his apprentices left him to his utter dismay. Ọ̀rúnmìlà suspected that something was wrong and quickly travelled back home where he discovered what Ọ̀sunlẹ́yọ̀ had done and the consequences of her action. He later humbled himself before Ọ̀rọ̀-mọ̀gìmọ̀gì, pleading with her to show him the way out of his plight.

This narrative shows that, despite Ọ̀rúnmìlà's status as a well-versed diviner, he needed the cooperation of his two wives in order to succeed in his endeavor. The import of the narrative is, therefore, a questioning of the position of most radical Western feminist critics who argue that the African man should be seen as the enemy of the African woman and suggest the need to create a separate world of women.

### *Conclusion*

In this chapter, we have examined some differing positions on gender related issues, and much as we agreed that gender stratification and discrimination is a reality in our present society, we contended that gender issues in Africa should not be looked at from the spectacles of the Western society. Eurocentric or radical definition of feminism has the agenda of liberating women for women only such as defining African women in ideologies of domesticity. Radical feminist limits the role of the African woman to sexual and commercial labour as satisfying the sexual needs of the African man, tending to children and preparing food under somewhat harsh conditions. Therefore, as the chapter has shown, the idea of feminism in African thought connotes a social transformation agenda that encompasses women's self-consciousness, self-expression or conditions of struggle.

Against the idea of radical Western feminism, which does not recognize the need for integration and communality in African socio-cultural milieu, the paper have shown that the idea of feminism in Africa does not suggest a struggle for emancipation of women in the midst of male antagonists or accommodate notions of innate male superiority. Rather, feminism in the African context is a call for humane recognition, freedom and opportunity for women, which requires the concerted efforts of all – male and female alike. Significantly, textual evidences from *Ifá* literary corpus were drawn to show the shortcoming of the separatist agenda, which does not leave room for African men to participate in the African feminist agenda and is, therefore, not representative of the idea of feminism in Africa. *Ifá* as a repository Yorùbá philosophy provides us with an insight that the issues confronting Africa, including the problems the African woman faces, require the efforts of both genders.

### *References*

Acholonu, C. 1995. *Motherism: The Afrocentric Alternative to Feminism.* Owerri: Afa Publication.

Akintunde, D.O. 1999. Violence against Women: Threat to Nigerian Society. *Orita: Ibadan Journal of Religious Studies*, Vol. XXXI, No. 1: 122 – 133.

Frank, K. 1987. Women Without Men: The Feminist Novel in Africa.

E.D. Jones, E. Palmer and M. Jones (Eds.). *Women in African Literature Today.* Trenton, N.J: African World Press: 14 – 34.

Iheanacho, N. 2009. Cultural Patterns of Gender Checks-and-Balances in Africa and Women's Influence on Men: The Etche Paradigm. *Journal of Intra-African Studies*, No. 2.

Kolawole, E.M. 1997. *Womanism and African Consciousness.* New Jersey: African World Press.

Mwaura, P. and Kimani, E. 2009. Gender-Based Violence: A Pastoral Challenge for the Church in Africa. *Orita: Ibadan Journal of Religious Studies*, Vol. XLI, No. 1: 23-36.

Ndibe, O. 1991. *African Commentary.* Amherst, Mass.

Nfah-Abbenyi, J.M. 2005. Gender, Feminist Theory and Postcolonial (Women's) Writing. *African Gender Studies: A Reader.* Oyewumi, O. (Eds) New York: Palgrave Macmillan: 259 – 278.

Oyewumi, O. 1997. *The Invention of Women: Making an African Sense of Western Gender Discourses.* Minneapolis: University of Minnesota Press.

Sen, G. and Grown, C. 1987. *Development Crises and Alternative Visions.*

New York: Monthly Review.

Steady, F.C. 2004. An Investigative Framework for Gender Research in Africa in the New Millennium. In *African Gender Scholarship: Concepts, Methodologies and Paradigms*. Dakar: CODESRIA: 42 – 60.

Wyrod, R. 2008. Between Women's Rights and Men's Authority: Masculinity and Shifting Discourses of Gender Difference in Urban Uganda, Gender and Society. 22. No. 6 .

# *Conclusion*

A book of contributions of this nature has the advantage of presenting diverse thematic and contextual perspectives and in the process offering the reader the opportunity of understanding the subject matter from diverse angles in one text. When such anthology focuses on the intersections of gender, culture and identity, and at different historical epoch; on the way men and women define themselves and are defined by diverse peoples and cultures across time and space, the book further privileges itself above a single authored text. This collection of chapters, I believe, has achieved this privilege. The discussions presented in this anthology primarily focus on 'being' as a state, defined by sex identity, and how this identity shifts, assuming diverse meanings in disparate societies and contexts over time. The text is also about how the perception of the self in cultural and historical contexts has informed actions and at some other times shaped interpretations given to historical facts. Changing economic realities also shape the definitions and constructions of social and relational issues in Sub-Saharan Africa. Indeed, African history is not complete without a recollection of how Islamic religion, colonial encounters and Christian missionary activities have shaped the worlds of the peoples of the region and impacted on gender relations.

But, before these trajectories, what were those structural imbalances that defined women's subordinating positionality in specific contexts? Elizabeth Kyazike and Oluwakemi Abiodun Adeisina in Chapters Four and Five respectively examined women's lack of involvement in political participation in specific cultural contexts, and those indigenous social structures that ensure and resist change. Kyazike's position that women's domestiticty is foregrounded in her socialization, and this has resisted modernity in

Muganda society of Uganda, while for the Ikale Yoruba women of southwest Nigeria, modernity has not succeeded in changing the way Ikale women perceive their place in society. Silence therefore prevails and defines women's attitude to their subordination in these contexts. Chapters Two and Three of this collection raise the question of validity of representation, and the politics of knowledge production. And so, for Sabine Jell-Bahsen, women's involvements in owu masquerade among the riverine Igbo of southeast Nigeria have been under-theorised, and subsequently women are presented as victims, passive participants. One of the issues that emerged from the paper is that a mis-representation or inadequate interpretation of a cultural practice can give rise to a misconception. A similar position is sustained by Akwi in his problematisation of modernity and migration in colonial Cameroun. Women's role as the conduit of modernity and participants in the evolution of modernity through migration deserves a reinterpretation, which Walter Gam Nkwi's paper achieved. In similar vein, the identity of Muslim women of northern Nigeria through three historical epochs reveals that Islam has not always subjugated women but that men have thwarted the process to their advantage. Aisha Balarabe Bawa's position is that the subjugation of women in Hausaland is men's attempt to privilege their position rather than following the dictates of Islam.

Technological innovation shapes culture and at the same time re-structures gender relations. In Orile-Owu, southwest Nigeria, the employment of technology in palm oil production, culturally structure the roles of men and women, and define their identities in the rural Orile-Owu community. Cultural construction of masculinity changes with the economic down turn in specific Sub-Saharan African societies. Among the members of rural community in patriarchal Nanka society, Igbo southeast Nigeria, men's inability to provide for the household reshapes cultural construction of masculinity as women in such households assume the responsibility of bread winners. Rural Igbo women's reinvention of long distance trading involves travelling across regions of Nigeria, and transforming such women into major bread winners in their households, and subsequently redefining women's identity. Cultural boundaries shift to accommodate the new realities. Women gain power of decision-making at the household level without commensurate power shift at the public spaces for such women. In some societies in Africa, religion plays a crucial role in determining the level of women's participation in politics. In Zimbabwe, Tapiwa Praise Mapuranga notes that Christianity and African Traditional Religion have highly influenced women's participation in politics in the country. [delete 'change is also partly instrumentalised by religion and defines women's participation in diverse sectors such as politics in Zimbabwe, as Tapiwa Praise Mapuranga's paper has revealed'.

Kwame Edwin Otu's exploration of how homosexuality and homo-erotism came to be repackaged as 'un-African' through the re-reading of African Holocaust, noted that homosexuality has existed in Africa (Uganda) prior to colonial contact. Otu's position is that homosexuality had long existed in Africa prior to colonial contact. The conclusion that can be drawn from the paper is that the portrayal of some Western countries as sexually superior and inclusive, while Africa is constructed as 'homophobic', particularly in reference to Uganda, represents a mis-interpretation of history. Anwesha Das's, paper provides an answer to what happens in moments of encounter as she rethinks 'moments of encounter' and the inter-relations among "thought" and "place". For her, when people from diverse cultures, or those from similar culture with contrasting views meet, it is that very moment of encounter which reshapes their selves, their identities, at the same time, questioning the politics of such perplexed encounters, which forces one to engage in a critical reading of one's own self along with that of the other. For Das, this is healthy as an engagement in dialogue with each other helps in bringing discordant views into focus and leads to mutual respect and understanding, even among different genders. It is in the light this that Omotade Adegbindin's paper titled "Gender Advocacy in Africa: Insights from Ifá Literary Corpus" recommends a paradigm shift in gender advocacy in Africa, and suggests inclusiveness in gender advocacy. Such a shift, he argues, promotes a human, rather than a woman agenda, and discourages any separatist agenda to resolving gender issues in Africa. Such balanced advocacy will help in resolving not only gender issues, but also impacts on the search for possible solutions to the problems confronting the African woman on the one hand, and Africa on the other, which requires the efforts of both genders.

'Being' and 'becoming' are a 'state' and a 'process' respectively, and involve the preservation and transformation of the self and meanings ascribed to that self in a social context. Undoubtedly, gender dynamics in Sub-Saharan

Africa is a product of cultural encounters and cultural reproductions, and the changing cultural paradigms they initiate. Not in all cases and circumstances, however, have these brought about the expected change or in fact brought a change at all. In some situations, resistance to change continues to emanate from within and define identity, while in some others, a shift is successfully carried through. Receptivity and resistance are the two ends of the continuum within which gender identities are constructed.

In sum, the contributions of the authors whose works are included in this collection evidenced some of the ways women and men and critical discourses on issues that pertain to gender, culture and identity in disparate societies in the sub-Saharan African societies, including their 'being', and at other times, their 'becoming', are constructed.

# *Notes on Contributors*

**Abosede Priscilla Ipadeola** lectures in the Department of Philosophy, University of Ibadan, Nigeria. Her areas of specialisation include: Gender Studies, Social and Political Philosophy, Ethics and Epistemology. She attended the Gender Institute of Council for the Development of Social Science Research in Africa (CODESRIA) in June 2010. She also attended the Gender Mainstreaming workshop at the University of Ibadan in August 2010. She holds a Ph.D in feminist theory and social and political Philosophy.

**Kwame Edwin Otu Kwame** is a Ph.D student in Anthropology at Syracuse University, with a certificate in Women's and Gender Studies. He is also a Carter Woodson Fellow (2014-2016) at the University of Virginia. Kwame's dissertation, which is titled, 'Reluctantly Queer: Sassoi and the Shifting Paradigms of Masculinity and Sexual Citizenship in Postcolonial Ghana' is underway and should soon be nearing completion.

**Anwesha Das** holds a Ph.D in English Literature from the English and Foreign Languages, University Hyderabad, India. anwesha.english@gmail.com Presently an Assistant Professor (Jr.) in the Department of English at VIT University, Chennai, India. She is interested in teaching and researching in varied areas related to literatures in English. Her research interests focus on postcolonial studies, and African literature in English. Apart from presenting quite a few papers in national and international conferences in India and abroad—such as the Igbo Studies Association, USA, and MELUS/MELOW, India— her articles based on postcolonial literatures have been published in international journals like *Igbo Studies Review; Subaltern Speak: An International Journal of Postcolonial Studies;* and *Language in India*. Her interview of the African author Thomas Obinkaram Echewa will be published in *Research in African Literatures*, 45.1 (2014). A few of her poems have been published in the online journal *Muse India*. She has been a member of the Igbo Studies Association, USA, and *Muse India*.

**Sabine Jell-Bahlsen,** Ph.D, is an anthropologist, writer and documentary film maker, Director, *Ogbuide Films;* Former Editor-in-Chief, *Dialectical Anthropology*; studies African Cultures with a focus on Igbo Culture. Her particular interests are socio-economic and political organization, gender studies, art and spirituality, as well as cultural transformation. Her ethnography is based on long-term field research that includes participant observation and oral literature translations in specific Riverine Igbo communities, began with her initial introduction to the area by Prof. Ikenna Nzimiro in 1978, developed in conversations with Flora Nwapa and other authors and scholars, and is further expanded, updated and supplemented by library, archival and literary research. Her publications include a book on *Mammy Water in Igbo Culture* (Ezu Books, 2014), *The Water Goddess in Igbo Cosmology* (Africa World Press, 2008), numerous articles in anthologies, refereed journals and African Profile magazine, as well as several documentary films, among them *Mammy Water: In Search of the Water Spirits in Nigeria* (1989) and *Owu: Chidi Joins the Okoroshi Secret Society* (1991).

As Editor-in-Chief of the Journal, *Dialectical Anthropology*, I have edited and published in cooperation with Dr. Chudi Uwazurike a "Special Triple Issue, In Memory of Six Eminent Igbo Scholars." (31) 1-3, 2007. I have taught at the *Rhode Island School of Design*, RI, USA; at the *Papua New Guinea University of Technology*; and at *Ball State University*, Indiana, USA; I have curated exhibitions of Artifacts from Papua New Guinea in Germany, and presently serve on the editorial board of refereed journals, consult with publishers and exhibitors, and review candidates for publication. Her current research interest centres on socio-cultural transformations and their artistic expressions, such as in architecture, landscape and masquerade performances. Sabinejb@aol.com ; www.sabinejb.com Phone: +1-646-2398519 (USA); +49(0)8054-302 (Germany)

**Walter Gam Nkwi** holds a Ph.D in Social History/Social Anthropology from the Universiteit Leiden, The Netherlands, and teaches at Department of History, University of Buea, Cameroon. He has published quite widely in peer review journals, books and book chapters. His latest book is *University Crisis and Student Protests in Africa: The 2005-2006 University Students' Strike in Cameroon* Dr. Nkwi was a senior researcher in the International Institute of Social History, Amsterdam from September 2012 to February 2013. He also held public lectures in the University of Africa at the Department of History, University of Buea, Cameroon. (www.ubuea.net) Dr. Nkwi has a passion for social, indigenous conflict management, cultural history and global labour historical issues of Africa. E- mail:nkwiwally@yahoo.com

**Chinyere Ukpokolo** holds a Ph.D in African Studies (Anthropology) from the Institute of African Studies, University of Ibadan, Ibadan, Nigeria, and teaches in the Department of Archaeology and Anthropology, University of Ibadan, Nigeria. She has received trainings on gender issues both within and outside Nigeria. She attended CODESRIA Gender Institute, Dakar, Senegal (2009), and a participant in the University of Ibadan Gender Mainstreaming Project and workshops sponsored by University of Ibadan and MacArthur Foundation between 2010 – 2012. Dr Ukpokolo was a member of the research team that participated in the formulation of University of Ibadan Gender Policy, and University of Ibadan Sexual Harassment Policy. She is a resource person on gender issues and a receiver of MacArthur Foundation Research Grant Award, 2009. Her research interests include gender issues, higher education, ethnic studies and ethnography. She has published in reputable journals within and outside Nigeria, and has a submission, 'Women in Yoruba Land' in *Yoruba Encyclopaedia* (University of Indiana Press). She co-edited the book, *Space, Transformation and Representation: Reflection on University Culture*, published in the USA. Contact: fcukpokolo@gmail.com +234 0802 3415 265.

**Tapiwa Praise Mapuranga,** Ph.D, is a senior lecturer in the department of religious studies, classics and philosophy of the University of Zimbabwe. She offers courses on 'women and religion' and 'sociology of religion' at both undergraduate and postgraduate levels. Her research interests are in the areas of religion and gender. Her latest publication on religion, gender and politics is entitled 'Religion, Politics and Gender: The Zimbabwean experience with special reference to the period 2000-2008', Ezra Chitando (ed.), *Prayers and Players: Religion and Politics in Zimbabwe*, SAPES Books: Harare, 177-188. She has also attended an APSA workshop on Religion and Politics, held in July 2013 in Burkina Faso, Ouagadougou. This has increased her experience in writing on religion and politics. Apart from these, she has over 30 publications in the area of religion and gender. Some of these areas of research include women and Pentecostalism, women in Islam, women in music, among other themes that are influenced by religion. Mapuranga has had significant training on gender issues. Some of this training includes CODESRIA workshops which are the Gender Institute of 2009 held in Dakar Senegal, as well as the CODESRIA-SEPHIS Workshop on gender and sexualities held in 2010. Apart from these workshops, she is also an alumni of OSSREA and the H.F Guggenheim Foundation. Mapuranga has also been to Zambia, Botswana, South Africa, Tanzania, Uganda, Namibia, Geneva and Germany, among other countries for different workshops and training in the area of religion and gender.

**Aisha Balarabe Bawa** is a lecturer with the Department of History at Usmanu Danfodiyo University, Sokoto. Her principal research interests lie in the field of Gender History. She has published a number of articles and chapters in books. Her recent work is *Engendering Democratisation: The Changing Political 'Images' of Women in Post colonial Nigeria.* Currently, she is a PhD candidate.

**Omotade Adegbindin,** PhD, teaches Philosophy at the Department of Philosophy, University of Ibadan. His areas of research include African Philosophy, Epistemology and Cultural Studies. A seasoned writer and consistent researcher in the field of Yoruba oral tradition, he is a member of the Philippine National Philosophical Research Society. He has published in both local and international journals. He is the author of *Ifá in Yoruba Thought System*, published by Carolina Academic Press, Durham, USA.

**Elizabeth Kyazike,** PhD, is a lecturer in the department of History and Archaeology at Kyambogo University in Kampala, Uganda. She is also an African Humanities Dissertation completion Fellow (F12) and wrote her article while in her AHP fellowship at the University of Ibadan in 2013. Elizabeth holds a Master of Arts (History) from Makerere University and a PhD in Archaeology obtained from the University of Dar es Salaam. This chapter is derived from her M.A thesis entitled, 'Culture and Development: The Case of Kiganda Traditional Women Education: 1900-1972'.

**Samuel Oluwole Ogundele** is a professor of Settlement and Public Archaeology with an emphasis on Nigeria. He began his career in 1982 as a graduate assistant and rose to the rank of full professor in October 2007, in the Department of Archaeology and Anthropology, University of Ibadan, Nigeria. Professor Wole Ogundele has solely authored five books covering different areas of African Archaeology and Anthropology. This is in addition to his contributions in local and international journals, as well as books. Professor Ogundele was a Visiting Scholar to the prestigious University of the Witwatersrand, Johannesburg, South Africa in 2000, and 2002 - 2003. Professor Oluwole Ogundele who obtained his doctorate from the University of Ibadan in January 1990 served as Visiting Professor to the University of Ghana, Legon between 2006 and 2008. He is currently on his Sabbatical at the same university (Legon) where he teaches Archaeology at the undergraduate and postgraduate levels. **E-mail: oluwoleogundele@yahoo.com**

**Oluwakemi Abiodun Adesina,** PhD, is a historian with research interests in African history, migrations, international commercial sex trade, gender and women's studies.

She teaches at the Osun State University, Osogbo, (Ikire Campus), Nigeria. She has published in local and international journals and books. Most notable amongst her publications are: 'Putting Africa on the Map: Contemporary Migrations, Livelihoods and the Socio-Economic Landscape' in *The Nigerian Journal of Economic History,* Nos. 7 & 8, 2005, pp.69-80, 'Between Culture and Poverty: The Queen Mother Phenomenon and the Edo International Sex Trade' in *Jenda: A Journal of Culture and African Women Studies.* Issue 8, 2006 pp. 1-31. She is currently a 2013/14 Fellow of the American Council of Learned Societies (ACLS). E-MAIL: oluwakemiadesina@yahoo.com Alternate email: oluwakemiadesina@gmail.com

# Index

www.ingramcontent.com/pod-product-compliance
Lightning Source LLC
Chambersburg PA
CBHW022305280326
41932CB00010B/985

* 9 7 8 1 9 4 2 8 7 6 0 7 6 *